Transnational Archipelago

Perspectives on Cape Verdean
Migration and Diaspora

Edited by Luís Batalha and Jørgen Carling

AMSTERDAM UNIVERSITY PRESS

Cover design: Neon, design and communications, Sabine Mannel
Layout: The DocWorkers, Almere

ISBN   978 90 5356 994 8
NUR   741 / 763

© Amsterdam University Press, Amsterdam 2008

Contents

Foreword

This is the first book to present a comprehensive exploration of Cape Verdean migration and transnationalism. It is also one of very few anthologies that presents a range of geographical and thematic perspectives on any single diaspora. The book emerged out of a conference organised at the Centro de Estudos de Antropologia Social (CEAS), at the Instituto Superior de Ciências do Trabalho e da Empresa (ISCTE), in Lisbon, April 2005. The conference comprised forty presentations by researchers from a dozen different countries. The chapters in this book include substantially revised versions of selected conference papers, chapters that merged individual conference papers, as well as newly written chapters. The conference itself was trilingual (Portuguese, Spanish and English) and several chapters have been translated into English. While there is a growing literature on Cape Verdean migration in Portuguese, our ambition with this book was to make high-quality research on Cape Verdean migration accessible to an international English-speaking audience.

Most of the research presented in this book would not have been possible without the contributions of Cape Verdean informants involved in the diaspora and on the islands. We are all grateful for the willingness of so many Cape Verdeans to generously share their experiences for the benefit of our research. There are, unfortunately, no academics from Cape Verde among the contributors to this volume. However, it is promising to see that higher education and research is developing rapidly in Cape Verde, and that increasing numbers of Cape Verdean students overseas are doing graduate research linked to migration.

The conference in Lisbon was supported by the Fundação para a Ciência e a Tecnologia (FCT), and the Fundação Luso-Americana (FLAD). We are also grateful to Antónia Lima, who while acting as Chair of the CEAS, promptly agreed to discuss with the board the organisation of the conference as part of its annual programme, and for Isabel Cardana's contribution to the organisation of the conference. The chapters in the book have been peer reviewed and commented upon by several anonymous referees, whose efforts we greatly appreciate. We would also like to thank our editor at the University of Amsterdam Press, Erik van Aert for his encouraging support, and Achim Lewandowski for permission to use the cover photograph of children playing in front of the old secondary school in São Vicente.

Lisbon and Oslo, December 2007
Luís Batalha and Jørgen Carling

Notes on contributors

LISA ÅKESSON is Director of Studies in Social Anthropology at the School of Global Studies, Göteborg University. Her PhD in Social Anthropology addressed the meanings of migration in Cape Verde and was based on extensive fieldwork in São Vicente during the period 1996–2003. She is currently doing research on remittances to Cape Verde with a focus on rural Santo Antão. She has also done fieldwork among Cape Verdeans in Sweden. Her research, teaching and supervision also covers family and kinship, ethnic and cultural diversity, and human trafficking.

JACQUELINE ANDALL is Senior Lecturer in Italian Studies at the Department of European Studies, University of Bath. Her research interests are on labour migration, female migration, second generations and Italian colonialism/postcolonialism. She is author of *Gender, Migration and Domestic Service* (Ashgate, 2000), editor of *Gender and Ethnicity in Contemporary Europe* (Berg 2003) and co-editor (with Derek Duncan) of *Italian Colonialism: Legacy and Memory* (Peter Lang, 2005). Her current research is on Ghanaian migration to Italy's industrial districts.

LUÍS BATALHA is a social anthropologist and Associate Professor at the Instituto Superior de Ciências Sociais e Políticas, Universidade Técnica de Lisboa. He has done ethnographic work among Cape Verdeans in Portugal, the U.S. and Cape Verde exploring issues relating to ethnicity, race and identity construction. He has published a book about the presence of Cape Verdeans in Portugal, *The Cape Verdean Diaspora in Portugal: Colonial Subjects in a Postcolonial World* (Lexington Books, 2004) as well as several articles and book chapters on related issues. He is currently working on the presence of the Cape Verdeans in Mozambique's late colonial period as middle-men civil servants.

HUUB BEIJERS is manager of transcultural psychiatry for Symfora group Mental Health Care in the Netherlands. He has a background in medical anthropology and social psychology. He was responsible for the development of the *Apoio* project, a community mental health care initiative for Cape Verdeans in Rotterdam. His research in the Cape Verdean community in Rotterdam focused on experiences of psychosocial distress, explanations of distress, pathways to health, and experiences of exclusion and discrimination in mental health care. He is currently developing research on experiences of Cape Verdean girls sexually abused by relatives.

JØRGEN CARLING is Senior Researcher at the International Peace Research Institute, Oslo (PRIO) in Norway. He holds a PhD in human geography based on a case study of Dutch-Cape Verdean transnationalism. He has done research on several aspects of migration and transnationalism, including human smuggling, migration control, transnational families and remittances. He has extensive fieldwork experience from Cape Verde, and among Cape Verdeans in the Netherlands and Italy. He has published in most of the leading journals in migration studies, including the *International Migration Review, Ethnic and Racial Studies, Global Networks* and *Journal of Ethnic and Migration Studies*.

RUI CIDRA is a researcher and doctoral candidate at the Instituto de Etnomusicologia, Universidade Nova de Lisboa, Portugal. He has carried out fieldwork on the islands of Santiago and São Vicente, and in the Metropolitan Area of Lisbon, on Cape Verdean Music and on Hip-hop. He is preparing a PhD dissertation on the creative processes of Santiago's young musicians. He is co-editor of *Enciclopédia da Música em Portugal no Século XX*, where he has written forty entries on musical genres, processes and musicians from Portugal, Cape Verde and other Lusophone African countries.

JULIANA BRAZ DIAS is Professor of Anthropology at Universidade Federal de Mato Grosso, in Brazil. She holds a doctoral degree in Social Anthropology from Universidade de Brasília. Her research has focused on popular culture and social identity in Cape Verde. She has extensive fieldwork experience, studying several aspects of Cape Verdean society, since 1998. Her teaching and research activities also cover kinship, migration, colonialism and museums.

ROCIO MOLDES FARELO is Associate Professor of Sociology at the Universidad Europea de Madrid. She holds a PhD in political science and sociology from the Universidad Complutense de Madrid. Her dissertation is an ethnographic study of Cape Verdean communities in Spain, based on extensive fieldwork in the years 1995–1998. Her current research is concentrated on the sociology of labour and migration and on human resource management. She is the author of *Prevenir el racismo en el trabajo en España* (IMSERSO, Diciembre 2000) and the co-author of *Paro, Exclusión y Políticas de Empleo. Aspectos sociológicos* (Tirant Lo Blanch, Octubre, 2004).

CLÁUDIA DE FREITAS is a PhD candidate in Social Sciences at the Utrecht University, The Netherlands. She has a background in Clinical Psychology and holds a MA in Migration and Ethnic Studies from the University of Amsterdam, based on a study of Cape Verdeans' perceptions of care providers, access to health care and transnational health care seeking. She is currently writing her dissertation on Cape Verdeans' participation in mental health care and recovery. She is the author of *Em Busca de Um Bom Médico – Quando a Saúde Não Tem Fronteiras: Percepções dos Caboverdianos Sobre Profissionais de Saúde na Holanda* (Lisbon: ACIME, 2006).

GINA SÁNCHEZ GIBAU is Associate Professor in the Department of Anthropology at Indiana University–Purdue University Indianapolis. She earned a PhD in Anthropology from the University of Texas at Austin, specializing in the African diaspora. She conducted fieldwork on identity formation among Cape Verdeans in Boston, Massachusetts, and in the islands. Her current research focuses on the construction of Cape Verdean diasporic identity in cyberspace. She has published articles in *Transforming Anthropology, Identities*, and *The Western Journal of Black Studies*.

LUZIA OCA GONZÁLEZ is Lecturer of Applied Anthropology at the Universidade de Trás-os-Montes e Alto Douro, Portugal. She holds a Master's Degree in applied anthropology from the Universidad de Santiago de Compostela. Her research and fieldwork is linked with social intervention, primarily with the Cape Verdean community in Galiza (Galicia), on which she has published various articles in Portugal and Spain. She has also done fieldwork on the island of Santiago, from where the community originates. She has created the anthropological exhibition *Badias: cabo-verdianas na Galiza*. She currently manages a participatory research with women in Santiago's fishing communities.

MARILYN HALTER is Professor of History and Research Associate at the Institute on Culture, Religion and World Affairs at Boston University. Her books include *Between Race and Ethnicity: Cape Verdean American Immigrants, 1860-1965* (University of Illinois Press, 1993) and with Richard Lobban, *The Historical Dictionary of the Republic of Cape Verde* (Scarecrow Press, 1988 edition) as well as *Shopping for Identity: The Marketing of Ethnicity* (Schocken Books, 2000) and *New Migrants in the Marketplace: Boston's Ethnic Entrepreneurs* (University of Massachusetts Press, 1995). Her current research project, 'The Newest African Americans', is a study of recent West African immigrants and refugees to the U.S.

JOANNE HOFFMAN is a doctoral candidate at the City University of New York Graduate Center. She is completing a PhD in ethnomusiciology which examines the Cape Verdean musical landscape from a social perspective, including race, class and gender, but also including issues of post-independence politics, colonial history, and migration. Her research has primarily been based in the islands themselves, but also includes the Dutch and American diaspora communities. She is the author the chapter 'O papel da Independência, da Emigração e da Música Mundial no Estrelato Ascendente das Mulheres de Cabo Verde' in the edited volume *Género e Migrações Cabo-Verdianas* (Imprensa de Ciências Sociais, 2007).

MEMORY HOLLOWAY teaches 20th-century art history at the University of Massachusetts Dartmouth, where she is on the executive board for the Center for Portuguese Studies and Culture. She holds a PhD from the Courtauld Institute of Art, London University. Holloway has published widely on contemporary Portuguese art including *Secrets Devoilés: Dessins et gravures de Paula Rego.* (Fundaçao Calouste Gulbenkian, 1999.) She is also the author of *Making Time: Picasso's Suite 347* (Peter Lang, 2006) on the late work of Picasso. Her current research is on the African diaspora in the Atlantic and includes Cape Verde and Brazil.

ANDRÉA DE SOUSA LOBO is Director of the Instituto Sociedade, População e Natureza (ISPN) in Brasília. She holds a PhD in Social Anthropology from the University of Brasília. Her doctoral research addressed family organization in the context of female emigration from the Islands of Boavista, Cape Verde. The dissertation was based on intensive fieldwork from 2004 to 2005. She previously conducted fieldwork in the city of Praia about the concept of landscape in Cape Verde, and its relation with cultural identity. This research was based on an analysis of documents from the time of discovery until after Independence.

MARTA M. MAFFIA is Senior Researcher of the National Scientific and Technical Research Council of Argentina (CONICET) and Associate Professor of Research Methods and Techniques of Sociocultural Anthropology at the Universidad Nacional de La Plata. Her doctoral research addressed the migration, kinship and family of Cape Verdean immigrants and their descendants in Argentina. Fieldwork in Argentina was complemented by travels to Cape Verde, Portugal and Brazil. She has published numerous articles on Cape Verdeans and other immigrant communities in Argentina. She is editor of *Mapeo sociocultural de grupos de inmigrantes y sus descendientes en la Provincia de Buenos Aires* (Al Margen, 2002).

SÓNIA MELO is a PhD candidate at the Theory, Culture and Society Centre, Nottingham Trent University, United Kingdom. Her thesis *Connections @ Cape Verde: Postcolonial Globalisation through the Internet* examines the practices of production, circulation and usage of the Internet among Cape Verdeans within the framework of postcolonial globalisation. Her work is trans-disciplinary, intertwining technology and communication studies with studies of migration and transnationalism and their dynamics of spatialisation. She has carried out fieldwork in Cape Verde, Portugal and the U.S. Her interests also include the links between research and policy.

AUGUSTO NASCIMENTO is a Researcher at the Instituto de Investigação Científica Tropical, Lisbon. His PhD focused on colonial society in São Tomé and Príncipe. He has conducted fieldwork about Cape Verdean migration to São Tomé and Príncipe in the 20th century. His current research addresses several aspects of political and social history of equatorial islands. Nascimento is the author of *Desterro e Contrato: Moçambicanos a Caminho de São Tomé e Príncipe* (Arquivo Histórico de Moçambique, Maputo, 2002), *O Fim do Caminhu Longi* (Ilhéu Editora, 2007) and *Ciências Sociais em S. Tomé e Príncipe: A Independência e o Estado da Arte* (Centro de Estudos Africanos da Universidade do Porto, 2007)

MÁRCIA REGO is a Mellon Fellow at the Duke University Writing Program. Her PhD dissertation in Cultural Anthropology is based on extensive fieldwork in Cape Verde and explores issues of language use and language ideology from early settlement to the postcolonial present. Her research and teaching interests also include ethnographic writing, anthropology of the body, and the complexities of intercultural communication and translation.

KARIN WALL is a sociologist and a Senior Research Fellow at the Institute of Social Sciences (ICS) of the University of Lisbon. She has carried out national and cross-national research on family patterns and interactions, migrant women and families, gender and family, the reconciliation of work and family life, and family policies in Europe. She is currently working on four projects: family life from the male perspective; family trajectories and social networks; leave policies in Europe; social care in families of workers under pressure. She recently co-authored *Famílias em Portugal* (ICS, 2005) and edited *Família e Género em Portugal e na Europa* (ICS, 2007).

Chapter 1
Cape Verdean Migration and Diaspora

Jørgen Carling and Luís Batalha

Few countries in the world have been as profoundly shaped by migration as Cape Verde. The archipelago of Cape Verde was populated by immigrants, and later experienced emigration on a massive scale in relation to its population. Ties with the diaspora were a critical lifeline for the newly independent country, and instrumental in the transition to multiparty democracy. While the emigrants have been central to Cape Verdean nation-building, they have nonetheless been an elusive minority in most of the places they have settled. Cape Verde is a remote country that most people in other parts of the world have never heard of. Cape Verdean immigrants have been mistaken for Surinamese in the Netherlands, Somalis in Sweden and Puerto Ricans and Dominicans in the U.S.[1] They have faced the challenge of carving out a place for themselves within ethnic, racial and national categories that did not easily accommodate people of puzzling African and Portuguese mixed origin.

The book is divided into two parts. The first part portrays eight Cape Verdean diaspora communities on four continents. The second part contains eleven chapters, each one focusing on a particular aspect of Cape Verdean migration or transnationalism. The remainder of the introduction starts with a discussion of Cape Verde's diverse connections to the outside world and the different frames of reference for a national identity. This is followed by a brief overview of the migration history of Cape Verde, a discussion of diaspora politics, and an account of Cape Verdean transnationalism and its relationship with the development of the archipelago. The introduction ends with a short discussion of the potential contribution of the Cape Verdean case, and this book, to the study of migration and diaspora processes.

Locating Cape Verde

The Cape Verde Islands are an archipelago in the Atlantic Ocean, about 500 km off the coast of Senegal. The islands were named after the closest point on the mainland, Cape Verde (Cap-Vert), which was allegedly where seafarers first saw greenery on land after sailing along the arid coast of the Sahara. The islands were uninhabited until a small group of Portuguese, Spanish and Genoese people settled there in the 1460s, only a few years after the discovery of the archipelago in 1456.[2] Over the next 150 years, Cape Verde became an important transit point in the Atlantic slave trade. During this period, the European settlers – who were almost exclusively male – and women brought as slaves from West Africa, produced a population of mixed origin that soon became the majority among the inhabitants.

Being settled by colonialists and developed on the basis of slavery and a plantation economy, Cape Verde's history has much in common with the West Indies. A striking parallel today, which also has implications for migration and transnationalism, is its flexible family structure. In Cape Verde and the Caribbean alike, nuclear families consisting of a couple and their children are the exception rather than the norm. Families are built primarily around the mother-child tie, and the role of fathers is much more variable (Smith 1995). Notwithstanding the historical parallels, there is minimal contact between Cape Verde and the Caribbean islands today.

The Portuguese-speaking (Lusophone) world is another important frame of reference for locating Cape Verde. The islands remained a Portuguese colony until 1975. Under Portuguese colonial rule, Cape Verdeans had an ambiguous middle-men role (Batalha 2004). As early as the 15th century, Cape Verdeans were sent to the Guinea coast, where they functioned as intermediary traders for Portuguese and later for other European merchants. Lisbon's need for qualified Cape Verdean administrators in the other colonies led to the establishment of the empire's first 'overseas' secondary school in the archipelago. While independence in 1975 by definition entailed a rupture with Portugal, it also reinforced ties with the other former Portuguese colonies in Africa, and thus did not do away with Cape Verde's identification with the Portuguese-speaking world. In particular, the independence struggles of Cape Verde and Guinea-Bissau were very closely linked. Amílcar Cabral (1924-1973), born in Guinea-Bissau of Cape Verdean parents, is considered the founding father of both countries. During the first fifteen years of independence, Cape Verde was a single party-state with a Marxist-leaning government. Initially, the same party, PAIGC (*Partido Africano para a Independência da Guiné e Cabo Verde*), was in power simultaneously in Cape Verde and Guinea-Bissau. In 1980, this unusual setup ruptured and the party renamed itself PAICV (*Partido Africano para a Independência de Cabo Verde*).

In terms of geography, Cape Verde is a West African country. At the time of independence, the country's African identity was also given great political importance. The adopted flag had colours typically African – red, yellow and green – and political and economic ties with the

African mainland were emphasised. Cape Verde is part of the Economic Community of West African States (ECOWAS), which includes a protocol on the free movement of people.

The first multiparty elections were held in 1991, after a new constitution had been adopted the previous year. The political transition involved a reorientation of Cape Verde's regional identity. The liberal-democratic *Movimento para a Democracia* (MpD) climbed to power and maintained it in the 1996 elections. One of the most symbolically important changes introduced under the MpD government was the new flag, designed in red, white and blue, with a circle of ten yellow stars representing the islands of the archipelago. The more European and American layout of the new flag matched a redirection of the country's foreign policy and development strategies. A privatisation programme for state-owned companies was introduced, and many are now under Portuguese ownership. Trade links with Portugal were also intensified; imports from Portugal accounted for 50-60 per cent of total imports in the early 2000s, up from around 30 per cent a decade earlier.[3]

The recent revival of economic ties with Portugal adds to a sustained Portuguese influence in many spheres of Cape Verdean society since independence. The institutions of the state and civil society are decidedly inspired by Portuguese models. In everyday life in Cape Verde, perhaps the most obvious example of Portuguese presence is football. Almost every man, and many women, in Cape Verde is a staunch supporter of one of the three main football clubs in Portugal: Benfica, Porto, or Sporting. Portuguese television shows and Brazilian soaps (*novelas*) are also important cultural influences from other parts of the Lusophone world.

Since the political transition in 1991, Cape Verde has sought to develop a new regional identity as part of the North Atlantic group of archipelagos known as Macaronesia (the Azores, Madeira, the Canary Islands and Cape Verde).[4] The other three archipelagos are European, and Macaronesian unity thus reinforces Cape Verde's links to Europe. In 2005, former Portuguese president Mário Soares and former late-colonial *Estado Novo* Overseas Minister Adriano Moreira launched a petition urging the European Union to start membership talks with Cape Verde, a plea that was supported by authorities from the other Macaronesian archipelagos. The following year, the Cape Verdean government announced that it would seek to suspend the ECOWAS protocol on free movement in order to suppress the use of Cape Verde as a transit country for undocumented migration from West Africa to the Canary Islands. This was a symbolically important step in terms of regional loyalties.

Island-specific transnational connections

The archipelago consists of ten islands, nine of which are inhabited (see figure 1.1). The islands are remarkably different from each other in terms of landscape, climate and natural endowments, and this has contributed to island-specific trajectories of development and migration. The largest island, Santiago, was home to the initial settlement, slave trade, and a plantation economy that supplied sailing ships. During the past decades, the interior of Santiago has remained one of the poorest regions in the country, but the capital city, Praia, has developed with astounding dynamism as the centre of an independent country.

The country's second largest city, Mindelo, on the island of São Vicente, has one of the best natural harbours along the Western Atlantic. It thrived in the era of steamships, when it was a coaling station of pivotal importance to international sea liners. This, in turn, stimulated emigration of seafarers from São Vicente and the neighbouring islands. In many countries, Cape Verdean communities are concentrated not in the capitals or the largest cities, but in the principal port cities. Rotterdam (the Netherlands), Antwerp (Belgium), Hamburg (Germany) and Gothenburg (Sweden) are cases in point. Elsewhere, ports remain the historical focal points of communities, though Cape Verdean populations are now more dispersed. That is the case with New Bedford, Massachusetts in the U.S., and Ensenada in Argentina.

Another transport revolution placed Sal, a small desert-like island, centre-stage in Cape Verdean development. The country's first international airport opened in Sal, in 1948, and has allowed Cape Verde to function as a transportation hub for decades now. Transatlantic flights from Europe to South America and from South Africa to North America required a fuelling stop half-way, and Sal's international airport served this purpose. The airport itself contributed significantly to the national economy, and also facilitated the development of international tourism in Cape Verde, centred on Sal's beaches.

The neighbouring island of Boavista, equally flat and dry, had a boom as a supplier of salt to the Portuguese empire in the 17th and 18th centuries but subsequently became a veritable backwater due to a population decline that made it the least-populated island. Since the early 1990s, however, Boavista has experienced renewed growth as a tourist destination, offering a yet unexplored alternative to Sal. On both islands, Italian investment has been fundamental to the tourist sector, and has coincided with substantial emigration to Italy. Large numbers of women, especially from Boavista, have departed for Italy as domestic workers. In chapter 11, Andrea de Sousa Lobo describes how the emigration of women has affected local society and family life.

A final example of the island-specific linkages to the wider world is offered by Brava, the smallest and least accessible island. Here the recruitment of crew members by American whaling ships on Brava laid the foundation for the large diaspora community in the U.S., as described by Marilyn Halter in chapter 2. Large-scale migration to the U.S. later came to include neighbouring Fogo as well. Even today, the links to the U.S. are decisive for sustaining the archipelago's population. While the rest of the islands have truly 'diasporic' connections with many emigrant destinations, Fogo and Brava are very strongly oriented towards the U.S.

Cape Verdean identity

Amidst the various affiliations with the outside world, Cape Verde has a distinct national identity. The children of European settlers and African slaves created the foundation for a Cape Verdean population soon after the islands were settled, but there was no assertion of a national identity as such until the 20th century. Not only was identification with the Portuguese empire dominant, but migrants who left Cape Verde often identified with their island of origin more than with the archipelago.

Today, language and music are the most important cultural markers of Cape Verdean identity. While Portuguese has remained the official language, Cape Verdean Creole (Kriolu) is the everyday language of the entire population. This is a language that differs substantially from Portuguese in terms of grammar, but relies almost exclusively on a vocabulary of Portuguese origin. Granting Kriolu official status is seen by many as an important step in asserting Cape Verdean nationhood. It is also a great challenge for the educational system that children be taught in a language that is not their mother tongue. There is still a long way to go before Kriolu is established as a written language and given official status. Substantial dialectical variation between the islands also makes the process of developing a standardised Kriolu politically complex. In chapter 12, Marcia Rego discusses the role of Kriolu for national identity in detail.

Cape Verdean music is the other key marker of Cape Verdean identity. Like the nation itself, Cape Verdean music is clearly shaped by influences from various parts of the world, but simultaneously constitutes something unique and distinct. The Cape Verdean music industry, the different musical styles and their relationship with migration are discussed in the chapters by Juliana Braz Dias, Rui Cidra and JoAnne Hoffman.

While music represents a national richness, Cape Verdean identity is also closely linked to the island's lack of natural resources and history

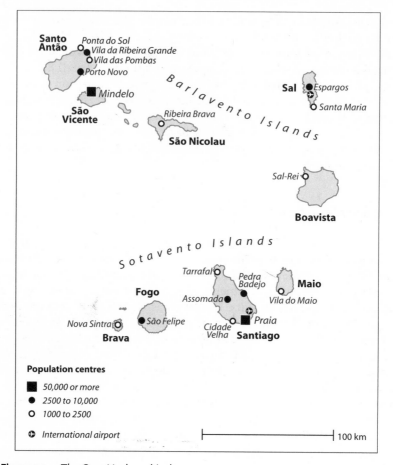

Santo Antão
Ponta do Sol
Vila da Ribeira Grande
Vila das Pombas
Porto Novo

B a r l a v e n t o   I s l a n d s

Sal
Espargos
Santa Maria

Mindelo

São Vicente

Ribeira Brava

São Nicolau

Sal-Rei

Boavista

S o t a v e n t o   I s l a n d s

Tarrafal
Pedra Badejo
Assomada

Maio
Vila do Maio

Fogo

Nova Sintra
São Felipe
Cidade Velha
Praia

Brava   **Santiago**

Population centres

■ 50,000 or more
● 2500 to 10,000
○ 1000 to 2500

✪ International airport   ├────────────────┤ 100 km

Figure 1.1. *The Cape Verde archipelago*

of extreme hardship. A series of devastating droughts, combined with negligence on the part of the Portuguese colonial power, have resulted in levels of famine mortality that are exceptional in human history (Drèze and Sen 1989; Patterson 1988). As late as the 1940s, about one quarter of the total population died in two consecutive famines (Carreira 1983). Today, less people live from subsistence agriculture, and international food aid provides a guarantee against widespread famine. Nevertheless, the scarcity and instability of rain is still a fundamental aspect of the people's image of homeland.

The Cape Verdean diaspora

After a century and a half of large-scale emigration, the Cape Verdean diaspora stretches across the four continents around the Atlantic Ocean (figure 1.2). The size of the diaspora communities is difficult to ascertain. It is widely claimed that the diaspora population is 'twice as large' as the resident population, but there is little demographic evidence for this claim (Carling 1997). Since much of the migration from Cape Verde happened during colonial rule, it is often impossible to identify

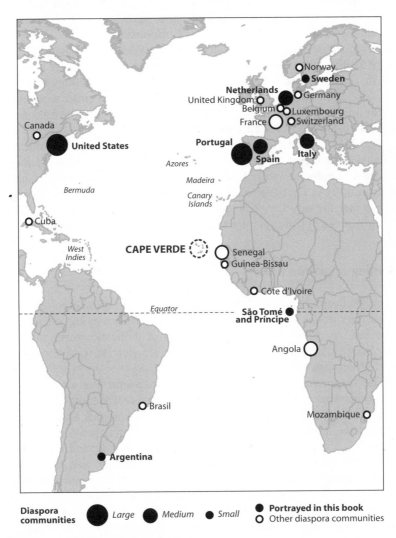

Figure 1.2.   *The Cape Verdean diaspora*

Cape Verdeans in historical migration statistics. Moreover, such statistics are altogether lacking in many of the destination countries. Finally, it is an open question who should be considered 'Cape Verdean'. In the U.S., for instance, the number of people who claimed Cape Verdean ancestry in the 1980 and 1990 censuses was only a fraction of the assessment of the size of the community offered by community leaders. In a recent article about the concept of diaspora, Rogers Brubaker (2005) convincingly argues against the notion of 'membership' of diasporas. According to him, many scholars have tended to exaggerate the importance of diasporas by, on the one hand, using loose definitions that make diasporas numerically large, and on the other hand, focusing on diasporic practices that only a small minority engages in. If we use an all-inclusive definition of who is a Cape Verdean in diaspora, we must therefore also accept that this large group of people may have little in common with one another. Narrowing the definition to those who are born in Cape Verde and/or maintain active links with Cape Verde might give the notion of diaspora a more substantive content, but also implies a much smaller number of people.

With these reservations in mind, the map (figure 1.2) only indicates a division into large, medium and small diaspora communities. The individual chapters contain further discussions about the size of each community. As for the total size of the diaspora, it is probably correct to say that the number of people of Cape Verdean origin outside Cape Verde outnumber the roughly 500,000 residents on the islands.

Shifting migration flows

Cape Verdeans have not only migrated to a large number of destinations, but under a diversity of conditions – with varying degrees of coercion, for employment niches spanning domestic work, mining, cranberry-picking and seafaring, and with a variety of legal and illegal immigrant statuses.

The shipment of slaves through the archipelago was Cape Verde's first experience with mass migration. Slaves were traded in Cape Verde before being shipped to the U.S., the West Indies and Brazil. It was around the time that slavery came to an end in Cape Verde, in the 1860s, that migration linked to the American whaling industry developed. The large-scale migration that followed can be seen as a small Cape Verdean component in the history of the great transatlantic migration. Between 1900 and 1920 approximately 20,000 Cape Verdeans, most of them males, entered the U.S. (Carreira 1983; Halter 1993). In chapter 10, Memory Holloway uses a series of photographs from 1904 to present the experience of Cape Verdean workers in the

New England whaling. Since migration is an intrinsic part of Cape Verdean identity, these migrant pioneers have come to play the role of cultural heroes. They are the forerunners of the tradition of migration, and they are crucial to the ideology of migration (Åkesson 2004).

Soon after the end of slavery in Cape Verde, the Portuguese colonial power started encouraging the migration of Cape Verdeans to other Portuguese colonies in Africa as indentured labourers. Cape Verdeans were primarily forced to migrate to the islands of São Tomé and Príncipe, in the Gulf of Guinea, where they worked on coffee and cacao plantations. Historians and anthropologists have discussed the exact degree of coercion, but in the popular memory, the migration to São Tomé and Príncipe is compared to slavery. The dreadful conditions on the plantations have been documented in detail by António Carreira (1983) and are discussed in chapter 3 by Augusto Nascimento. Between 1900 and 1970, approximately 80,000 women and men left Cape Verde for the islands in the south, while smaller numbers were sent to Guinea and Angola (Carreira 1983: 245).

While migration to the other Portuguese colonies happened with varying degrees of coercion, Dakar became an escape for many Cape Verdeans. The proximity of the West African mainland enabled Cape Verdeans to travel back and forth quite easily, and thus escape the surveillance of authorities. Since the Portuguese sought to drive labour to São Tomé and Príncipe, passports and travel permits were often not issued for other destinations. When the U.S. barred immigration, around 1920, a passage to Dakar became a new way for Cape Verdeans to leave their country. They were well regarded by the French colonialists. Women often worked as domestic servants in their homes, while men found jobs as artisans.

In the early 20th century, Argentina was a leading industrial power and a major source of immigration from Europe. Cape Verdeans were also part of this migration flow, especially from the 1920s onward. The Cape Verdean community in Argentina is portrayed by Marta Maffia in chapter 3. The migration flows to Argentina and Dakar continued until the 1950s. The flow of indentured labour to São Tomé was sustained until the end of colonial rule. In the post-war years, Angola was developing quickly and attracted migrants from Cape Verde. The status of Angola is reflected in the popular Cape Verdean song *Terezinha*, about a return migrant and his girlfriend: 'Oh Terezinha; the money from Angola is gone; I don't have a penny left; to spend with you'.[5] Even today, after several decades of civil war left much of Angola in ruins, the Cape Verdeans see hope in the country's vast economic resources and lack of professionals. 'Soon, Angola might be the best *abertura* (opening) for us', people say (Åkesson 2004: 35).

In the middle decades of the 20th century, migration to Portugal was the preserve of a relatively small colonial elite. They were students, merchants and administrators, welcomed without any bureaucratic hassle. The numbers were still small, however, in relation to later migration flows to Portugal. As described by Luís Batalha in chapter 5, labour migration was first facilitated by Portuguese construction companies working in Cape Verde which brought Cape Verdean workers to Portugal. This gave rise to a chain migration of low-skilled workers that increased rapidly in the 1960s and early 1970s. It was also around 1960 that Cape Verdean men began migrating to the Netherlands to find work as seafarers. The shipping industry was booming and Rotterdam was a recruitment hub for shipping companies from many European countries. In chapter 8, Jørgen Carling describes the subsequent development of a Cape Verdean community in the Netherlands, the largest in northern Europe. The recruitment of seafarers in Rotterdam played an important role for the settlement of Cape Verdeans in port cities throughout non-Western Europe, including the community in Gothenburg portrayed by Lisa Åkesson in chapter 9.

At the same time as Cape Verdean men were looking for work in the shipping industry of Rotterdam, increasing numbers of Cape Verdean women were travelling to Italy as domestic workers. As Jacqueline Andall describes in chapter 7, Capuchin friars based on the island of São Nicolau functioned as mediators for the first migrants. Through their contacts with Catholic parishes in Rome and elsewhere, they could place young girls as domestic workers in Italian families. Migration to Spain followed a completely different pattern. Chain migration into two localised niches – mining in León and fishing in Galiza – fuelled the development of a Cape Verdean population in Spain, in the 1970s and 1980s. This fascinating story is told by Rocío Moldes Farelo and Luzia Oca González in chapter 6. Only later did Cape Verdean women start working as domestic workers in Spanish cities.

As with Cape Verdean participation in the great transatlantic migration half a decade earlier, the northward migration in the 1960s and 1970s was also part of a larger migratory phenomenon. Cape Verdean workers arrived in non-Western Europe alongside migrants from Turkey, Morocco and other countries as part of the massive 'guest worker' migration. Cape Verdean migration to southern Europe contributed to the so-called 'migration turnaround' through which Portugal, Spain and Italy went from being countries of emigration to being countries of immigration (King et al. 1997).

The 1960s also marked the revival of Cape Verdean migration to the U.S., in response to a relaxation of immigration regulations. The new migrants met a Cape Verdean-American ethnic group whose members looked like them, but differed culturally. In chapter 19, Gina Sánchez

Gibau discusses how this diversity of immigration histories influences diasporic identity formation among Cape Verdeans in Boston.

A final important development in the Cape Verdean diaspora around 1960 resulted from Senegal's independence. Many Cape Verdeans had been employed by French colonialists and moved to France with their employers. This migration from Senegal to France was significant for the subsequent development of French-Cape Verdean communities. Paris, Marseilles and Nice are all cities with substantial Cape Verdean populations. The migration from Senegal to France is one of several migration flows *between* destinations in the Cape Verdean diaspora. Many Cape Verdean women left Italy for the Netherlands in the 1970s, and more recently there has been a substantial flow of Cape Verdeans from Portugal to the Netherlands. While this northward movement has been dominated by legally resident migrants (often Portuguese citizens) in search of better employment conditions, there has been a counter-movement of Cape Verdeans who have come to the Netherlands on tourist visas and subsequently left for Southern Europe, where it is easier to make a living without papers.

Diaspora politics

The diaspora played an important role in the struggle for Cape Verde's independence, but relations between the Cape Verdean government and the diaspora soon became strained. Emigrants were critical of the union with Guinea-Bissau and of the land reform that threatened their properties, and they were annoyed by the exploitative practices of customs officials and other government employees (Silva 1995). The PAICV government tried to improve relations with the diaspora in the mid-1980s by establishing the Institute for Assistance to Emigrants (IAPE, *Instituto de Apoio ao Emigrante*), which was given the task of helping emigrants with practical matters such as property development, imports, and pension rights. Nevertheless, many emigrants remained opposed to the PAICV government and helped bring about the transition to multiparty democracy in 1990. The country's new constitution gave emigrants the right to vote in parliamentary and presidential elections, six parliament seats reserved for diaspora constituencies, and the right to retain Cape Verdean citizenship upon naturalisation in the country of residence. These moves put Cape Verde in line with the many other countries of emigration that saw their diasporas as a national resource in need of strategic management.

After ten years of MpD rule, the PAICV was re-installed in the 2001 elections, and retained power in the elections of 2006. Many of the changes initiated by the MpD have been continued, including economic reforms and the policies of courting the diaspora. In the 2001-2006 programme of the PAICV government, for instance, the final section is devoted to the integration of emigrants in the development of the country. In a tone that is typical of policy statements related to the diaspora, one of the objectives is formulated as follows:

> To contribute to the unity and cohesion of the Cape Verdean nation, at whatever latitudes its children are found, stimulating community initiatives, abroad and in Cape Verde, thus capitalising on the great love of Cape Verdeans for their motherland (República de Cabo Verde 2001).

An important change instituted under this government was the termination of IAPE and the creation of the Institute of the [Emigrant] Communities (IC, *Instituto das Comunidades*). Responsibility for the more bureaucratically oriented assistance to individual emigrants was transferred to the municipalities, with varying success. The new national organ, the IC, was oriented directly toward the diaspora, with the dual aim of reinforcing ties with Cape Verde and assisting emigrant communities in need. The latter was an important development, constituting the latest addition to an expanding scope of policies vis-à-vis the diaspora. In an analysis of emigration policy in Cape Verdean government programmes, Katia Cardoso (2004) concludes that there have been seven main steps in this process: 1) Opening of diplomatic representation in countries with diaspora communities; 2) Signing of bilateral agreements on migration and social security; 3) Incentives for sending remittances; 4) Creation of a co-organising institution; 5) Incentives for political participation; 6) Encouragement of organisation and lobbying; and 7) Protection and assistance to the communities in greatest need.

This new initiative towards communities in need was initially oriented toward Cape Verdeans in São Tomé and Príncipe, many of whom were descendants of indentured labour migrants. However, it has also come to encompass consideration for the second generation in Europe and the U.S., where there is widespread concern for the descendants of Cape Verdean emigrants. Initiatives to promote a sense of Cape Verdean culture among the allegedly alienated youth are seen as beneficial to Cape Verde as well.

In terms of party politics, the power of the diaspora once again became evident in the January 2006 elections. In the national electorate, the 160,000 votes were split almost equally between the two presidential candidates, with a margin of only 24 votes in favour of Carlos Veiga, the candidate backed by MpD. In the diaspora, however, almost two-thirds of the 11,000 votes were in favour of Pedro Pires, who is affiliated with PAICV. Pires' lead in the diaspora thus outweighed Veiga's victory on the islands.

Transnationalism and the transformation of Cape Verde

Ever since the pioneering Cape Verdean migrants started a steady flow of packet-trade between the U.S. and Cape Verde, the archipelago and its diaspora have been linked via the exchange of goods, money and information. The changes in transnational activity over time have been affected by the development of particular diaspora communities, events in Cape Verde, and changes in the markets and technologies of transport and communication (e.g., Grassi 2003; Marques et al. 2001; Meintel 2000, 2002). In some cases, specific external influences have been decisive. As Marta Maffia writes in chapter 2, for instance, contact between the Argentinian-Cape Verdean community and Cape Verde flourished when Aeroflot provided a reasonably priced direct flight. When this was suspended, in 1998, visiting Cape Verde from Argentina became prohibitively expensive. For Cape Verdeans in Europe, meanwhile, the development of tourism in Cape Verde has meant an expanded choice of air travel, and better opportunities for holidays in Cape Verde.

One important consequence of the technological development has been the emergence of Cape Verdean transnationalism on the Internet. In chapter 13, Sónia Melo discusses how Cape Verdean web sites have become important for linking diaspora communities with each other, for maintaining ties with Cape Verde, and for the local politics of emigrant communities in their countries of residence. The desire to communicate with emigrants has created demand for Internet connectivity in Cape Verde, although it remains very expensive in relation to the local families income.

Transnational connections with Cape Verde are also changing in response to the social and demographic transformation of the diaspora communities. On the one hand, there has been a marked ethnic revival among Cape Verdeans in several countries, perhaps most notably in the U.S. This involves well-integrated immigrants with resources to engage with Cape Verde, for instance through holidays. On the other hand, most Cape Verdean diaspora communities are 'maturing' in the sense that recent arrivals constitute a progressively smaller proportion of the population, and that the second and subsequent generations become increasingly dominant. Estimates of emigration from the 2000 census in Cape Verde suggest that the major diaspora communities are only receiving a trickle of new migrants from Cape Verde compared to the size of the existing emigrant population.[6] The principal reason for this is the gradual tightening of immigration policies in the destination countries (Carling 2002, 2004). The wish to emigrate remains widespread in Cape Verde, but opportunities for doing so are severely limited. The falling proportion of 'fresh blood' in the diaspora communities is likely to affect the nature of ties with Cape Verde.

The propensity to engage in transnational practices such as sending remittances might wane over time – not because time itself seems to be particularly important in this respect, but because family members are reunited in the diaspora, or reach old age and die in Cape Verde. A large proportion of the elderly in Cape Verde are sustained by children abroad, and when they pass away, this flow of remittances will cease. The second generation is less likely to have close relatives to send remittances to in Cape Verde. Where intermarriage with non-Cape Verdeans has been common, as in Italy and Senegal, the Kriolu skills of the second generation are often rudimentary. Even in the Netherlands, where the vast majority of the second generation have two Cape Verdean-born parents, there is a clear intergenerational difference vis-à-vis Cape Verde. For many Dutch-born children of Cape Verdean descent, Cape Verde is first and foremost a holiday destination. This is evident every August, when the islands' beaches and discos are filled with emigrant youths. Their holidays are more akin to conventional tourism, whereas the first generation tends to see holidays in Cape Verde primarily as family visits.

The blurring of migrants' transnational travelling and commercial tourism is part of a broader transformation of the Cape Verdean society and economy. In the first decade after independence remittances and aid combined accounted for a staggering 80-90 per cent of GDP (Bourdet and Falck 2006). By the end of the 1990s, this had fallen to 25 per cent. Cape Verde has not only become less dependent on such gifts from abroad, but has also experienced solid economic growth through the 1990s and the early 2000s. Much of the current growth and optimism is, in fact, linked to the rapid development of tourism. The trends in tourism receipts and in remittances over the past decade are indicative of the transformation that Cape Verde is undergoing (figure 1.3). In 2006, tourism receipts were markedly larger than remittances for the first time ever. When opportunities for emigration are limited, many young Cape Verdeans see employment in the tourism industry as an alternative.

Over the past couple of decades, there has also been a marked change in how Cape Verdeans view emigration. Not least because of media coverage of the hardship of Cape Verdean emigrants in Portugal and elsewhere, the view that life abroad is a bed of roses is ridiculed and rejected (see Åkesson 2004). While many Cape Verdeans still wish to leave the islands, they are increasingly aware of the challenges awaiting them.

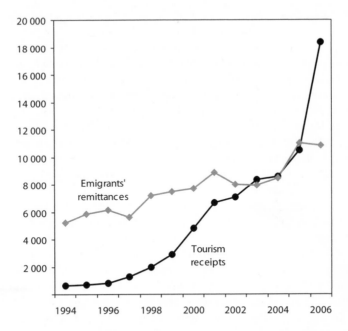

Figure 1.3.   *Emigrant remittances and tourism receipts 1994-2006 (CVE Million)*
Source: Banco de Cabo Verde.

Relations with the homeland are changing in response to the maturing of the diaspora communities, but the large Cape Verdean populations abroad maintain particular traditions and face particular challenges because of their Cape Verdean origin. Recent research on transnationalism has highlighted the need to differentiate between transnational identification (i.e., maintaining an identity linked to the country of origin) and transnational practices (i.e., actual activities through which migrants engage with people in their country of origin) (Snel et al. 2006; Vertovec 2004). Furthermore, transnationalism and integration should not be seen as opposites: those who have strong transnational links with the country of origin are not necessarily less integrated in the country of residence. In fact, maintaining a transnational lifestyle might require financial resources that can only be acquired through a good position in the labour market.

Two of the chapters in this book are concerned with the ways in which Cape Verdeans manage specific aspects of everyday life in the diaspora, and the significance of their Cape Verdean origins in this context. In chapter 17, Karin Wall discusses how Cape Verdean families in Portugal manage work and care for young children. The low wages, the absence of grandparents, and the income-earning pressure of the migration project itself makes it particularly difficult for Cape Verdean families to find adequate solutions for child care. In chapter 18, Huub Beijers and Cláudia de Freitas analyze how Cape Verdeans in the Netherlands manage their health problems, particularly those of a psychosocial kind. They show that although the incidence of such problems is particularly high among Cape Verdeans, they are among the groups that make the least use of available mental health services. The explanations for health and ill-health that Cape Verdeans use differ significantly from the dominant biomedical framework, and are often linked to their Christian-spiritual repertoire of health beliefs. Beijers and Freitas also show how Cape Verdeans make extensive use of their transnational networks in seeking healthcare that fulfils their expectations of good treatment. These two chapters vividly illustrate the meaning and reality of being Cape Verdean even after many decades abroad.

In Cape Verde, the increasing barriers to emigration, the maturing of the diaspora communities, and the consequent changes in transnationalism are facts of life. Nevertheless, the tradition of migration is a resilient one, as Lisa Åkesson shows in chapter 20. The history of Cape Verde is imbued with departures, and has resulted in a culture of migration that is central to the way the people view themselves and their nation. A quarter of the people in Cape Verde has a parent, spouse or child abroad, and can thus be regarded as part of a transnational family.[7] As Åkesson writes, there is a widely held notion that migration is a destiny that unites the Cape Verdean people. This is reproduced through personal experience and practices of popular culture, such as the singing of *morna* songs about departure and longing. The widespread desire to emigrate is not a rejection of Cape Verde, but, on the contrary, connected to images of the good Cape Verdean life. The people who have returned from many years of hard work abroad and now live in a house of their own, surrounded by family and friends, can be said to lead such a life. In the diaspora, many Cape Verdeans have eventually decided against returning, or have simply ended up not doing it. Among Cape Verdeans in Europe, the second generation will probably soon outnumber the first generation. It remains to be seen how they, as adults, will manage their Cape Verdean heritage and ties with Cape Verde. The experience from the U.S., with an ethnic revival among third- and fourth-generation Cape Verdean-Americans suggests that the diaspora will survive regardless of immigration policies which might make emigration less of an option for future Cape Verdeans than it has been in the past.

The Cape Verdean case and the study of transnationalism

The *New York Times* started a recent series of articles on international migration with a front-page story about Cape Verde. The rationale behind this choice was that 'the intensity of the national experience makes this barren archipelago the Galapagos of migration, a microcosm of the forces [...] remaking societies across the globe' (DeParle 2007: 1). The ubiquity of migration in Cape Verdean society, cultural heritage and family life facilitates the study of processes that are also present in other parts of the world, but often in a more subtle way. Moreover, Cape Verde represents an astounding diversity of migration experiences, as illustrated by the chapters in this book. These features of the Cape Verdean case invite reflection on the interaction of the general and the specific, which lies at the heart of research on migration and transnationalism. There are striking commonalities in migration-related processes across cultures that are also evident in Cape Verde. These include the moral obligations to remit money, the creation of diasporic spaces on the Internet, intergenerational tensions in the emigrant communities, and the investment in houses in the country of origin – construction project of both symbolic and material importance.

There are also factors that make the Cape Verdean case unique, not to say peculiar. Cape Verde does not have a regional 'neighbourhood' of countries with similar migration histories. Although the West African mainland is geographically close, it is distant in terms of society and history. Cape Verde is basically alone at sea, with its distinctive mix of African, European and Caribbean traits. This may, in some contexts, have made life easier for Cape Verdean migrants in the encounter with xenophobic destination societies. They have faced a challenge of invisibility, but they have also, in general, been less vulnerable to the sweeping ethnic stereotypes attributed to Arabs, Africans or Latinos. Portugal is an exception in this respect, since post-independence migration from Cape Verde has been part of a broader inflow of people from the former colonies in Africa, often grouped together as Africans in popular discourse.

Cape Verde departs from common assumptions in the migration literature with its loose and flexible family structure. Since the mother–child tie is generally strong throughout life while conjugal relations are often unstable, the 'nuclear family' is more of an exception than a norm in Cape Verde, not least when migration is a factor.[8] In the cases where there is a breadwinner migrant supporting a family on the islands, the migrant is often a woman.

This book draws together a range of perspectives that testify to the diversity of Cape Verde's migration experiences. There are contrasts between the different islands of origin, between the range of migration destinations in Europe, Africa and the Americas, and between the historical periods through which Cape Verdean migration has evolved. Despite the contrasts, the migrants in different parts of the diaspora and the non-migrants on the various islands relate to a shared notion of Cape Verdean identity. This book contributes to the literature on migration and transnationalism by exploring this fusion of unity and difference in a world of movement.

Notes

[1] Misunderstandings about Cape Verdean Identity in the U.S. is the topic of Claire Andrade-Watkins 2006 documentary *Some Kind of Funny Porto Rican?* See: www.spiamedia. com.

[2] The islands may well have been visited by mainland Africans, some of whom may have stayed for some time, but there was no indigenous population on Cape Verde.

[3] Calculated based on statistics from the International Monetary Fund (IMF).

[4] This is an old idea exposed in the literary journal *Claridade* (1936-67).

[5] Terezinha is written by Gregório Gonçalves. It appears on Cesária Évora's 1999 CD *Café Atlântico* (Lusafrica).

[6] Both existing emigrant populations and emigration flows are hard to determine. The census data, based on questions about persons who migrated from the household during the past five years, nevertheless suggest that the annual inflow of migrants to the seven most important destinations (Portugal, U.S., France, Netherlands, Spain, Italy and Luxembourg) amounts to less than one percent of the resident emigrant population.

[7] Calculated based on data from Instituto de Emprego e Formação Profissional (2002-2003).

[8] This is similar to Sana and Massey's (2005) argument that the tight-knit family presumed in the so-called new economics of labour migration is typical of Mexico but not of the Dominican Republic.

References

Åkesson, L. (2004) *Making a Life: Meanings of Migration in Cape Verde*, Ph.D. thesis, Gothenburg: Department of Social Anthropology, Göteborg University.

Batalha, L. (2004) *The Cape Verdean Diaspora in Portugal: Colonial Subjects in a Postcolonial World*. Lanham, MD: Lexington Books.

Bourdet, Y.; Falck, H. (2006) 'Emigrants' remittances and Dutch disease in Cape Verde'. *International Economic Journal* 20(3): 267-284.

Brubaker, R. (2005) 'The "diaspora" diaspora'. *Ethnic and Racial Studies* 28(1): 1-19.

Cardoso, K. (2004) *Diáspora: A (Décima) Primeira Ilha de Cabo Verde. A Relação entre a Emigração e a Política Externa Cabo-Verdiana*. Unpublished Master's thesis, Lisbon: Instituto Superior de Ciências do Trabalho e da Empresa.

Carling, J. (1997) 'Figuring out the Cape Verdean Diaspora'. *Cimboa* 4(2): 3-9.

Carling, J. (2002) 'Migration in the Age of Involuntary Immobility: Theoretical Reflections and Cape Verdean Experiences'. *Journal of Ethnic and Migration Studies* 28(1): 5-42.

Carling, J. (2004) 'Emigration, Return and Development in Cape Verde: The Impact of Closing Borders'. *Population, Space and Place* 10(2): 113-132.

Carreira, A. (1983) [1977] *Migrações nas Ilhas de Cabo Verde*. Praia: Instituto Caboverdiano do Livro.

DeParle, J. (2007) 'In a World on the Move, a Tiny Land Strains to Cope', *New York Times*, 24 June.

Drèze, J.; Sen, A. (1989) *Hunger and Public Action*. Oxford: Clarendon Press.

Grassi, M. (2003) *Rabidantes. Comércio Espontâneo Transnacional em Cabo Verde*. Lisbon/ Praia: Imprensa de Ciências Sociais/Spleen Edições.

Halter, M. (1993) *Between Race and Ethnicity: Cape Verdean American Immigrants, 1860-1965*. Urbana and Chicago, IL: University of Illinois Press.

Instituto de Emprego e Formação Profissional (2002-2003) Observatório de Migrações e Emprego 1/2002, 2/2002, 3/2002, 4/2002, 1/2003. Unpublished statistics. Praia: IEFP.

King, R.; Fielding, A.; Black, R. (1997) 'The International Migration Turnaround in Southern Europe', in *Southern Europe and the New Immigrations*, R. King and R. Black (eds.), Brighton: Sussex Academic Press, pp. 1-25.

Marques, M.M.; Santos, R.; Araújo, F. (2001) 'Ariadne's Thread: Cape Verdean Women in Transnational Webs'. *Global Networks* 1(3): 283-206.

Meintel, D. (2000) 'Transnationalité et renouveau de la vie festive capverdienne aux États-Unis'. *Revue Européenne des Migrations Internationales* 16(2): 77-90.

Meintel, D. (2002) 'Cape Verdean Transnationalism, Old and New'. *Anthropologica* 44: 25-42.

Patterson, K.D. (1988) 'Epidemics, Famines and the Population in the Cape Verde Islands, 1580-1800'. *International Journal of African Historical Studies* 21(2): 291-313.

República de Cabo Verde (2001) *Programa do Governo para a VI Legislatura (2001-2005)*. Praia.

Sana, M.; Massey, D.S. (2005) 'Household Composition, Family Migration, and Community Context: Migrant Remittances in Four Countries'. *Social Science Quarterly* 86(2): 509-528.

Silva, L.A. (1995) 'Le rôle des émigrés dans la transition démocratique aux Îles du Cap-Vert'. *Lusotopie*, pp. 315-322.

Smith, R.T. (1995) *The Matrifocal Family: Power, Pluralism, and Politics*. London: Routledge.

Snel, E.; Engbersen, G.; Leerkes, A. (2006) 'Transnational Involvement and Social Integration'. *Global Networks* 6(3): 285-308.

Vertovec, S. (2004) 'Migrant Transnationalism and Modes of Transformation'. *International Migration Review* 38(3): 970-1001.

Section I
Diaspora Community Portraits

Chapter 2
Cape Verdeans in the U.S.

Marilyn Halter

History of migration

For well over a century, the U.S. has hosted the largest proportion of the world-wide Cape Verdean diaspora residing in any one nation, a population that includes immigrants and their descendants, and it continues to do so to this very day (Halter 1993; Carling 2002).

Always plagued by scanty and erratic rainfall, the effects of the dry climate in the Cape Verde Islands was exacerbated by colonial mismanagement of the land, so that by the end of the 18th century, the people of the islands were experiencing severe and recurrent droughts with related famines and high mortality rates. Unable to escape overland to more favourable conditions, the young Cape Verdeans seized the chance to leave home in search of a better life as crew members aboard the U.S. whaling ships that were beginning to arrive at the archipelago's protected harbours, particularly on the island of Brava. American merchant vessels were already a familiar sight, as by this time the islands had become a regular stopover in the trade with the west coast of Africa, the Canaries, Brazil, and other parts of the world. Beginning in 1816, the U.S. established consuls on two of the islands, Santiago and São Vicente. Furthermore, in the 1840s and 1850s, in an effort to curtail the imports of slaves, the U.S. formed its African squadron, a fleet of sailing cruisers used to further the antislavery mission by boarding suspected ships and seizing their human cargoes. Some of these vessels were based in Cape Verdean ports.

Ship captains began looking to the Cape Verde Islands in order to recruit hands that could be paid lower wages than their American counterparts especially as Yankee seamen began to lose interest in whaling due to decreasing profits. At the same time, because of the impoverished conditions, the men of the archipelago were eager to obtain a berth on a whaler, no matter what the pay, as a means of escaping their constant suffering. The Cape Verdean seamen earned a reputation as disciplined and able crews. Despite their skill and desirability as whalers, however, they were routinely allotted the lowest rates in the division of profits and were frequently subject to harsh treatment in the mariners' hierarchy because of discrimination based on race and ethnicity (Busch 1985). Their exploitation at sea foreshadowed a similar prejudice that they would face once the immigrants began to settle more permanently in the U.S. (see chap. 10)

By the late 19th century, with the advent of the steamship and the decline of the whaling and sealing industries, the old sailing vessels had become obsolete and were available at a very low cost. Some of the early Cape Verdean migrants took advantage of this opportunity to buy up these old Essex-built 'Gloucester Fishermen'. They pooled their resources and converted them into cargo and passenger ships, used as packet boats that regularly plied between the Cape Verde islands and the ports of New Bedford, Massachusetts and Providence, Rhode Island. Before long, Cape Verdean-American settlers came to own a fleet of these vessels. Thus, in a situation unlike that of most immigrant groups, black or white, the Cape Verdeans came to have control over their own means of passage to the U.S. Indeed, though relatively small in numbers, these Afro-Portuguese settlers are of particular significance as the only major group of immigrants prior to the late 20th century to have voluntarily made the transatlantic voyage from Africa to the U.S.

During this same period, cheap sources of labour were being sought for the expanding textile mills, on the cranberry bogs, and in the maritime-related occupations of southern coastal New England. Increasing numbers, including women and children, were arriving to fulfil the demand, as they fled their land of continual hunger. In the first decade of the 20th century, drought conditions became even more intolerable, accelerating the economic disintegration of the islands. The people booked passage on the packet ships, with the hope of surviving by emigrating to the U.S. The movement continued steadily until the time of the National Quota Act in 1924, which curtailed the influx. After Cape Verde became an independent nation in 1975 and with the concurrent liberalisation of immigration policy in the U.S., migration picked up once again.

Demographic patterns

As a by-product of a society that is organised on the basis of a rigid binary racial structure, official U.S. government records, such as those compiled by the U.S. Census or the Bureau of Immigration, have been hopelessly deficient regarding multiracial populations such as the Cape Verdeans. Historically, entrenched standards of 'black' and 'white' formed the basis of classification when Cape Verdeans began arriving in larger numbers during the latter part of the 19th century. Routinely grouped under other broader categories, those looking phenotypically the most European or 'white' were listed as 'Portuguese' while the remainder were grouped under the labels of 'black Portuguese', 'African Portuguese', or 'Atlantic Islanders'. It should also be noted that many of the Cape Verdean newcomers of this period did not initially identify themselves as originating from the Cape Verde Islands. Rather, they were more likely to see themselves as native to their particular island of origin – as 'Bravas' and 'Fogos'. By the end of the 20th century, government record-keeping had improved somewhat. However, even with reforms in the 1980 and 1990 federal censuses, which for the first time allowed respondents to list their race and their ancestry, measures that were instituted especially to assist in accounting for mixed-race populations, many Cape Verdean Americans continued to identify themselves as Portuguese, African American or Hispanic; thus, ancestry tabulations continue to represent severe undercounts.

Nonetheless, estimates based on packet ship passenger lists from the period 1820-1924 show that in those years, approximately 40,000 immigrants arrived from Cape Verde (Halter 1993). During the half-century between implementation of the 1924 Quota Act in the U.S. and the attainment of independence, in 1975, by Cape Verde, migration went into steep decline. Even after 1965, when the U.S. passed the Hart-Cellar Act, which again opened the doors to large-scale immigration, Cape Verdeans were not able to take advantage of the liberalised policy because it was so difficult to navigate the crumbling Portuguese colonial bureaucracy or even get to a diplomatic post to make an application. All that changed considerably when Cape Verde became independent and a U.S. Embassy was established in Praia, greatly facilitating the process of obtaining a visa.

In the 30 years since the Cape Verdean archipelago became an independent nation, approximately 60,000 Cape Verdeans have emigrated to the U.S. The number of Cape Verdeans and their descendants living in the U.S. today stands at several hundred thousand, possibly even more than the total population of the home country itself. In the 2000 census, however, only 77,000 people reported having Cape Verdean ancestry. Not more that 26,600 people were registered as born in Cape Verde.

One demographic difference between past and present flows is that contemporary migrants have more diverse island origins. While the influx from the last century came almost entirely from the islands of Brava, Fogo and São Nicolau, today there are newcomers from all of the islands with increasing numbers coming especially from Santiago and São Vicente, now that it is no longer necessary to apply under Portuguese immigration policy. Still the largest population of Cape Verdeans hails from Fogo. These arrivals represent both those who are starting new chains of migration and those who relocate under family reunification allotments. Another significant demographic shift concerns the gender composition of the diaspora. Whereas men overwhelmingly predominated in the first wave, today the gender ratio is more balanced.

Settlement and integration patterns

Cape Verdeans in the U.S. are still heavily concentrated in the New England region, especially the states of Massachusetts and Rhode Island with smaller communities in Connecticut (See map, figure 2.1). The city of New Bedford, Massachusetts, remains the historic hub of the Cape Verdean American community while areas around the smaller towns of upper Cape Cod are populated by residents of Cape Verdean descent. However, the post-1975 newcomers began to migrate into the city of Boston, Massachusetts especially the Dorchester and Roxbury neighbourhoods, metropolitan areas where low-income and minority populations are concentrated. They also began settling in large numbers in the city of Brockton, which lies southeast of Boston, as well as in Pawtucket, Rhode Island. After Cape Verde's independence, employment in maritime-related work, the cranberry industry and textiles – the jobs that had brought the earlier influx to southeastern New England – had all but disappeared so that the post-1975 wave gravitated to the larger urban centres hoping to find work in manufacturing and

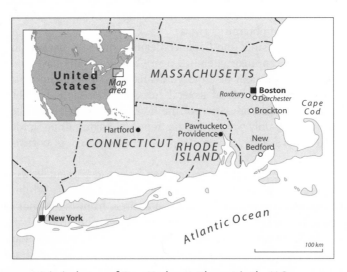

Figure 2.1.   *Principal areas of Cape Verdean settlement in the U.S.*

other industries. Immigration picked up dramatically in the 1980s when the Massachusetts economy was dynamic but has continued strong right throughout the 1990s until the present day.

As of the 2000 census tabulations, 87 per cent of Cape Verdean-Americans lived in New England. Outside this region, the state of California is home to clusters of Cape Verdeans in the Sacramento, San Francisco, and Los Angeles metropolitan areas, while Cape Verdeans from New England have in recent years been relocating to central Florida. Though highly assimilated into local cultures, a Cape Verdean presence also exists in Hawaii.

Cape Verdeans, past and present, have been pushed and pulled by similar factors. Economic necessity at home and economic opportunities abroad as well as family reunification have driven the dynamics of the diaspora. However, the desire to seek a better education plays more of a role today in motivating migration than it did a century ago. Moreover, recent Cape Verdean arrivals are already better educated – most adults enter having completed a high school education in Cape Verde – than those who came in the first wave. At that time, there were only two high schools on the entire archipelago, one in Mindelo, São Vicente, and one in Praia, Santiago. Neither island was home to the great majority of Cape Verdeans who actually immigrated to the U.S. in those days. Thus, only the children of the wealthiest would have had the opportunity to be sent to another island or abroad for a high school education. As a result, on average most of the immigrants in the past arrived with minimal schooling, usually only a fifth grade education. Women were even less likely to be educated whereas, since Independence in Cape Verde, girls are going to school right alongside the boys. With secondary schools in place on all of the islands today, unprecedented numbers of young people of both sexes complete high school. In addition, current newcomers are much more likely to speak English since English language classes are a required part of the curriculum in Cape Verdean schools beginning in ninth grade. Once in the U.S., like their Cape Verdean-American counterparts, many more are going on to college. Consequently, for the first time in the history of Cape Verdean settlement in the U.S., a significant proportion of young adults are receiving higher education.

One constant of the Cape Verdean experience has been the predominance of Catholicism as the primary religious affiliation. However, recent immigrants are more likely than in the past to become evangelical Christians, who have experienced an ongoing and unprecedented surge in Africa and in other parts of the developing world. Thus, the long-standing Cape Verdean Protestant minority is being joined today by newcomers who experience religious conversion and become active members of Pentecostal, storefront congregations.

Employment patterns between the old and new immigrants have shifted largely because of changes in the socio-economic structure of American society. Cape Verdeans of the first immigration wave filled the need for low-wage labour working the cranberry bogs and the docks, although they sometimes procured manufacturing jobs in the textile mills of industrial America. Today new immigrants are still finding employment in factories housed in old mill buildings but the nation's increasingly post-industrial, service-oriented economy often requires other kinds of technical and occupational skills. Since the 1970s, increasing numbers of Cape Verdean Americans have become successful as professionals, in management positions or in civil service jobs.

Although Cape Verdeans have not established an ethnic employment niche such as the West Indian immigrant population has done in the healthcare industry, one aspect of their occupational structure that has changed significantly in the current period has been the development of a robust Cape Verdean business sector. The first wave of Cape Verdeans was rarely self-employed and when they did operate small businesses they were in the traditional category of personal services to the co-ethnic community such as barbershops and funeral parlours. These were enterprises that white proprietors shunned because the level of intimate contact with minority customers that they required was too great. Contemporary migrants are much more entrepreneurial, in some cases, arriving with enough resources and a systematic business plan that enables them to open up shop without much difficulty. These are typically small-scale establishments, often family-owned and catering to the immigrant community. Nonetheless, their proliferation is noteworthy in the changes they have brought to the urban landscape. Cape Verdeans are establishing bona fide ethnic enclaves where residential concentration in combination with the existence of a versatile business district enables the immigrants to work and live in close proximity.

Identity matters

The Cape Verdean settlers of the first wave brought with them a distinctive cultural identity, migrating freely to New England as Portuguese colonials, thereby initially perceiving themselves in terms of ethnicity; they were Portuguese. However, they migrated to the U.S. at the turn of the last century, to a society entrenched in fixed notions of black and white and because of their mixed African and European ancestry, they were looked upon as an inferior racial group. Throughout this phase of adaptation, the strategy of being recognised as a distinctive cultural group – as Cape Verdean Americans – was met with stiff resistance as it coincided with a period in American history when racial segregation was at its height.

Issues of identity have continued to figure prominently in the Cape Verdean-American experience, but today the range of affiliations has broadened, making the permutations of multiple identifications more multifaceted and complex. Moreover, contemporary migrants are settling into a society where the cultural climate has become more accepting of cultural hybridity, making the possibility of upholding a uniquely Cape Verdean identity much more viable today. In the post-Independence period, the changing socio-political dynamics in Cape Verde as well as the demographic and cultural transformations in the U.S. continue to complicate issues of ethnic identification. Either to migrants from the earlier period or to contemporary arrivals, identity concerns have been paramount in the life stories of members of the Cape Verdean diaspora. The legacy of both colonialism and creolisation has continued to divide the population over conceptions of race, colour and ethnicity. As was the case a century ago, many Cape Verdeans today still wrestle with these fundamental questions of identity and their individual biographies reflect complex diasporic histories.

Among the long-standing American-born population, there are those, especially of lighter skin colour, who continue to refer to themselves as ethnically Portuguese while others, particularly those who live in predominantly black communities who identify themselves as black. The position of being 'in-between peoples' (Barrett and Roediger 1997) continues to manifest itself among the current wave. And despite thirty years as an independent African nation, the great majority of both immigrants and the American-born still resist the label of African. There are some exceptions, however, especially among those families who were active in the revolutionary struggle or who have lived in continental Africa enroute to migrating to the U.S.

Faced with the complexities of ethnoracial social dynamics, in a variation of what social scientists have termed situational ethnicity, individuals sometimes have used several different identity strategies simultaneously in the course of negotiating daily life (Gans 1979; Okamura 1981; Waters 1990). Such levels of internal diversity can result in intragroup segmentation that challenges the creation of a cohesive community. The deepest divisions are generational. Given that there was a 50-year hiatus in migration flows, differences related to education, culture and social levels separate those families who have been in New England for generations and those who immigrated after the independence of Cape Verde. The results of recent ethnographic research on identity structures among the Cape Verdean diaspora in Boston also underscores the division between immigrants and the American-born

(Gibau 2005; see also chapter 19 of this book). For starters, the immigrant community tends to continue to converse in Cape Verdean Kriolu while the American-born residents speak English. But the fragmentation is much more complex than that.

The first Cape Verdean immigrants tended to identify with their particular island of origin forming social organisations such as the Brava club and the São Vicente Sporting Club. An additional source of tension in the years of the protracted armed struggle for independence from Portugal was the stance the immigrant community took on the revolutionary movement. The revolutionaries did find some support for their cause among Cape Verdean Americans but there was also much resistance to the idea of Cape Verde breaking its long-standing ties with Portugal and switching to an African-identified political and cultural ideology. While island rivalries still exist today, they are far less pronounced among recent immigrants, largely because of the greater numbers among this population who have attained higher levels of education. Especially among college students, such cliquishness is minimal. Differences based on the politics of Cape Verde remain persistent, however. Loyalty to the African Party for the Independence of Cape Verde (PAICV) versus the Movement for Democracy (MpD) can shape the shared vision of the diaspora population and influence how alliances are built on this side of the Atlantic.

An equally important element of cultural fragmentation, then, is the extent to which diaspora Cape Verdeans identify as Portuguese versus as African Americans. The 1960s were watershed years for Cape Verdean Americans as the rise of Black Nationalism and its attendant emphasis on pride in one's African heritage had a transformative effect on many. Thus, the struggles for liberation from Portuguese colonialism on the continent of Africa coincided with turbulent social change on the domestic front. The process of rethinking racial identifications touched most Cape Verdean-American families in this period, often creating intergenerational rifts between the parents and grandparents, who were staunchly Portuguese, and their children, who were beginning to ally themselves with the African-American struggle, not only in political thought but also in cultural expression. More recently, the intergenerational struggles have centred, instead, on what is viewed as an erosion of traditional family controls. The past decade has witnessed a significant upsurge in drug and gang-related violence among Cape Verdean youth, especially in the cities of Boston and Brockton, which is attributed to this generation's lack of respect for its elders and the community itself.

Finally, maintaining a strong transnational, dual identity has become much more feasible for the Cape Verdean diaspora in recent years. The government of Cape Verde now defines a Cape Verdean as someone born on the islands or having a parent or grandparent born there. Citizens in the diaspora community can vote in Cape Verdean national elections and have representation in the National Assembly. Indeed, Cape Verdean presidential candidates routinely include southern New England on their campaign trails. The vast majority of people in Cape Verde have relatives abroad, and remittances from emigrants continue to be enormously important to the islands' economy.

Intergroup relations

During the last two decades, the demography of southern New England, still the overwhelming destination of the recent Cape Verdean diaspora, has been dramatically transformed from communities comprised primarily of people of European descent to a much more diverse and multiracial social landscape. Whereas the first Cape Verdeans were accompanied primarily by Azorean immigrants to southern New England, today the contemporary flow includes migrants from several other African nations as well as a variegated Caribbean and Latino diaspora that includes a large and increasing Brazilian population.

During the initial settlement, although the Cape Verdeans sought recognition as Portuguese-Americans, white society, including the other Portuguese immigrants in the region, excluded them from their social and religious associations. At the same time, Cape Verdeans chose not to identify with the local African-American population (Halter 1993). Today, the relationship between Cape Verdeans, Azoreans and mainland Portuguese remains uneasy. Furthermore, despite some mutual residential aggregation, Cape Verdeans still resist identification with African-Americans as well as foreign-born populations of African descent such as those in the Haitian or Dominican communities whose cultural backgrounds and native languages differ from the Cape Verdean heritage; such circumstances have not been conducive to building alliances. And while increasing numbers of immigrants from West Africa, especially Liberians, are settling in New England, Cape Verdeans do not associate with these groups either. Not surprisingly, given their mutual histories of Portuguese colonialism, the only other African population with whom Cape Verdeans interact is the sprinkling of Angolans in the region.

Although not a case of full-blown integration, on the level of other ethnic groups in New England, Cape Verdeans are beginning to form connections with the burgeoning Brazilian population, particularly in the area of cultural exchange. One basis of affinity has grown out of the shared legacy of Portuguese colonial rule and a common resentment of the power and control that the Portuguese government has wielded over them in the past. Another commonality is in religious participation, not only because of the overarching influence of the Catholic Church, but also because many Brazilians worship at the same new evangelical congregations that Cape Verdeans belong to and where Portuguese-speaking pastors conduct services. There are also cases of collaboration in business start-ups, as well.

In the arena of musical performance, the contemporary cachet of Cape Verdean and Afro-Portuguese rhythms and sounds, as well as the intersecting cultural forms represented by both the world music and hip-hop genres, has brought Brazilians and Cape Verdeans together. Finally, participation in sports, especially soccer, has facilitated closer intergroup relations. For instance, Brockton supports four soccer teams made up primarily of Cape Verdean players, but also Brazilians and Angolans, while interleague play between Cape Verdean and Brazilian teams naturally attract fans from both groups.

The ethnic revival

American society has certainly changed in many ways over the decades between the arrival of the first wave of Cape Verdean immigrants and the contemporary influx, particularly with regard to the incorporation of ethnoracial populations. One of the most striking contrasts concerns attitudes toward ethnic differences and the vision of what it means to be an American. The Cape Verdean newcomers a century ago arrived at a time when the foreign-born were expected to suppress their cultural distinctions and shed their old world customs, either through conformity to the Anglo-Saxon way of life, or by fusing and melding such differences into a unified American character.

By the mid-1970s, after decades in which assimilation was the leading model for the incorporation of diverse populations, the notion of cultural pluralism, advocating the preservation of the immigrant's heritage, emerged to take its place as the reigning paradigm. The ethnic revival and the emphasis on cultural pluralism were just beginning to take hold when Cape Verdeans began to arrive again in larger numbers in the wake of independence at home and a more liberal immigration policy in the U.S. Thus, post-1975 newcomers have been migrating in an age of multiculturalism where claims of a hyphenated identity have become the norm or even fashionable. Furthermore, the influx of large numbers of nonwhite immigrants from many parts of the globe over the past two decades combined with the increase in rates of mixed-race marriages and reproduction have transformed the U.S. from a largely black and white world into a kaleidoscopic ethnoracial landscape where the boundaries between groups are becoming less and less sharp.

Some call it the browning of America – a canvas on which Cape Verdean brush strokes much more readily blend in.

In this current environment of ethnic pride and reclamation of roots as well as greater acceptance of multiracial identities, the more recently immigrated Cape Verdeans have had less difficulty asserting their cultural distinctiveness than those who settled in the U.S. in the early 1900s, when notions of racial identity were rigidly cast in black and white.

At the local, regional and national levels, Cape Verdean-Americans are proudly calling attention to their cultural heritage. Like many other third-and fourth-generation immigrants who have lost their native language skills, American-born Cape Verdeans are eagerly signing up for Kriolu language classes. On New England college campuses, Cape Verdean student groups have organised conferences, fundraisers and social events to celebrate their ancestry and promote greater awareness of Cape Verdean history. Usually at least one program on the school calendar pays tribute to the legacy of Amílcar Cabral as young Cape Verdeans today, whether new immigrants or American-born, are likely to be familiar with the monumental role that Cabral played in the history of Cape Verdean independence.

Indeed, the most public displays of the political culture of recent African immigrant groups are Independence Day festivities that mark the overthrow of colonialism in their respective home countries. Thus, the most widely celebrated holiday among Cape Verdeans in the U.S. occurs on 5 July, Cape Verdean Independence Day, which commemorates the successful ousting of Portuguese colonial rule in 1975. Parades, picnics, pageants and cultural performances are held in Cape Verdean-American communities throughout the country. The occasion provides an opportunity to acknowledge the historic significance of the event but, increasingly, also to highlight and legitimise Cape Verdean culture to the broader community.

A century before the notion of the browning of America gained popularity, as a way of describing the increasingly mixed complexion of the U.S. during the past three decades as changes in immigration policy transformed the nation from a largely black and white society to a multiracial one, the Cape Verdean diaspora was testing the waters of American pluralism. Always in flux, their mixed African and Portuguese heritage continues to defy rigid social classification, challenging notions of race, colour, ethnicity and identity.

References

Barrett, J.; Roediger, D. (1997) 'Inbetween Peoples: Race, Nationality and the "New Immigrant" Working Class'. *Journal of American Ethnic History* 16(3): 3-44.

Busch, B. C. (1985) 'Cape Verdeans in the American Whaling and Sealing Industry, 1850-1900'. *American Neptune* 45: 104-16.

Carling, J. (2002) 'Migration in the Age of Involuntary Immobility: Theoretical Reflections and Cape Verdean Experiences'. *Journal of Ethnic and Migration Studies* 28(1): 5-21.

Gans, H. (1979) 'Symbolic Ethnicity: The Future of Ethnic Groups and Cultures in America'. *Ethnic and Racial Studies* 2 (1): 1-20.

Gibau, G. Sánchez (2005) 'Contested Identities: Narratives of Race and Ethnicity in the Cape Verdean Diaspora'. *Identities: Global Studies in Culture and Power* 12(3): 405-438.

Halter, M. (1993) *Between Race and Ethnicity: Cape Verdean American Immigrants, 1865-1960.* Urbana: University of Illinois Press.

Okamura, J. (1981) 'Situational Ethnicity'. *Ethnic and Racial Studies* 4(4): 452-65.

Waters, M. (1990) *Ethnic Options: Choosing Identities in America.* Berkeley and Los Angeles: University of California Press.

Chapter 3
Cape Verdeans in Argentina

Marta Maffia

Immigration history

According to oral testimonies, the first Cape Verdeans arrived in Argentina towards the end of the 19th century, in connection with the South Atlantic whaling industry. During the first half of the 20th century, Cape Verdeans arrived as passengers, crew members or stowaways on ships. Migration increased in the 1920s, coinciding with one of the most serious famines in Cape Verde's history (Carreira 1977). The migrants came in small groups or individually, mostly from the islands of São Vicente, Santo Antão and São Nicolau, and, to a lesser extent, from Fogo and Brava.

Documentary sources on Cape Verdean migration to Argentina are practically non-existent. It is therefore necessary to depend on oral sources. Historical statistics are also unavailable because Cape Verdeans either immigrated with Portuguese passports or entered illegally and were not registered.

Most of the current Cape Verdean community leaders in Argentina arrived between the mid-1940s and the 1960s, or are children of migrants who came during this period. In the 1960s, Cape Verdean emigration to Argentina declined at the same time as flows to Portugal and other European countries increased. In 1979, an estimation of the size of the Cape Verdean population was carried out with the help of the honorary consul at the time, Joaquim dos Santos, and various community members (Lahitte and Maffia 1981). The study concluded that there were approximately 4,000 Cape Verdean natives and descendants in Argentina.

Most of the Cape Verdean migrants settled in maritime, industrial environments near the Mouth of the Río de la Plata. The most important locations were Ensenada, the neighbourhoods of Dock Sud, La Boca, and the city of Avellaneda. Here they found work linked to the shipping industry, the navy, or in the area's factories and shipyards. In terms of regional origin, the community in Ensenada was dominated by migrants from Santo Antão, while São Vicenteans were particularly numerous in Dock Sud.

Within the ethnic neighbourhoods, social networks developed among Cape Verdeans. These were based first on kinship and second on shared nationality. New migrants from Cape Verde were accommodated by these networks, charged with sheltering them, finding employment or finding a wife. The networks represented a far more effective solidarity than the one institutionalised in the Portuguese Consulate (Maffia 1986). They were also the origins of the associations which mirrored the collective undertakings by the larger immigrant groups, such as the Spanish and Italians.

The birth of Cape Verdean associations

The first Cape Verdean association, the Asociación Caboverdeana de Cultura y Deportes (Cape Verdean Culture and Sports Association), was founded in Ensenada in 1927. It still exists, with 182 members, including several who are not of Cape Verdean origin. Five years later the Sociedad Caboverdeana de Socorros Mutuos de Dock Sud (Cape Verdean Society of Mutual Help, Dock Sud) was founded. The association was founded after one of the Cape Verdean migrants died. Like the majority of Cape Verdeans, he was single and without family in Argentina. The other migrants collected money for a proper burial so that his body would not be taken away by the Municipality to be incinerated. This event inspired the creation of an association for mutual help and self-protection (Correa 2000).

The creation of the first Cape Verdean associations between 1927 and 1932 must be understood in light of the world-wide economic crisis at the time, with its high levels of unemployment. The principal needs they covered were related first and foremost to employment, shelter, medical and funeral services and, secondly, to recreation.

The associations were open to all Cape Verdeans, irrespective of island or place of origin. This contrasted with the situation in the U.S., Portugal and the Netherlands, where the much greater Cape Verdean presence facilitated a broad diversity of associations.

Identity and invisibility

Compared to some Cape Verdean communities in the U.S., Portugal, and elsewhere, the Cape Verdean population in Argentina has not formed closed, distinct groups. They speak perfect Spanish and they have not taught Kriolu to their children – who, for the most part, understand it but do not speak it. They do not eat Cape Verdean food on a regular basis – only on festive occasions – and they have not maintained traditional life cycle rituals, such as *guarda cabeça* or wedding and funeral rites. The majority of Argentineans of Cape Verdean origin has married outside the group, and the descendants of Cape Verdean migrants know little or nothing about their family's place of origin. As will be shown below, however, this has changed in recent years.

Many people of Cape Verdean origin do not interact much with other Cape Verdeans, preferring people of mixed ancestry, especially Italian or Spanish. There are several reasons why people choose not to associate with the Cape Verdean community. For some, their memory of Cape Verde is so traumatic that they wish to do away with any element that may trigger it. Others deny their African, Black, Cape Verdean origin, and regard themselves as Portuguese. Finally there are those who, having advanced in socio-economic terms, do not wish any contact with those in lower positions.

Surveys of the Cape Verdean population in 1979 and 1998 have shown a great movement away from the traditional places of settlement (Lahitte and Maffia 1981; Maffia 2003). More than half of the population studied had moved away from the industrial port Ensenada to the nearby city of La Plata, or from the working-class neighbourhoods of La Boca and Dock Sud, which are surrounded by heavy industry, to other areas in the Greater Buenos Aires area. The reasons given were the desire to improve their socio-economic situation and to give their children a better education. A young second-generation woman in an interview noted:

> What I have always heard and continue to hear is that Dock Sud [laughter] is an infectious focus and that the people who could, left the place... they did not want to be identified with that neighbourhood. [...] The Dock is drugs, alcohol, bad environment; the Dock was always looked down upon; those who could leave, left.

Although some Cape Verdeans within the old generation of immigrants continue to live in the ethnic neighbourhoods, their Argentinean-born children and grandchildren have denied their traditional Cape Verdean values and have 'Argentinized' themselves. In many cases, this leads to intergenerational conflicts accompanied by profoundly ambivalent feelings regarding ethnic identities.

Cape Verdean immigration and the Argentinean state

Cape Verdean migration to Argentina took place in the context of powerful state initiatives to 'nationalise' immigrants, first and foremost through the school system and mandatory military service (Devoto 2003). As early as 1902 and 1910, legislation that allowed for the expulsion or rejection of socially undesirable immigrants was introduced. This was partly a result of the political elite's concern about urban labour movements led by foreigners (Donghi 1976). Even in the context of assimilationist policies, many groups of immigrants, including Italians, Poles, Lithuanians, Germans, Danes and Jews, had ethnic schools where the language and culture of their country of origin was taught. Cape Verdeans not only did not have such institutions, but also did not transmit their language and culture to their descendants within their own homes.

The invisibility of Cape Verdeans is also related to the fact that they came from a Portuguese colonial regime that sought to understate Cape Verde's cultural links with mainland Africa, and that they entered an Argentinean society in which the presence of Blacks was denied in practice and discourse. This is reflected in the words of an elderly informant who came to Argentina in the 1920s: 'The Cape Verdean has a European character, a fully Portuguese mind, a white mind, a white people's mind, a distinct mind, but, of course, they have mixed too much'. Many Cape Verdeans in Argentina tried to ascribe themselves to the Portuguese segment of the population, but few were accepted in the Portuguese social environment. In practice, this was limited to the elite group whose parents had excellent relations with the colonisers in Cape Verde. In their interactions with European immigrants outside the ethnic neighbourhoods, however, many Cape Verdeans said they were Portuguese and were treated as Portuguese.

The Cape Verdeans' adaptive strategies as 'Cape Verdean Portuguese' or 'Cape Verdean Argentine' led to the group's invisibility at an early stage. The strategies were adopted with the conscious or unconscious objective of accomplishing integration and social reproduction with the least possible conflict, although with little social mobility. It is important to remember that they arrived clandestinely, remained in the margins of the social structure without a recognised presence, and were essentially invisible to the state. At the same time, any collective political participation through the association was perceived negatively and could undermine their position vis-à-vis the state and society at large. Not only was there a fear of 'subversive ideologies', but strong ties between the military government in Argentina and the Salazar regime in Portugal meant that any criticism of Salazar or of Portugal entailed a risk of persecution. On many occasions, Cape Verdean associations became the targets of investigation. A regional PAIGC committee was established in Buenos Aires in 1964, but pro-independence activity was fervently opposed by Cape Verdeans who were against political participation or who favoured maintaining Portuguese rule. The regional committee was led by Joaquim José dos Santos, who later served as Cape Verde's honorary consul in Argentina from 1976 to 1991.

Identity politics and ethnic revival

The dilution of Cape Verdean identity and community is currently being reversed by some groups of young people of the second and third generations. They have been rethinking invisibility in terms of discrimination and of political struggle in an effort to present claims together with other minorities. They see themselves as Argentineans of African descent and seek to reclaim their origins and diaspora affiliations. Some Cape Verdean activists are now associated with Afro-Argentinean organisations and intellectuals and have links with Black communities in the U.S. (Correa 2000). Some young people adopt a Cape Verdean/African identity focused on being Black, and expressed through material elements such as African hairstyles and clothes, and through an emphasis on African heritage and pan-African politics. Descendants of Cape Verdeans have also drawn upon memories that are not their own, memories which legitimise them as Cape Verdeans, recovering and reinventing traditions.

Cape Verdeans have played an important role in the Afro-Argentinean movement. In 1995, two Cape Verdean Argentineans founded Casa de África in Buenos Aires with the objective of improving communication between Argentine authorities and different African peoples. The movement gained impetus after the World Conference Against Racism in Durban, in 2001. One important issue has been the adaptation of future population censuses to give a better picture of the Argentinean population of African descent.

The Cape Verdean associations in Ensenada and Dock Sud organise cultural events, with the participation of groups of dancers, choirs, musicians, art exhibitions, craft pieces and videos made by descendants of Cape Verdeans on themes related to the islands. The associations have also established their own radio broadcasts in Avellaneda and Ensenada.

Transnational ties with Cape Verde

To many first-generation immigrants, Cape Verde assumes the ambiguous character of ungrateful and beloved homeland. This is strongly manifested in the literature, accounts and letters of Cape Verdeans in Argentina. As one informant, an elderly woman, put it 'I remember beautiful things in my life, very beautiful things... at the same time, I remember Cape Verde as a sad place, sadness due to lack of work. If there was work nobody would have left'.

First-generation migrants frequently sent letters and goods to Cape Verde, and occasionally small amounts of remittances. When relatives in Cape Verde found an opportunity, they sent traditional Cape Verdean products such as *grogue, ponche,* coconut jam, goat cheese or *kuskus.* While such exchanges have existed ever since the arrival of the first Cape Verdean migrants, transnational links gained pace in the 1990s.

Argentina's relations with Africa improved greatly after the end of the military dictatorship in 1983. Four years later, the first Cape Verdean state visit to Argentina took place, led by President Aristides Pereira. Political contacts increased throughout the 1990s. In 2003, the essay contest *Olhares de Descendências* organised by the Instituto das Comunidades, in Cape Verde, was won by the Argentinean granddaughter of immigrants from Cape Verde (Mateo 2003).

The establishment of direct flights between Argentina and Cape Verde in 1989 was an important impetus to Cape Verdean-Argentinean relations. The Russian national airline Aeroflot used Sal as a convenient refuelling stop on flights from Moscow to Buenos Aires and sold tickets from Argentina to Cape Verde at very low prices. This made it possible for many Cape Verdeans and their descendants to travel to the islands. In the 1990s, telephone communications also improved as a result of privatisation in both Argentina and Cape Verde.

Coupled with the increased possibilities for travel and communication, increasing unemployment in Argentina, and the encouraging news about developments in Cape Verde, made many young Cape Verdean descendants who did not even know their ancestors' homeland consider the possibility of 'returning' in search of new opportunities. Those who went found it difficult to integrate into the labour market, however, and virtually all of them eventually returned to Argentina.

After the turn of the millennium, the possibilities for travel and communication deteriorated with the deepening economic crisis in Argentina. Aeroflot withdrew in late 1998 and the price of telephone calls rose as a result of the currency devaluation in 2002. Meanwhile, the Internet remains the most accessible communication alternative, not only with Cape Verde, but also with other parts of the diaspora.

References

Carreira, A. (1977) *Migracões nas Ilhas de Cabo Verde.* Lisbon: Universidade Nova de Lisboa.
Correa, N. (2000) *Afroargentinos y Caboverdeanos. Las Luchas Identitarias Contra la Invisibilidad de la Negritud en la Argentina.* Tesis de Maestría, Universidad Nacional de Misiones.

Devoto, F. (2003) *Historia de la Inmigración en Argentina*. Buenos Aires: Editorial Sudamericana.

Donghi, T.H. (1976) 'Para Qué la Inmigración? Ideología y Política Inmigratoria y Aceleración del Proceso Modernizador: El Caso Argentino', in *Jahrbuch für Geschichte von Staat, Wirtschaft und Gesellschaft Lateinamerikas*, Colonia: Bohlau Verlag, pp. 437-489.

Lahitte, H.; Maffia, M. (1981) 'Presentación Estadística y Corroboración del Cálculo por el Tratamiento Analítico Descriptivo, en un Grupo Caboverdeano'. *Publicaciones Larda* 10: 1-23.

Maffia, M. (1986) 'La Inmigración Caboverdeana Hacia la Argentina. Análisis de Una Alternativa'. *Trabalhos de Antropología e Etnología* 25: 101-207.

Maffia, M. (2003) 'Estrategias de Inserción de Inmigrantes Caboverdeanos. Estudio de Casos', in *Cambios y Perspectivas en los Patrones Migratorios Internacionales: Su Impacto en América Latina Con Especial Referencia al Cono Sur*, E. Oteiza (ed.), Buenos Aires: EUDEBA.

Mateo, L.M. (2003) 'Os Caçadores de Heranças: Uma aproximação às Descendências Caboverdianas na Argentina, "Olhares de Descendências"'. Organized by Instituto das Comunidades do Ministério dos Negócios Estrangeiros, Cooperação e Comunidades de Cabo Verde. Unpublished.

Chapter 4
Cape Verdeans in São Tomé and Príncipe

Augusto Nascimento

Introduction

The Cape Verdeans were brought to São Tomé and Príncipe to work on the cacao plantations. In the aftermath of the Second World War there was an increase in the prices of colonial products, which forced plantation owners and local authorities to try to obtain large numbers of workers. At the same time, a succession of droughts caused thousands of deaths in Cape Verde. Though some cases of conscription still occurred, this was hardly necessary, since the harsh conditions pushed Cape Verdeans to accept work contracts in any place outside of the islands.

The demand for workers in the *roças* (plantations) was a factor that contributed to the absence of questions regarding the indigenisation being forced upon the Cape Verdean labour force.

There were some clashes between the Cape Verdean workers and the plantation owners. Slogans about the supremacy of the white 'race' probably fuelled the behaviour of the European employees and plantation owners. They also considered the fact that workers were constantly hungry and exhausted to be to their advantage. Despite being subdued by local conditions, the Cape Verdeans were very aware of the indignities imposed upon them by the plantation owners. Their willingness to resolve personal conflicts through violence was certainly due to the disrespect suffered at the hands of the plantation owners and foremen who were more accustomed to dealing with Angolans and Mozambicans, who were allegedly much easier to boss around.

At the end of the 1940s, the plantation owners still questioned the value of the Cape Verdeans as a workforce. But in April 1950, the recruitment of Angolans ceased, and restrictions would soon apply in Mozambique as well. This meant that the need for Cape Verdeans in São Tomé remained.

In the 1940s, recruitment sometimes took the form of conscription, but this was generally unnecessary since it came at a high political price. The usual lures associated with migrating played a part in attracting Cape Verdeans to São Tomé and Príncipe. Whereas many Cape Verdeans will say they never had a choice, others will say that they

were not conscripted. This would make them feel, more than anything
else, that they existed among the bottom rungs of society.

From indigenisation to wage-earning

The status of Cape Verdeans was lowered, both as a result of the recruitment practices (*arrebanhamento*) and of having to share their situation with people from mainland Africa (the *gentios*).

In 1947, the Cape Verde colonial authorities declared that the Indigenous People Statute and the Indigenous Regime were no longer applicable to Cape Verdeans. However, the colonial political framework
and the economic and social configuration of the equatorial islands created a wide berth between the law and the everyday forced indigenisation they were subjected to. Demands were made of them that were altogether incompatible with their degree of 'civilisation'.

Even in a colonial context, the social hierarchy based on racial classification was utterly called into question by the normal course of affairs.
For instance, one of the paradoxes of indigenisation was the fact that
some Cape Verdeans were actually asked to write letters for the white
illiterate employees.

Throughout the 1950s, faced with the perspective of no other source
of workers but from Cape Verde, some plantation owners started to
change their ways. Work and life conditions became recognisably better
in the following decade (see Meintel 1984:67). The freedom of movement for workers and families that came with this development eased
their plight. They managed to preserve some of their habits, and maintain a sense of community both in the *roças* (Eyzaguirre 1986: 268-9)
and in the whole of society in São Tomé.

Although conditions improved – small and occasional monetary
compensations, bonuses for renewal of contracts and temporary con-
cessions of small agricultural plots were also included – the offer of a
contract for the *roças* was quickly becoming less attractive. Furthermore, because of the broader possibilities of the labour market, Cape
Verdeans stopped looking for work in the *roças*. The last year for which
there is a record of Cape Verdeans arriving in São Tomé is 1970.

The instrumental use of Cape Verdeans

From the 1940s onward, the evolution of international relations and its
implications for the colonial regime led to the use of Cape Verdeans in
a variety of ways.

In the 1940s, many Cape Verdean women were put to work in the *ro-ças*. They were employed to even out the gender ratio and to satisfy the sexual demands that prevailed in the plantations. Though conditioned by the facts of life in the *roças*, some of them took the opportunity to take matters pertaining to their lives into their own hands, since they worked side by side with the men (Nascimento 2003: 227 ff.).

Another way Cape Verdeans were used concerned the establishment of a labour market through the creation of settlements. Governor Gorgulho had a scheme to favour the settlement by whole families of Cape Verdeans, a solution that he saw as cheaper in political terms than indentureship. They would not be allowed to produce anything that could be exported and would only deal in the items that were needed to supply the population of the city (Gorgulho 1948: 49-50). The land they received would not be enough to guarantee their subsistence, so they became dependent on the work they could find in the *roças*. But the owners rejected the notion of Cape Verdean settlement and continued to push for recruitment on the islands. The plans drawn up in the 1950s to settle the Cape Verdeans failed because the government could not obtain land from the plantation owners (cf. Eyzaguirre 1986: 271) and because São Tomé and Príncipe lost its attraction when compared to other destinations already available to Cape Verdean migrants. Certain abandoned areas in the *roças* were used for agricultural work and some Cape Verdeans became small suppliers to the urban markets, becoming somewhat locally integrated (Eyzaguirre 1986: 269). None of these events happened against the wishes of the colonial government or the hegemony of the plantation owners.

The presence of Cape Verdeans produced no economic and social changes, namely in what concerned land ownership. And this would influence what happened after the independence.

The course of prejudice

In a society marked by social segmentation, and from which a labour market was absent, the different groups – Europeans, natives, Cape Verdeans and other indentured workers from Angola and Mozambique – did not seem to have the drive to compete. Nonetheless, that was not enough to prevent the growth of reciprocal prejudices between natives and Cape Verdeans. These can be traced to the instrumental use of Cape Verdeans in the colonial project. The clear racial hierarchy on which colonial ideology was based produced constant friction between the groups.

Afraid of losing this intermediate social position the natives had good cause to resent the fact that Cape Verdeans sided with the Europeans in the 1953 massacre (Santo 2003: 345-6; see also Seibert 1996, 2002, 2006).

The natives may also have thought that if the Cape Verdeans started to settle, the redistribution of lands would, in the end, work to their disadvantage. Thus, the prejudices against Cape Verdeans may have been linked to the struggle for possession of the land. Though Cape Verdeans seemed tailored to work it, the land for the natives was politically priceless.

Among the Cape Verdeans there was a certain feeling of superiority towards the natives. They felt closer to Europeans namely because of crossbreeding and of a reputation for being hard workers (Eyzaguirre 1986: 312-3), a thought that could have been reinforced by the political changes in the final years of the colonial period, and by the efforts of the natives to set themselves apart from the people who worked as servants in the plantations.

There was no contribution by Cape Verdeans to the nationalist struggle in São Tomé and Príncipe. In fact, the impoverished Cape Verdeans who migrated to São Tomé were not generally politically conscious. Some were clearly aware of the injustices suffered, but were afraid to complain and lose their return trip to Cape Verde.

The community in post-independence São Tomé and Príncipe

In 1970, the population of São Tomé and Príncipe was 73,631 people. In 1975, there were some 15,500 Cape Verdeans in the archipelago, including 6,500 children (Eyzaguirre 1986: 343). Presumably, family bonds, a lifetime devoted to work in the roças and the nature of social relations in the final years of colonial power contributed to their stay.

When independence arrived, Cape Verdeans became victims of the same resentment they showed the white minority; they were seen in restricted circles as foreigners and not trustworthy.

Amidst the joy of independence, the Cape Verdeans were encouraged to side with the newly formed government. They were a necessary workforce that could keep the plantations running. Under the cover of African fraternity, the relative social positions were maintained. Local natives took the place of Europeans in the newly state-run roças. This solution prevailed over the division of the land into small plots, a step that would have accommodated the dreams of many Cape Verdeans and contributed to the economic development of the islands.

Statistically, the community became less important. In 1981, they comprised just 5 per cent of a total population of 97,000 people (Hodges and Hewitt 1988: 63). Their numbers decreased in percentage, except maybe in Príncipe where they may have increased.

Socially, the community was somewhat diluted through social integration and exogamy.

Economically, their situation became worse. The bankruptcy of the state-owned *roças*, where they worked as paid labourers, destroyed their means of subsistence, and impoverishment and extreme marginality struck the community.

After political liberalisation in the beginning of the 1990s, they lost the right to vote. Afraid of the political effect of their affectionate identity with the MLSTP (Movement for the Liberation of São Tomé and Príncipe), the winners of the first democratic elections denied the right to vote to Cape Verdeans, to other ex-servants of the *roças* and their non-citizen descendants.

This gratitude that the Cape Verdean ex-servants showed towards the MLSTP is somewhat paradoxical, since it was the economic policy of this party that brought about their impoverishment and affected the rest of the population as well. The sense of fraternity between the leaders of the two countries must not be underestimated. For many years, loyalty to the MLSTP was the duty of any Cape Verdean.

Social and political change

Today, São Tomé authorities will deny any accusation of segregation against the Cape Verdeans. They will point out, for instance, that the community is so well integrated that it is hard, if not impossible, to distinguish the Cape Verdeans from the rest of the population. They will say that, as any national from one of the former Portuguese colonies in Africa, they have full citizenship.

Nonetheless, abject poverty affects the Cape Verdeans and other former servants and their descendants. Impoverished and aged, they have little political leverage, which becomes even less when they try to use their ethnicity. As victims of social segregation and of extreme poverty, they seem altogether incapable of joining forces and creating any sort of representation for themselves. Some cultural manifestations, such as *tchabeta*, survive, performed by more or less informal groups and a sense of unity with the motherland. These associations show no visible activity and, until recently, their links with the diaspora were nonexistent.

The affirmation of the Cape Verdean identity or citizenship comes with the request for a return to the motherland – a wish that grows less insistent as the population ages. Their identity is manifested in the pride they have for their motherland, Cape Verde.

In the meantime, the *roças* were ruined by sheer lack of concern. This constitutes one more reason why many Cape Verdeans morally and politically condemn the natives and their behaviour after the independence. Because they have no economic power and no leadership, the Cape Verdeans are not in a position to voice a political stance and reap social benefits from it. While the elders resist the idea of giving up their Cape Verdean identity, the younger generation fits in with the local society and assumes a *de facto* native condition. This attitude is encouraged by the Cape Verdean authorities, but it does not mean that Cape Verdean identity can not be resuscitated at any given moment.

In São Tomé and Príncipe, many Cape Verdeans have no other asset than their passport, a document they will never use. They keep and treasure it so they can proclaim their nationality. Aged, and encountering terrible conditions, most of them will never again see their motherland.

References

Carreira, A. (1983 [1977]) *Migrações nas Ilhas de Cabo Verde*. Praia: Instituto Cabo-verdeano do Livro.

Eyzaguirre, P. (1986) *Small Farmers and Estates in São Tomé, West Africa*. Ph.D. dissertation, Yale University.

Gorgulho, C. de S. (1946) *Relatório Anual. Ano 1945*. São Tomé: Imprensa Nacional de São Tomé.

Gorgulho, C. de S. (1948) *Relatório do Governo da Província de São Tomé e Príncipe Respeitante aos Anos de 1946 a 1947*. São Tomé: Imprensa Nacional de São Tomé.

Hodges, T.; Newitt, M. (1988) *São Tomé and Príncipe: From Plantation Colony to Microstate*. London: Westview Press.

Meintel, D. (1984) *Race, Culture, and Portuguese Colonialism in Cabo Verde*. Syracuse, NY: Syracuse University.

Nascimento, A. (2002) *Poderes e Quotidiano nas Roças de São Tomé e Príncipe: De Finais de Oitocentos a Meados de Oitocentos*. São Tomé: SPI.

Nascimento, A. (2003) *O Sul da Diáspora: Cabo-verdianos em Plantações de São Tomé e Príncipe e Moçambique*. Praia: Presidência da República de Cabo Verde.

Santo, C.E. (2003) *A Guerra da Trindade*. s. l., Cooperação.

Seibert, G. (1996) 'São Tomé: O Massacre de Fevereiro de 1953'. *História* 19: 14-27.

Seibert, G. (2002) 'The February 1953 Massacre in São Tomé: Crack in the Salazarist Image of Multiracial Harmony and Impetus for Nationalist Demands for Independence.' *Portuguese Studies Review* 10(2): 52-77.

Seibert, G. (2006 [1999]) *Comrades, Clients and Cousins: Colonialism, Socialism and Democratization in São Tomé and Príncipe*. Leiden: Brill Academic Publishers (2nd ed., revised).

Tenreiro, F. (1961) *A Ilha de São Tomé*. Lisbon: Junta de Investigações do Ultramar.

Chapter 5
Cape Verdeans in Portugal

Luís Batalha

The 'community'

Despite being often referred to as a single, large 'community' (e.g., França 1992; Gomes 1999), Cape Verdeans in Portugal are scattered across several different, small communities, which exist mostly at the local level of the neighbourhood. This does not mean, however, that Cape Verdeans in Portugal do not share some features of a more general and global identity that they mutually understand as 'Cape Verdean'.

In fact, Cape Verdeans in Portugal (as elsewhere) are divided by race, ethnicity and education, factors which combine to construct their social position both within Portuguese society and among themselves. Education plays the most important role in dividing them; it operates in an objective way and is also subjectively recognised as a differentiating factor. Race and ethnicity work in more subtle ways and are not strictly enforced within Portuguese society at large; they are meaningful from within the minds of the actors more than from the outside as something imposed by strict legal or social rules.

For the sake of sociological simplification, I shall consider Cape Verdeans as divided between two different social worlds: the world of the relatively highly educated, whom I have referred to elsewhere as the 'elite' Cape Verdeans; and the world of labour migrants, who have little or no formal education (Batalha 2004a, 2004b). The highly educated belong to the middle- and upper-middle classes within Portuguese society. Most were born and bred during the last decades of colonialism and maintained their Portuguese citizenship when Cape Verde became an independent nation, in 1975. A few also retained a sense of Portuguese nationality, acquired by education and enculturation; this allowed them to incorporate their Cape Verdean identity as part of the mosaic of Portuguese colonial identities – being Cape Verdean as an expression of *portugalidade* (Portuguese-ness). Indeed, these elites see themselves both as Cape Verdean and as Portuguese. Some of these educated Cape Verdeans left their homeland at an early age to study in the schools and universities of the metropolis, and they never returned to Cape Verde. Education, even if only of a high school level, allowed them to achieve positions in the ranks of the colonial administration throughout the Portuguese empire – ironically, except in Cape Verde, where opportunities were few and far between. Thus, in the last decades of the colonial regime, most educated Cape Verdean elites went to work for the colonial administration in the other major Portuguese colonies in Africa – Guinea-Bissau, Angola, São Tomé and Príncipe, and Mozambique; only a few were living in Portugal at the time of decolonisation.

The other social world of Cape Verdean immigrants in Portugal is that of Cape Verdeans who have been arriving in Portugal as labour migrants since the 1960s. Many were illiterate; others had only attended elementary school, sometimes not even completing these first four years.

Cape Verdean migration to Portugal started in the mid-1960s and intensified throughout the 1970s and 1980s. In the beginning, it was mostly unskilled men coming from rural communities, sometimes with an intermediate stay in a local town only until they accumulated the financial means and necessary contacts to emigrate. The majority of these labour migrants came from the island of Santiago.

During the 1960s and early 1970s, a significant part of the Portuguese unskilled labour force was being drained to the highly industrialised European countries, particularly France, Germany and Luxembourg (Franco 1971; Rocha-Trindade 1975, 1979; Porto 1977; Serrão 1977; Poinard 1979). At the same time, the Portuguese economy was growing and was beginning to experience a shortage of cheap, unskilled labour. This colonial need for urban labour was certainly a 'pull' factor for many of the first wave of working-class Cape Verdean emigrants. Nonetheless, we cannot entirely explain the onset of Cape Verdean migration to the metropolis by referring only to Portuguese labour shortages, for in the 1960s and 1970s, a large number of Portuguese peasants still living in rural communities were looking for an opportunity to migrate to the metropolitan areas of Lisbon and Setúbal (Barreto and Preto 1996; Lopes 1998), thus making a domestic labour supply for the newly emerging cities readily available as well. Nonetheless, the rising demand for unskilled industrial labour began to drive up wages – Cape Verdean unskilled peasants offered a new, cheap supply.

The declining situation of the Cape Verdean economy, combined with the termination of indentured labour migration to the plantations of São Tomé and Príncipe, and the significant growth of the Portuguese economy in the late 1960s and early 1970s, triggered an increase in Cape Verdean migration to Portugal. When Cape Verdean labour migrants first began to arrive in the 1960s, only a small number of educated Cape Verdeans were already living in the metropolis. The latter had come in search of the education they could not get in Cape

Verde; after completing their studies, the vast majority found jobs in Portugal and the Portuguese colonies and never returned to live in Cape Verde. These educated Cape Verdeans assimilated easily within mainstream Portuguese society by adopting the ideals of colonial society, which they accepted and with which they identified. They had little in common with the mass of labour migrants who later arrived in Portugal.

The first Cape Verdean labour migrants came from the rural hinterland and had to adapt to urban life, changing from peasants to industrial workers. Although their worldview had to adjust to a new setting, they remained tied to the fundamental values and social representations of Cape Verdean society. Whereas these immigrants tried to reproduce their social world as it existed in Cape Verde, their descendants do not see themselves as belonging to that world. The children of Cape Verdean immigrants grow up in a liminal world: they neither fit in their parents' world nor have they gained a satisfactory place in the mainstream of Portuguese postcolonial society. The government-supported housing projects (*bairros sociais*) in which many of them live (and some still live in undeveloped slums) are spaces of liminality from which only a few ever leave. Education is the main avenue for integration within the middle-class mainstream, but most Cape Verdean teenagers drop out of school early and can thus only apply for low-paid and low-qualification jobs. Their aspirations to middle-class status are thereby compromised.

In Portugal, the mass media as producers of identity have created a negative image of Cape Verdean immigrants, and particularly of their descendants. While the first migrants were depicted as good workers – although 'hot-blooded' – their descendants are seen as dropouts and juvenile delinquents. In turn, Cape Verdean youths use media representations depicting them as 'disintegrated' and 'marginal' to blame the white mainstream for their situation, and to develop an oppositional identity that places little or no value on school and education. They see education as something for *tugas* (white Portuguese), and so their view of school and education becomes a self-fulfilling prophecy. Their main unit of identity is their neighbourhood, or *bairro*, which they see as their social territory; identity is rooted not in 'national' but 'neighbourhood' boundaries. What they carry in their hearts is not their parents' homeland but their neighbourhood. The importance of the *bairro* as an identity unit is presented to others via TV coverage and video documentaries about the creole and rap cultures now emerging in housing projects. These youths born in Portugal to Cape Verdean parents are classified by the white mainstream as '*jovens de origem africana*' (youths of African origin). Their identity has not been hyphenated as is common in Britain or the U.S.; the category of 'black Portuguese' does not exist as such. They are often seen as 'black' but only rarely as 'Portuguese'. Because they are perceived as 'Africans', their integration is difficult; reciprocally, because they see in their skin colour a reason for rejection, they tend to interpret their relation to the mainstream in terms of race, which in turn pushes them to develop an oppositional, 'African' identity that – both they and others believe – denies them the middle-class lifestyle and values of the white families who live in neighbourhoods surrounding theirs.

Most of the Cape Verdean 'elite' who see themselves as Portuguese-Cape Verdean (or Cape Verdean-Portuguese) felt compelled to abandon Cape Verde and the other Portuguese colonies after independence, in 1975, for political or employment reasons. Some were not happy with the political turnover that overthrew Portuguese colonialism in favour of the PAIGC – a Marxist party that instituted land reform and the nationalisation of many privately owned businesses, clearly threatening the economic interests of the old colonial-era upper class. Other elites feared that the archipelago would not survive independence because of its bleak economic and ecological situation. Others were shown they were not welcome under the new regime because of their previous involvement with the colonial administration. Still others, fearing they would lose their labour rights as civil servants, managed to maintain their Portuguese citizenship and were given new jobs in the Portuguese civil service. Those who had held jobs in the colonial private sector relocated to the colonial metropolis, where they found jobs commensurate with their educational level.

As this narrative implies, independence brought to the surface ethnic and racial divides that were latent during colonial times. Darker-skinned Cape Verdeans saw 'white' Cape Verdeans as too 'Portuguese' to embrace the postcolonial political project: a 'brotherhood' of the newly independent African countries. There was little room for 'white' Cape Verdeans in the aftermath of independence, especially for those who had thrived under colonialism and had not opposed it. These elite 'Portuguese-Cape Verdeans' now number just a few hundred and live in Lisbon or nearby cities. They reside in middle-class dwellings they purchased or rented, in some cases more than thirty years ago. Most of their descendants do not identify themselves with Cape Verde or 'being Cape Verdean'. The parents regret the fact that their children and grandchildren are no longer interested in anything related to Cape Verde and do not participate in the social life of their club – *Associação dos Antigos Alunos do Ensino Secundário de Cabo Verde* (AAAESCV, The Association of Former High School Students of Cape Verde). The club provides a space where a small group of Portuguese-Cape Verdeans meet weekly to recreate their vanished Cape Verdean world – a world that now exists only in their aging memories – and to discuss issues related to Cape Verde and its postcolonial situation. At the association meetings, they eat Cape Verdean food and listen and dance to Cape Verdean music (see Batalha 2004a, 2004b).

By contrast, the major part of the so-called 'Cape Verdean community' in Portugal consists of darker-skinned immigrants who have been arriving since the 1960s. Many of them are classified as *badiu* Cape Verdeans – the name given to Cape Verdeans from the island of Santiago, particularly those with darker skin and clearly of African ancestry. In contrast to the small minority of 'Portuguese-Cape Verdeans', they have not become invisible in postcolonial society but have instead gained a visibility they never experienced in Cape Verde. A conjunction of ethnicity, race, class, and cultural practices has worked to segregate them in the social world of shantytowns and, lately, in government-sponsored housing projects. It is these immigrants who those in white, mainstream Portuguese society consider as constituting 'the Cape Verdean community'. In the eyes of that mainstream, they are 'Cape Verdean', 'black', or 'African' – but rarely 'Portuguese'. This holds true not only for the immigrants themselves, but also for their descendants – who, despite having been born in Portugal and often having Portuguese nationality, are viewed by others as 'Africans'.

It was during the period that Carreira (1982: 74) defined as the 'third phase' of Cape Verdean emigration that Portugal became an important destination to Cape Verdeans. This 'third phase' occurred between 1946 and 1973, a period during which Cape Verdean emigration reoriented towards Europe because of the restrictive quota immigration policy adopted by the U.S. between 1924 and 1965 (see Joppke 1999). Migrants who had basic education and some labour market skills headed to the most developed countries in Europe, where they could find better-paying jobs. Some would come to Lisbon and stay for some weeks or months until they gained access to broader migration networks, and then headed to other countries. Throughout the 1960s and 1970s, Portugal was the likely destination for illiterate peasants coming from the rural hinterland of Cape Verde, mainly from the island of Santiago. A lack of political interest by the colonial government of Portugal to promote the necessary infrastructural investments to create jobs in Cape Verde made things worse on the islands throughout the 1960s. While in Cape Verde, the 'push' factor, in the forms of drought and famine, had its effects on migration until the early 1970s. In Portugal, the 'pull' factor only became significant in the 1960s, when the country experienced considerable economic growth, industrialisation, and growing urbanisation (Barreto and Preto 1996). Migration to Portugal and other European destinations, as well as indenture on the Portuguese colonial plantations in São Tomé and Príncipe, helped ease the economic and political pressure caused by famine and chronic underdevelopment in Cape Verde. Cape Verdean migration to Portugal went into full swing in the 1960s, when some Portuguese construction companies secured contracts for infrastructure projects in Cape Verde, including electrification, a plant for the desalinisation of sea water, public fountains, roads, airfields, and docks. These companies began offering local workers employment in the metropolis. Once settled, these workers passed the word along to other *patrícios* (country fellows) back in Cape Verde whenever more workers were needed. It was via this chain migration that the number of Cape Verdean immigrants to Portugal increased rapidly, reaching a peak in the early 1970s.

In the late 1950s, industrialised countries in Europe such as France, Germany, Belgium, and Luxembourg began to attract Portuguese unskilled labour for the construction industry, cleaning, food catering, and other jobs typically scorned by the locals. Attracted by better wages, some of the Portuguese peasantry who had been drawn to the urban littoral of Portugal since the 1950s began to head for these northern European nations whose economies were recovering and expanding following the end of World War II and the implementation of the Marshall Plan. The Portuguese workers headed to northern Europe, while Cape Verdeans headed to Portugal as a replacement labour force. As Carreira wrote, 'they were workforces of the same kind, both containing a high percentage of illiterates, and differentiated only by their skin colour' (1982: 83). The majority of the Cape Verdean workers were of black and mixed complexion. Most did not initially speak Portuguese and never managed to learn it properly. After a few years they were able to understand Portuguese in the context of their work, but, outside of their jobs, their command of Portuguese was very limited, and many did not feel at ease speaking it. The fact that they were black and could not speak Portuguese easily confirmed the stereotype that many Portuguese had of a 'black' person: someone who lived in Africa, was unmannered, irreligious, and for these reasons was to be mocked. Class was confused with race: instead of being seen as 'uncultured peasants', these working-class Cape Verdean immigrants were classified by Portuguese whites as 'uncultured blacks'. Most of this first wave of urban labourers lived in barracks provided by their employers at the construction sites. Those immigrants willing to spend money on accommodations could rent a room in cheap boardinghouses, and some Cape Verdeans, particularly those who adapted more easily to Portuguese working-class ways, also rented rooms from Portuguese working-class families in some urban areas.

In the 1970s-80s, many of these working-class Cape Verdean immigrants began moving to shantytowns in Lisbon's metropolitan area. In part, they did so because of a scarcity of affordable housing; in some cases, racist white landlords who were unwilling to rent to Cape Verdean tenants were also a factor. But the move to shantytowns was also partly an active decision on the part of the immigrants: they recognised that they could more easily stay together in shantytowns than in rented accommodations, where they had to be dispersed. Moreover, not only were the accommodations in shantytowns free – once they built their own shack with materials brought from the construction sites they worked at – but they could more easily reproduce the cultural life and physical environment they were used to in Cape Verde.

As in the case of other migration fluxes, in its beginning stages, Cape Verdean migration consisted mainly of single or married men who had left their families behind on the islands. Women only started to arrive a few years later, when their men had already found stable jobs, and realised that they were going to stay for a longer period than they had originally planned. As they moved into shantytowns, it was not difficult to accommodate women and other family members: they could always add an extension to their home-made dwelling, or build a new one. However, not all Cape Verdean immigrant workers moved to shantytowns; a small number of men and families managed to get housing in urban and suburban quarters, usually in the more run-down areas. In the 1970s-80s, some of these families occupied rooms, and sometimes an entire floor, in the Lisbon boroughs of Campo de Ourique, Estrela, and São Bento.

Migrant numbers and the labour market

At the end of 1962, about 70,000 Portuguese immigrants were living in France; only ten years later, that number had increased more than tenfold, to about 750,000 (Barata 1975: 39). In 1972, an additional 69,000 Portuguese 'guest-workers' were living in Germany. Between 1950 and 1968, more than 900,000 people left Portugal to live and work in other European countries (Barata 1970: 16). This high level of migration meant that the population of Portugal between 1961 and 1970 actually decreased – by more than 1 million people.[1] This statistically significant outflow of the Portuguese labour force created, in large measure, the conditions for the inflow of Cape Verdean migrants.

According to Carreira's figures (1977: 125-6), between 1900 and 1952, the number of Cape Verdeans who left Cape Verde for Portugal, the Azores, and Madeira was only about 8,500, which is less than the 9,920 registered in 1971 (1972 was the peak year, with 14,375). For the period 1955-73, the total number of Cape Verdeans arriving in Portugal was about 87,000, but this included migrants, students, transients migrating to other destinations, and other short-term sojourners. It is not possible to figure out just how many of this figure that Carreira gives

were actually labour migrants. In the years after Cape Verdean independence, the number of Cape Verdean migrants to Portugal continued to grow steadily. Cape Verdeans were employed in the construction
industry as builders (the underground subway system, roads, ditches
for electricity and telephone cables, etc.). The main employers of Cape
Verdean labour were construction companies and the mining com-
pound of Panasqueira. J. Pimenta was responsible for the construction
of Reboleira Sul – several quarters of apartment buildings for middle-
class dwellers in what is now the city of Amadora. Pinto & Bentes employed Cape Verdeans to do the hard work of digging the ditches for
water pipes and telephone cables. In the early 1970s, the large increase
in the number of Cape Verdean arrivals led the Portuguese authorities
to set up an office to help them find appropriate employment – the
Centro de Apoio aos Trabalhadores Ultramarinos (CATU) (Centre for
the Aid of Overseas Workers).

The vast majority of these Cape Verdean workers stayed in Lisbon
and the nearby municipalities of Amadora, Sintra, Oeiras, and Almada,
where labour demand was higher than elsewhere in the country, but
some headed south to the Algarve, where the construction industry
was beginning to blossom because of the growing tourist industry. In
the beginning, the Cape Verdean workers were not welcome in the Algarve, where local, white residents were even less used to seeing black
people around than they were in Lisbon. Most Cape Verdeans lived segregated from their Portuguese co-workers, mainly in shacks they built
themselves on waste lands, with materials provided by their employers;
while some rented accommodations from local residents. However, in
the beginning, renting was rare because the local white property owners were reluctant to rent to 'blacks'.

Although the influx of Cape Verdeans to Portugal was never compar-
able, for instance, to that of Caribbean migration to Britain or the U.S.
in the post-Second World War period, it was very significant at the cultural level, since Portugal had not experienced a migratory influx for a
long time, with the exception of the movement of transitory Jewish refugees escaping Nazism during the Second World War. According to
figures compiled by Carreira (1982: 89), between 1969 and 1973, some
11,000 Cape Verdean workers seeking employment either in Portugal
or the colonies registered with the CATU. But these figures are far below the actual number of arrivals in Lisbon during that period. In
1976, there were about 30,000 Cape Verdeans in Portugal, a much
greater number than the 5,539 workers registered with the CATU.

Estimates for the number of Cape Verdeans currently living in Portugal vary between about 50,000 and 80,000, depending on the
source. Portuguese authorities usually give a lower figure and the Cape
Verdean representatives (embassy or Cape Verdean organisations) a

higher one. In 2004, according to the Serviço de Estrangeiros e Fronteiras (SEF) (Service of Foreigners and Frontiers), there were about
55,590 Cape Verdeans in Portugal with residence permits. As of September 2006, the Instituto Nacional de Estatística (INE) (the National
Statistics Bureau) estimates the number of legally resident Cape Verdeans at 56,433. Both figures, however, only count Cape Verdean nationals, while the number of those who consider themselves Cape Verdean is much higher. The latter includes Cape Verdean immigrants
who, despite having acquired Portuguese citizenship, continue to identify themselves primarily as Cape Verdean, as well as the descendants
of Cape Verdean immigrants who, despite being Portuguese citizens,
identify themselves as Cape Verdean. Furthermore, there also undocumented Cape Verdean workers not accounted on the statistics. Lastly,
we could also include those Portuguese nationals who still identify
themselves as 'Portuguese Cape Verdean' – the old colonial minority
mentioned earlier.

In recent years, Portugal has witnessed a significant influx of Eastern European and Brazilian migrants; nevertheless, Cape Verdeans
continue to be the largest group with temporary permits (*autorização
de permanência*). Ukrainians and Brazilians, now the two largest groups
of immigrants, are mostly on temporary permits – they are allowed to
stay for only a limited number of years, and only if they have a work
contract. According to the INE, in 2005 there were 64,337 Ukrainians
and 37,765 Brazilians with temporary permits. If we consider foreigners on long-term residence permits, in 2005, the Brazilians were on
top with 13,976 (30.0%), followed by Ukrainians with 8,295 (17.8%)
and Cape Verdeans with 5,942 (12.7%). Cape Verdeans live and work
mostly in the three large administrative areas of Lisbon (36,971), Setúbal (11,936) and Faro (3,506).

Whereas there was a strong demand for male labour in the construction industry, one cannot say there was a specific demand for Cape Verdean female labour in any particular sector of the Portuguese economy.
During the first period of Cape Verdean migration it was mainly the
men who came, but as Cape Verdeans began moving to shantytowns,
the women began joining them. The women in Cape Verde did agricultural and domestic work. Throughout the 1980s and early 1990s they
peddled fish in the streets, or pulled crates in the wholesale fish markets of Lisbon (e.g., Doca Pesca) (see Fikes 1998, 2000). In the 1990s,
the government imposed legal restrictions so that Cape Verdean women could no longer peddle fish, and so they turned to cleaning jobs.
Cleaning is now their main occupation, either in private homes, shopping malls, or public buildings. However, in the last decade, a significant number of immigrant women from Eastern Europe (mostly the
Ukraine) and Brazil have also taken cleaning jobs. The arrival of these

women has kept wages low and has made it more difficult for Cape Verdean women to find jobs. In the last decade, Cape Verdean men have also faced competition from Eastern European migrants in the construction industry. Most of these jobs are now given to Eastern Europeans, with a small minority of Cape Verdeans acting as middlemen subcontractors. Fewer and fewer Cape Verdean men actually work as builders nowadays.

Cape Verdean youth from the shantytowns show high school drop-out rates. Many do not even complete their compulsory education, which should be completed by the age of fifteen. Others remain behind in school until they are able to complete the required schooling, however, when they finish their schooling they are still 'functional illiterates'. But, one cannot say that this is a particular predicament of the children of Cape Verdean immigrants. School failure has a significant effect on the Portuguese lower-middle and lower classes in general as well. Thus, Cape Verdean youths in Portugal are being affected by factors not specific to the Cape Verdean community; in fact, they are common to an increasing number of families, particularly those who live on the margins of the newly emerging 'affluent society'.

Notes

[1] For the quinquennium 1966-70, the negative balance was about 700,000 people, which nearly doubled the 400,000 from the previous quinquennium 1961-65.

References

Barata, Ó.S. (1970) 'O Problema Demográfico Português'. *Separata da Revista Militar* 5: 3-26.

Barata, Ó.S. (1975) 'A Emigração e o Êxodo Rural em Portugal'. *Separata do Boletim da Sociedade de Geografia de Lisboa* 93(1-6): 37-69.

Barreto, A.; Preto, C.V. (1996) *A Situação Social em Portugal, 1960-1995*. Lisbon: Instituto de Ciências Sociais, Universidade de Lisboa.

Batalha, L. (2004a) *The Cape Verdean Diaspora in Portugal: Colonial Subjects in a Postcolonial World*. Lanham, MD: Lexington Books.

Batalha, L. (2004b) 'Contra a Corrente Dominante: Histórias de Sucesso entre Caboverdianos da 2ª Geração'. *Etnográfica* 8(2): 297-333.

Carreira, A. (1977) *Migrações nas Ilhas de Cabo Verde*. Lisbon: Universidade Nova de Lisboa.

Carreira, A. (1982) *The People of the Cape Verde Islands: Exploitation and Emigration*. London: C. Hurst & Co. (trans. by Christopher Fyfe).

Fikes, K.D. (1998) 'Domesticity in Black and White: Assessing Badia Cape Verdean Challenges to Portuguese Ideals of Black Womanhood'. *Transforming Anthropology* 7(2): 5-19.

Fikes, K.D. (2000) *Santiaguense Cape Verdean Women in Portugal: Labor Rights, Citizenship and Diasporic Transformation*. Ph.D. Dissertation, University of California, Los Angeles.

França, L. (ed.) (1992) *A Comunidade Caboverdiana em Portugal*. Lisbon: Instituto de Estudos para o Desenvolvimento.

Franco, A.L.S. (1971) *A Emigração Portuguesa no Último Decénio: Causas Problemas e Soluções.* Guimarães, PT: Edição da Assembleia de Guimarães.

Gomes, I.B. (co-ordinator]) (1999) *Estudo de Caracterização da Comunidade Caboverdiana Residente em Portugal.* Lisbon: Embassy of Cape Verde.

Jopkke, C. (1999) *Immigration and the Nation-State: The United States, Germany, and Great Britain.* Oxford: Oxford University Press.

Lopes, J. da S. (1998) *A Economia Portuguesa Desde 1960.* Lisbon: Gradiva.

Poinard, M. (1979) 'Le Million des Immigrés: Analyse de l'Utilisation de l'Aide au Retour par des Travailleurs Portugais en France'. *Revue Géographique de Pyrénées et du Su-Oest* 50(2): 511-39.

Porto, M. (1977) 'Emigration and Regional Development in Portugal'. *Boletim da Comissão de Planeamento da Região Centro* 5.

Rocha-Trindade, M.B. (1975) 'Portuguese Rural Migrants in Industrialized Europe'. *Iberian Studies* 4(1): 9-14.

Rocha-Trindade, M.B. (1979) 'Portugal', in *International Labor Migration in Europe,* R.E. Krane (ed.), New York: Praeger, pp. 164-172.

Serrão, J. (1977) *A Emigração Portuguesa: Sondagem Histórica.* Lisbon: Livros Horizonte (3rd ed.).

Chapter 6
Cape Verdeans in Spain

Rocío Moldes Farelo AND *Luzia Oca González*[1]

The history of Cape Verdean migration to Spain

The history of Cape Verdean migration to Spain illustrates the role of migrant networks in creating diaspora communities in unlikely places. It is striking that people from specific villages in the African archipelago became employed as miners in the hills of León and as fishermen on the coast of Galiza (Galicia). The Cape Verdeans in León were in fact pioneers in African migration to Spain, migrating ten years before the subsequent settlement of other Sub-Saharan African groups.

The arrival of Cape Verdeans in Spain is closely linked to the successive waves of Cape Verdean migration to Portugal. The first Cape Verdeans settled in Spain in the mid-1970s (França 1992). Their aim was to migrate to the richer countries of northwestern Europe, such as France and the Netherlands. Some were not allowed to cross the Franco-Spanish border in the Pyrenees and remained in Basque country, where there was great demand for construction workers. These migrants eventually sought work in other parts of Spain, often working in public works or factories. Networks between these migrants and their relatives, who were anxious to leave Portugal and Cape Verde, facilitated the migration of others.

Just over 3,500 Cape Verdean-born people were registered as residents of Spanish municipalities in 2005 (Instituto Nacional De Estadística 2006). Of these, almost 80 per cent were Spanish citizens. Moreover, there are also an unknown number of undocumented Cape Verdeans in Spain. According to the Consulate of Cape Verde in Madrid, the total size of the community is approximately 6,000 people.

Today, the vast majority of Cape Verdean citizens are concentrated in four autonomous regions (Secretaría de Estado de Inmigración y Emigración 2006; see map, figure 6.1). Madrid (38%) has especially attracted Cape Verdean women, many of whom are domestic workers. Castilla and León (20%) and Galiza (11%) are home to the oldest Cape Verdean communities in Spain, which will be described in detail below. Finally, Aragón (13%), and especially the city of Zaragoza, has more recently attracted numerous Cape Verdeans, who are often internal migrants escaping unemployment in Galiza.

Figure 6.1. *Important locations in Cape Verdean Migration to Spain*

Madrid stands out as the community with the highest proportion of women, in contrast to the communities that developed based on the demand for male workers. Nevertheless, almost 60 per cent of the Cape Verdean-born population in Spain as a whole is female (Instituto Nacional De Estadística 2006). The communities also differ from each other in terms of origin. Cape Verdeans in Madrid and León come primarily from the Barlavento islands, while those in Galiza and Zaragoza are mainly *badiu* from Santiago.

The Cape Verdean communities in León and Galiza provide fascinating case studies of how a series of coincidences and the dynamics of local labour markets have shaped the development of the Cape Verdean diaspora.

The Cape Verdean mining communities in León

The arrival of Cape Verdeans in León was not so much the result of conscious decisions, as of a series of circumstances and the struggle for survival (Moldes 1998). A small group of Cape Verdeans in Lisbon were allegedly deceived by a fellow countryman who promised to take them by car to the Netherlands but abandoned them en route. As they tried to make their way back to Lisbon with limited means, they were encouraged by a Portuguese immigrant in Galiza to try their luck as miners in León. In this province, the Cape Verdeans eventually settled in the towns of Bembire in the area of El Bierzo and Villablino in the

Laciana valley. Also here there was an element of segregation by island of origin, with people from São Nicolau in Bembire and people from Santo Antão in Villablino, although this distinction has faded with time. Most of the Cape Verdeans who started working in the mines joined the company Minero Siderúrgica de Ponferrada (MSP) in the years 1975-76. The only requirement for working in the mine was the absence of any notable physical deficiency.

The Cape Verdean immigrants were mainly young men who arrived on their own, with the idea of working for a time and saving as much money as possible. Their lack of knowledge about work in the mines, the harshness of this work, and the inhospitable climate led them to see their situation as purely transitory. Approximately four to six years after the men settled, however, family reunification began. Women arrived from a variety of places, especially Madrid, Lisbon, and Rome, but rarely from Cape Verde. In some cases, it was a matter of couples who had lived in different places who were now reunited in León. In other cases, the men working in the mines formed new relationships with Cape Verdean women who had initially migrated to other parts of Southern Europe. It is worth noting that in both instances, the gender-segregated labour markets of Europe led men and women to migrate to different destinations before they were united in the mining areas. The men then moved out from company boardinghouses and rented flats with their families. The small town of Villaseca outside Villablino became a principal area of settlement, where Cape Verdeans eventually came to constitute 6 per cent of the population.

Unlike their husbands or partners who established relationships with colleagues at work that facilitated their integration and improved their language skills, the women often remained largely isolated from the community. Even after living in the valley for almost twenty years, their sphere of activity has often been limited to the home and the care of their children. An association of Cape Verdean women was formed in the early 1990s, modelled on Spanish women's associations. This initiative did not contribute to the women's emancipation and integration, however. The reasons for the failure were partly associated with the community's concern about its own reputation as hard-working immigrants. Many women in the community felt that traditional notions of the 'good Cape Verdean women' were integral to this image. They resisted the promotion of a more independent role, which was seen as subversive to their primary role as wives and mothers.

The chain migration through family networks continued in the 1990s, but under different conditions. Many of those who arrived in this decade were male teenagers or young men, often nephews or children (fidj' fora[2]) of the men in the community. These newly arrived Cape Verdeans faced a much more difficult labour market, who were at a disadvantage because of their lack of qualifications and because they often worked or resided illegally. They often ended up working without contracts in the construction sector, or in the illegal coal mines which are widespread in the area.

Cape Verdeans in Galiza: men at sea, women on land

Only a couple of years after the arrival of Cape Verdeans in León, another community was developing on the coast of Galiza (González 2006). In 1977-78, a large group of Cape Verdean men were working on the construction of the Alúmina-Alumínio metallurgical plant. Once this construction was completed, however, they were not accepted as permanent workers and some left the area in search of work elsewhere. Those who stayed eventually became an important substitution force in a different sector: the fisheries. Many locals were offered better jobs in the plant and left vacancies in the fishing industry, which the Cape Verdeans filled. The men were later joined by wives and children, and a stable community developed on the coast of the province of Lugo, known as the Marinha. The majority of Cape Verdeans in the area come from Santiago, especially the western and northern coasts. The principal areas of origin are the villages of Porto Rincão and Porto Mosquito, with which there are strong migratory networks based on kinship. In the second half of the 1980s, many Cape Verdean families also arrived from Lisbon.

Deep-sea fishing is an extremely dangerous occupation, and rest periods are often limited to four- or five-hour periods. The workers do not have a fixed salary, but are remunerated according to the traditional system of redistribution of the catch. Over the last few years, a clear ethnic division of labour has emerged on the ships: a few native men get the best paid and least dangerous jobs, while Cape Verdeans, Peruvians and other immigrants have the hardest and the most poorly paid jobs.

From the beginning, the Cape Verdean communities in León and Galiza were focused on the men's work. In Galiza, the men's absence while working at sea has made the community on land the women's realm. The women's lives change considerably when their husbands are back on land. The women's autonomy is restricted by the permanent attention they must pay their husbands. Since the men are absent much of the time, the socialisation of children is taken on almost entirely by women. This is, in fact, similar to the solitary motherhood that one encounters in Cape Verde, where they live the major part of their lives as emigrants' wives. As fishermen's wives in Galiza, the women help each other and reproduce the solidarity network experienced in their homeland.

The women in Marinha are not only wives and *de facto* heads of the families but also the community representatives. Women's work outside the domestic sphere has existed since they arrived in Marinha, although some of these Cape Verdean women have never had access to the local labour market. Those who are employed work in low-paid jobs, usually in sectors that are known for their precariousness, temporariness and exploitation: domestic work, cleaning, hotels and or algae collection in the coast. In some of these cases, they engage in clandestine work. Subsistence agriculture is also an important activity and a source for modest savings. Women's work in the kitchen gardens is also the basis for the reproduction of the main *badiu* diet, which is based on corn. The agricultural work reproduces the *djuntamon* system brought from Cape Verde and reinforces relations between local families.

Most of the women come to Spain as wives and depend on their husbands for the renewal of their residence permits. This also limits their access to the labour market. The reliance on their husbands for their legal status also forces women to endure hardships created by their partners, since they are not protected by the law.

The women play an essential role in the fostering of relations with Cape Verde and the diaspora, and via the socialisation of the second generation as Cape Verdeans. This involves the preservation of the *badiu* identity and the recreation of *badiu* cultural practices. Kriolu is the mother tongue of virtually all of the descendants.

Relations with the majority population are mostly limited to the sphere of work, while personal relationships are directed to the community. Mixed marriages have been very unusual in the community's thirty-year history.

In the gender-segregated Cape Verdean community of Galiza, many second-generation girls are resisting the female role models of their mothers. They strive for greater autonomy and are the ones who most frequently have friendships or relationships with white Spaniards. The boys, by contrast, favour traditional gender roles in which they have a privileged position, and tend to prefer endogamous relationships.

The transformation of the Cape Verdean communities

The development of the mining and fishing industries has continued to have a profound impact on Cape Verdean communities. Since the early 1990s, the mining industry has undergone a severe crisis. The gradual termination of EU subsidies for mining and the progressive worsening of working conditions caused ongoing labour conflicts in the valleys of León. An early retirement plan for workers aged 55 or over became effective in 1997, and within three years all of the Cape Verdeans who had been hired between 1975 and 1978 had retired. The retirement wave dramatically altered the community's situation. It raised new issues such as the 'invention of leisure' and the prospect of a return to Cape Verde or migration to other parts of Spain. For the Cape Verdean miners in León, planned leisure was basically nonexistent. The little free time the workers had was primarily spent resting or in bars. After retirement, some of the men worked on small allotments, went for walks, or even assumed larger roles in the housework.

Faced with a more hostile attitude towards immigrants and fewer opportunities for their children in the labour market of the valleys, many Cape Verdeans eventually migrated to other parts of Spain. Some moved to the regional centre of Ponferrada where there are better employment opportunities. Others went to the city of Torrevieja on the Costa Blanca, just south of Alicante, where there is a small but rapidly growing Cape Verdean community. Many Cape Verdeans have found work in the city's bakeries, restaurants and bars, and the climate is more pleasant than in the valleys.

The overriding factor for remaining in the valleys has been house ownership. Those who managed to buy a house in the past know that they could sell it at a loss. In a sense, they remain involuntarily chained to the area, and are concerned about the implications for their children's future. The sharp drop in the Cape Verdean population has also made it difficult to maintain communal activities.

The idea of returning to Cape Verde is a constant aspect of conversations among the migrants. The islands are often presented in a nostalgic light, as a lost paradise of egalitarianism, solidarity and friendliness. Although the 'myth of return' is kept vividly alive, very few have actually returned. When asked, they generally refer to their children's future as the reason for staying in Spain. Some have managed to build or restore houses in Cape Verde, but are often prevented from actually returning because of the expensive fares and their large families.

In Galiza, the restructuring of the fishing industry has led to a shortage of work for Cape Verdeans since 1993. There were no employment opportunities for men other than the fishing industry, and the lack of employment precipitated a wave of out-migration of Cape Verdeans from the region. Most migrated to the city of Zaragoza, where there is now a substantial community of *badiu* origin. Almost half of the Cape Verdean families in the Marinha left during the 1990s, mirroring the massive out-migration from the mining areas of León. The crises in the two communities were also reflected in the remittances to Cape Verde: from 1992 to 1994, remittances from Spain dropped by half, while the flow from other European countries grew by almost 20 per cent (Banco de Cabo Verde 1990-2001).

However, since the turn of the century the Galizan community has seen a remarkable revival. Renewed demand for labour in the port of Burela has led to an inflow of Cape Verdean workers greater than ever before. This coincides with the development of a new migrant community of Peruvian fishermen. While the Peruvians are actively recruited and have all their paperwork handled by an agency, there is no formalised recruitment from Cape Verde. The migration of Cape Verdean workers is facilitated only by family networks and the private services of a lawyer. While the new inflow is driven by the demand for male workers, women and children are arriving through family reunification. This is now subject to tight legal restrictions and high financial costs, which only adds to the emotional strain of the migration process. The renewed immigration has led to rapid growth in the size of the community in Burela, from some 140 people in 1998 to circa 250 only six years later.

In contrast to the situation in León, few Cape Verdeans in Galiza have reached the retirement age. The few fishermen who have retired so far have in fact opted to return to Cape Verde. Many of the Cape Verdeans who came to Galiza in the 1970s and 1980s will retire in the coming decade, and it remains to be seen what kind of choices they make upon retiring.

The two traditional communities exhibit interesting parallels and differences. Both emerged via strong family networks after an initial foothold was gained more or less by chance. Furthermore, the histories of both communities have been closely linked to the cornerstone industries that only employed men. Changes in these industries have profoundly affected the communities. In Galiza as well as in León, the gender-segregated labour markets have affected the integration process, but in somewhat different ways. The miners' wives in León have been largely confined to the domestic sphere and have failed to organise collectively. Meanwhile, the women in Galiza have, in the absence of their husbands who work at sea, become the foundation of the community on land and have managed to reproduce some of the *badiu* traditions of collective action. The differences between the two communities reflect not only the characteristics of the socio-economic environments in which they are inserted, but also their origin from very different areas of Cape Verde.

Several decades after Cape Verdean settlement in Spain, the second generation now serves as an important component of the Cape Verdean population. The integration of the descendants is important to the future development of the Cape Verdean communities. Although education is often perceived as the sole vehicle of social mobility and improving one's living conditions, dropout rates remain high. When they enter the labour market, most of the descendants end up in jobs with working conditions very similar to what their parents experienced.

New directions in the immigration of Cape Verdeans, along with substantial internal migration, have led to dramatic changes in the geography of Cape Verdean settlement in Spain. In the early 1990s, the traditional communities in León and Galiza accounted for almost two-thirds of the registered Cape Verdean population in Spain. By 2005, however, their proportion had fallen to less than one-third. Significant internal migration by Cape Verdeans in Spain, the growth of the second generation, and the arrival of new groups of migrants, has resulted in the fact that the Cape Verdean population in Spain is now moving towards greater diversity so that the traditional communities in Galiza and León are becoming progressively a smaller part of the total picture.

Notes

1 Some of Luzia Oca González's earlier published material on this issue appear under her previous name, Luzia Fernández González.
2 Literally 'outside children', i.e., children by other women than the man's wife or long-time partner. It is also common among Cape Verdean men who were formally married or have had a life-long relationship with one woman, to have additional children by other women.

References

Banco de Cabo Verde (1990-2001) Remessas de Emigrantes por Países e por Concelho. Unpublished statistics, Praia: BCV.

Franca, L. (ed.) (1992) A Comunidade Caboverdiana em Portugal. Lisbon: Instituto de Estudos para o Deselvolvimento.

González, L.F. (2006) 'Evolução da comunidade cabo-verdiana residente no Litoral Lugués', in As Migracións em Galiza e Portugal: Contributos Desde as Ciencias Sociais, Matés, R. V. and R. L. González (eds.) Santiago: Edicións Candeia, pp. 217-235.

Instituto Nacional de Estadística (2006) Revisión del Padrón Municipal 2005. Madrid: Instituto Nacional de Estadística.

Moldes, R. (1998) Relaciones Etnia Clase: Inmigrantes Caboverdianos en las Cuencas Mineras del Valle de Laciana. Madrid: Editorial Complutense.

Secretaría de Estado de Inmigración y Emigración (2006) Extranjeros Con Tarjeta o Autorización de Residencia en Vigor a 31 de Diciembre de 2005. Madrid: Ministerio de Trabajo y Asuntos Sociales.

Chapter 7
Cape Verdeans in Italy

Jacqueline Andall

Cape Verdean migration to Italy is characteristic of the emergence of new trends in migration patterns to Europe. It is significant for at least three principal reasons. Firstly, no colonial relationship existed between Cape Verde and Italy – a migratory pattern which had characterised earlier post-war migrations from Africa to Europe. Secondly, when Cape Verdeans began to migrate to Italy, in the 1960s, the migration consisted of an exclusively female single-sex movement. This was a novel departure in terms of previous patterns of migration from Cape Verde, but it was also novel from a European perspective, marking, as it did, the growing incidence of female single-sex migration for paid live-in domestic work. Finally, the migration of Cape Verdean women to Italy was also important as it signalled Italy's transition into a country of immigration.

Following a period where women were either overlooked in migratory processes or included primarily within a dependency paradigm, much more focused attention has been paid to the role of women in migrations in recent times (Morokvasic et al. 2003; *Feminist Review* 2004). In particular, the labour migration of women for domestic work has led to female single-sex movements in a wide range of countries (Gamburd 2000; Andall 2000; Parreñas 2001). A global care chain analysis has been developed to account for the consequences of this type of movement in relation to the care of children but the long-term consequences of female single-sex migration in other areas still needs further elaboration. In this overview of the situation of Cape Verdeans in Italy, I examine the consequences of female single-sex migration in relation to the labour market, geographical mobility and the second generation.[1]

Moving between invisibility and visibility

It is estimated that by the end of 1972 some 3,500 Cape Verdean nationals had legally migrated to Italy (Carreira 1982). In the 1960s, young women, or girls in some cases, were recruited by Capuchin fathers serving on the island of São Nicolau to work as live-in domestic

workers in Italy. The Capuchin fathers were responding to demand
from within Italy. As alternative employment options became available
for Italian women or the choice of domesticity as a housewife became
viable even for Italian women from traditionally poorer backgrounds,
families accustomed to employing live-in help were forced to look elsewhere for their workers.

The early departures of Cape Verdean women to Italy were thus organised and included employment contracts and air travel. Moreover,
given that this recruitment was organised primarily by Catholic organisations – the Capuchin fathers based in São Nicolau and Italian Catholic organisations such as the Order of Santa Zita and the association
Tra Noi – attention was also paid to the moral and social welfare of
these young women. This included the presence of a social worker, Lea
Manzone, who was sent out to Cape Verde from Italy (Carreira 1982).
In the 1970s, commentators were still not clear what significance to ascribe to this movement of young women to Italy. There were concerns
about their marriage prospects and even suggestions that they should
be guided to other countries given that Italy only accepted the migration of Cape Verdeans for domestic work. The migration to Naples began in the 1970s and involved primarily young women from São Vicente and Sal (Monteiro 1997). In the 1970s, women migrating to Italy
generally had low levels of education (De Lourdes Jesus 1989) however,
those Cape Verdeans based in Rome were able to benefit from the establishment of a Portuguese school in Rome, in 1971. The objectives of
the school were to assist Portuguese-speaking workers abroad and it
provided a range of educational courses, from literacy to the school
leaving examination. At its peak year of enrolment, the academic year
1980/1, some 358 students were registered.

Cape Verdeans frequently featured as a case-study group in some of
the earliest studies of immigration to Italy. By the early 1990s, the local
official in charge of the regional immigration office based in Rome
confidently asserted that Cape Verdeans in Italy were fine and had
settled without any major problems. In 2005, an Italian academic who
had studied Cape Verdeans in Naples some fifteen years earlier maintained that Cape Verdeans were no longer central in the Neapolitan
context. Both statements are revealing as they share an assumption of
the unproblematic nature of Cape Verdeans' presence in Italy. However, the virtual disappearance of Cape Verdeans as a subject of Italian
immigration research suggests that Cape Verdeans have become an increasingly invisible component of the Italian immigration landscape.
Social and political invisibility had characterised their presence in the
1960s and 1970s, as they were literally enclosed within Italian families'
homes. By the 1980s, they had gained some visibility as the general increase in labour migration forced Italy to acknowledge its transition

into a country of immigration. More recently, Cape Verdeans appear to have moved towards renewed invisibility as the number and diversity of labour migrants to Italy has increased substantially. In fact, Cape Verdeans have never constituted a large group in Italy. In 1990, there were 4,991 Cape Verdean legal residents in Italy, of whom only 622 were male (Andall 2000). In 2000, there were 4,004 documented Cape Verdean nationals living in Italy and although the current gender balance is not as stark as it had been in earlier decades, in 2000, some 77 per cent of Cape Verdean nationals were women.

Unlike Moroccan or Albanian nationals, who are currently present in all of Italy's twenty-one regions and who represent two of the largest ethnic minority groups in Italy (respectively 227,940 and 233,616), Cape Verdeans are not a nationally known ethnic group in Italy (Caritas 2004). Rather, Cape Verdeans are only present in a few specific regions. Their geographical settlement is concentrated primarily in just two cities – Rome and Naples. Much smaller settlements are present in Palermo and Milan. This geographical distribution has remained virtually unchanged over the years. Monteiro's (1997) data collected in 1995 from the Italian Ministry of the Interior demonstrated that Rome was still the major city of settlement, with 2,057 Cape Verdean residents in Rome, of whom 82.5 per cent were women. Data for 2000 confirms the geographical stability of Cape Verdean settlement in Italy (table 7.1).

As one might expect with a migrant labour group, in 2000, the overwhelming number of Cape Verdeans were in the 19-40 age category (2,351) and the 41-60 age category (1,367). However, the fact that in 2000 they still only numbered 4,004, slightly less than in 1990, suggests that Italy is not a particularly attractive destination for Cape Verdeans. Although their long-term presence in Italy means that some have gained Italian citizenship and thus no longer appear in the fig-

Table 7.1.   *Cape Verdean residents in selected cities in Italy (2000)*

City	Number	Distribution (%)
Rome	1904	47.6
Naples	944	23.6
Palermo	200	5.0
Milan	164	4.1
Florence	126	3.1
Genoa	94	2.3
Other	572	14.3
Total	**4004**	**100.0**

Source: unpublished data, Ministero degli Interni.

Table 7.2.   *Cape Verdean residents in Italy, by age group (2000)*

Age group	Number			Proportion female (%)
	Female	*Male*	*Total*	
0–18	100	78	178	56.2
19–40	1917	434	2351	81.5
41–60	1137	230	1367	83.2
61+	7	7	14	50.0
Total	**3255**	**749**	**4004**	**81.3**

Source: unpublished data, Ministero degli Interni.

ures of Cape Verdean nationals, compared to other migrant groups their numerical presence in Italy has not increased significantly. However, this does not mean that they have been a static group. To the contrary, there has been much movement in and out of Italy and between European countries, especially between Cape Verde, Portugal, Italy and the Netherlands (Andall 1999).

The geographical settlement of Cape Verdeans in Italy is important to note because Cape Verdeans are not present, or are present in negligible numbers in those Italian regions whose economic profile is both more dynamic and more diverse. For example, in regions such as Tuscany and Emilia Romagna, which are renowned for the economic dynamism of their industrial districts, the collective presence of Cape Verdeans is less than 500. Instead, Cape Verdeans primarily reside in cities such as Rome, which has a large tertiary sector, access to which is often restricted to Italian citizens, or Naples which has a large informal economy.

Mapping Cape Verdeans' geographical settlement onto regional labour market opportunities reveals that their working opportunities, in terms of variety of economic niche, are limited. In the economically dynamic northeastern part of the country, 53 per cent of all migrant workers are employed in industry, compared to 22 per cent in services, 13 per cent in agriculture and 12 per cent in the domestic work sector. In the central and southern regions of the country, where almost 90 per cent of Cape Verdeans live, 50 per cent and 57 per cent respectively of migrant workers are employed as domestic workers. In the specific situation of Campania, where the second largest concentration of Cape Verdeans reside, some 72 per cent of migrant workers are legally employed in the domestic work sector, with only 11 per cent employed in industry, nine per cent employed in services and 8 per cent in agriculture (Bisogno and Tanturri 2000: 80).

The dominance of the domestic work sector

Despite the long time they have spent in Italy, paid domestic work has remained a central occupation for Cape Verdean labour migrants. This is partly because domestic work or care work for the elderly constitutes an important occupational niche for migrant women in general in Italy. While in the 1990s, factory work also became available to migrant women in several of Italy's northern regions, Cape Verdean women were not able to benefit from this as they were geographically settled in the centre and south of the country.

Cape Verdeans have generally been well regarded as employees in the domestic work sector and do not face the same obstacles and discrimination that has been noted for some other groups, such as Moroccan women (Scrinzi 2004). Within the domestic work sector, wages are higher in northern Italy, but this has not led to significant internal migration within the country. Rather, Cape Verdean women's internal mobility has been constrained by other factors, such as the need for and importance of proximity to friends and family (Altieri 1992; Andall 1999).

The majority of Cape Verdean women are no longer employed as live-in domestic workers and they have shifted instead to hourly paid domestic work. In the early stages of their migration, their incorporation into the live-in sphere had significant ramifications for their family life. Italian legislation organised their labour as live-in work and not only did they earn lower wages than Italian nationals but they were additionally tied to employers in a way that would have been unthinkable for Italian women. The young women worked long hours and had limited time off as there were only slow improvements in general working conditions in the sector. Where Cape Verdean women found good employers and working conditions however, they demonstrated remarkably high levels of stability, often living-in with the same family for many years.

In the cities and regions where Cape Verdean women initially settled, paid domestic work was a buoyant and secure employment sector. Indeed, in the 1970s, female migrants in Italy were viewed as having more stable employment opportunities compared to men and this partially explains the huge gender imbalance amongst Cape Verdeans in Italy. The dominance of domestic work reduced the incentive for family reunification where male partners would be more precariously incorporated into local labour markets. In the early years, some Cape Verdean men were also employed alongside their wives and they worked as a 'couple' with the men working as gardeners or drivers. Others worked in the construction sector. The limited numbers of Cape Verdean men migrating to Italy has not facilitated the internal mobility of

Cape Verdeans towards the northern industrial regions, where, in the 1980s, male migrants from other African countries began to find employing in the heavy industry.

The stable employment conditions of Cape Verdean women in the domestic work sector are, however, increasingly coming in jeopardy. The implications of limited employment diversification are becoming increasingly evident in light of the evolution of Italian migration trends. Cape Verdean women now face greater employment competition, particularly given the increased intensity of East European migration to Italy. This transformation has been rapid and substantial. For example, in 1999, in the Naples region, there were only 681 legally resident Ukrainian labour migrants, compared to 1,010 Cape Verdeans (Caritas 2000). In 2000, Ukrainians numbered 1,355, overtaking the number of Cape Verdeans (Caritas 2001). Following an immigration regularisation policy in 2002, Ukrainians, in 2003, emerged as the largest ethnic minority in the region, numbering 31,042. Eighty per cent of Ukrainian nationals in the region are women and are primarily employed in the domestic work sector (Caritas 2004). The competition they pose to Cape Verdean women is not simply the result of more migrant women supplying domestic or care work but it is also intimately tied to their form of labour supply. For example, in Naples first Polish and then Ukrainian women developed forms of rotational labour, where they worked for a family for a few months and were then replaced by a female relative or an acquaintance (De Filippo 1994; Spanò and Zaccaria 2003). Some East European women's mobility was therefore less focused on settlement, which inevitably had an impact on labour market conditions and the opportunities available to Cape Verdeans. In fact, the Cape Verdeans who were interviewed in Naples, in 2005, confirmed that work was scarcer in Naples as a result of the presence of East European women.

Gender and generation

The consequences of living in a community of nationals that was predominantly female and largely restricted to the domestic work sector has also had an impact on the lives of Cape Verdean women. Consular data on marriages contracted in Italy between 1977 and 1996 showed that almost 40 per cent of Cape Verdean marriages were with non-Cape Verdeans (Monteiro 1997). Monteiro's overview of Cape Verdeans in Turin found that approximately half had married Italians, while others were married to Eritreans, Congolese and Cameroonians. Altieri (1992) has also noted the higher percentage of mixed marriages with Italians in Milan compared to other regions in Italy.

Live-in domestic work, moreover, reduced the opportunities for socialisation. Just as their initial migration had originally been organised by
Catholic organisations, so too were their social encounters in Italy. In
Rome, for example, when Cape Verdeans had time off on Thursday
and Sunday afternoons it was frequently spent at the *Tra Noi* Catholic
association. According to one Cape Verdean's description of this association: '*Tra Noi* allowed friends and family the opportunity to meet
up; we heard news of our families from the newly arrived; we read and
wrote letters for our friends who were illiterate; we had parties with
Cape Verdean music and, before we went back home, we went to
Church' (De Lourdes Jesus 1989: 85). In Rome, the central train station
Stazione Termini initially emerged as an alternative meeting point for
Cape Verdean women and later clubs such as *Criola* became popular
meeting places. An official Cape Verdean Association was founded in
Italy, in 1975, which aimed to support Cape Verdean immigrants and
provide information about their employment rights, but it also focused
on cultural activities often organised in conjunction with the various
communities of Cape Verdeans in Italy. In 1988, the Organisation of
Cape Verdean Women in Italy was formed to address new issues facing
Cape Verdeans (Pimentel 1989).

Although Cape Verdean migration was initially composed of single
women, many of them were also mothers at the time of their migration. In Milan, it was estimated that approximately half of them had
children (Monteiro 1997). This was a particularly relevant factor in the
Italian context, where single-parent families were uncommon and in-
frastructures for supporting single, working mothers were undeveloped. In addition, live-in work was simply incompatible with family
life and mothering responsibilities. In the recent past, this type of work
was in fact done by single Italian women without children. The care of
their own children has thus been a particularly serious issue among
Cape Verdeans in Italy. Some women who migrated had left their children behind to be cared for by relatives in Cape Verde. Others gave
birth to children in Italy and either sent them or took them back to
Cape Verde to be raised. For those who kept their children in Italy, the
use of residential homes as a way to reconcile their family and work
obligations developed into a common practice. Of the estimated 500
Cape Verdean children in Italy, in the late 1980s, at least 200 had been
placed in residential homes (De Lourdes Jesus 1989). Thus, the second
generation of Cape Verdean origin is not a uniform body in Italy. It includes not only children born in Italy but also those born in Italy and
sent back to Cape Verde for a significant part of their childhood. It includes children who may have spent time in Cape Verde, Portugal or
the Netherlands before a suitable arrangement could be found for
them in Italy. It includes children born or brought to Italy but who

then grew up temporarily or largely in residential homes, particularly in Rome. It includes children born in Italy who grew up with their mothers in the employer's home. It also includes those who were the product of mixed marriages in Italy. This diversity reflects the difficulties that Cape Verdean women have encountered in trying to fulfil their roles as mothers in Italy. Indeed, some of the movement away from Italy to cities such as Rotterdam was in part motivated by the desire of these women to live independently and to have a more regular family life. In any case, this variation makes it difficult to generalise about the second generation. The first generation has certainly attempted to encourage cultural attachment to Cape Verde through the organisation of various cultural activities. However, the second generation is also geographically settled in areas of Italy where employment prospects for young people are often poor or precarious. More detailed and systematic research is still needed to fully assess the wider consequences of their experiences in Italy.

Conclusions

Two dominant factors have characterised the situation of Cape Verdeans in Italy: the significant gender imbalance amongst Cape Verdean nationals and their concentration in the domestic work sector. While these factors have restricted Cape Verdeans' internal mobility within Italy, leading to a geographical concentration in some of the less economically dynamic areas of the country, these factors have simultaneously led to a secondary movement out of Italy to countries like the Netherlands. To date, Italy has provided Cape Verdean women with stable employment. However, current trends may mean that this situation will change in the future. Moreover, their renewed 'invisibility' as a small migrant community in Italy may well be obscuring the long-term ramifications of gender imbalance combined with a concentration in the domestic work sector.

Notes

[1] My analysis draws on primary qualitative data conducted with Cape Verdean female migrants in Rome, in the early 1990s, the second generation of Cape Verdean origin in Milan in 2000 and with the first and second generations in Naples, in 2005.

References

Altieri, G. (1992) 'I Capoverdiani', in *L'arcipelago immigrazione*, G. Mottura (ed.), Rome: Ediesse, pp. 185-201.

Amaturo, E. and Morlicchio, E. (1993) 'Immigrazione e identità femminile: il caso della comunità di Capoverde a Napoli', in *Immigrazione in Europe*, M. delle Donne, U. Melotti and S. Petilli (eds.), Rome: CEDISS, pp. 471-480.

Andall, J. (1999) 'Cape Verdean Women on the Move: 'Immigration Shopping' in Italy and Europe'. *Modern Italy* 4(2): 241-57.

Andall, J. (2000) *Gender, Migration and Domestic Service: The Politics of Black Women in Italy*. Aldershot: Ashgate.

Bisogno, E.; Tanturri, M.L. (2000) 'Gli immigrati stranieri nel mercato del lavoro ufficiale: la Compania nel contesto nazionale', in *Gli Immigrati in Campania*, A. Pane and S. Strozza (eds.), Torino: L'Harmattan Italia, pp. 75-92.

Caritas (2000) Immigrazione. Dossier Statistico 2004. Rome: Anterem.

Caritas (2001) Immigrazione. Dossier Statistico 2004. Rome: Anterem.

Caritas (2004) Immigrazione. Dossier Statistico 2004. Rome: Anterem.

Carreira, A. (1982) *The People of the Cape Verde Islands: Exploitation and Emgiration*. London: C. Hurst & Co (trans. by Christopher Fyfe).

Crowley, H.; Puwar, N.; Kofman, H.; Raghuram, P. (eds.) (2004) *Feminist Review – Special Issue: Labour Migrations*, vol. 77, no. 1.

De Filippo, E. (1994) 'Le lavoratrici "girono e notte"', in *Le mani invisibili. La vita e il lavoro delle donne immigrate*, G.Vicarelli (ed.), Rome: Ediesse, pp. 65-72.

De Lourdes Jesus, M. (1989) 'La Nostra Emigrazione in Italia', in *Capo Verde. Una storia lunga dieci isole*, OMCVI (ed.), Milan: D'Anselmi, pp. 85-88.

Feminist Review (2004) *Special Issue on Labour Migrations: Women on the Move*, 77.

Gamburd, M. (2000) *The Kitchen Spoon's Handle: Transnationalism and Sri Lanka's Migrant Housemaids*. Cornell, NY: University Press.

Monteiro, C.A. (1997) *Comunidade Imigrada, Visão Sociológica: O Caso da Itália*. São Vicente: Gráfica do Mindelo, Lda.

Morokvasic, M.; Erel, U.; Shinozaki, K. (eds.) (2003) *Crossing Borders and Shifting Boundaries: Gender on the Move* (vol. 1). Leske & Budrich: Opladen.

Parreñas, R. (2001) *Servants of Globalization*. Stanford, CA: Stanford University Press.

Pimentel, C. (1989) 'Fino al giorno che ci incontreremo', in *Capo Verde. Una storia lunga dieci isole*, OMCVI (ed.), Milan: D'Anselmi, pp. 89-91.

Scrinzi, F. (2004) 'Professioniste della tradizione. Le donne migranti nel mercato del lavoro domestico', *Polis* 1: 107-136.

Spanò, A.; Zaccaria, A. (2003) 'Il mercato delle collaborazioni domestiche a Napoli: il caso delle ucraine e delle polacche', in *Percorsi migratori tra reti etniche, istituzioni e mercato del lavoro*, M. La Rosa and L. Zanfrini (eds.), Milan: F. Angeli, pp. 193-224.

Chapter 8
Cape Verdeans in the Netherlands

Jørgen Carling

The Dutch-Cape Verdean community has an ambivalent position in the Cape Verdean diaspora. On the on hand, the Netherlands retains its reputation from the 1960s as a wealthy and orderly land of opportunities. On the other hand, people in Cape Verde increasingly associate the Netherlands with drugs and other social problems. The Cape Verdean minority has also acquired an ambiguous image in Dutch society. It was traditionally seen as a hard-working, inconspicuous immigrant population. More recently, the Dutch-Cape Verdean community is being discussed in more critical terms.

The Netherlands has the third largest population of Cape Verdeans in diaspora, after the U.S. and Portugal. The Dutch-Cape Verdean community has also been important as a stepping-stone for the expansion of the Cape Verdean diaspora in northern Europe. At the beginning of 2005, the legally resident population of Cape Verdean origin was 20,100.

Seafarers and the creation of a migrant community

Migration from Cape Verde to the Netherlands started in the 1950s and gained pace in the early 1960s. Young men, primarily from Santo Antão, São Vicente and São Nicolau, came to Rotterdam in search of work as seafarers. After the first handful of men arrived on their own, a classical chain migration system developed. Brothers, nephews and friends were assisted by those who had arrived before them. The vast majority were housed in Cape Verdean pensions when they were not at sea. Elderly men who worked at sea in the 1960s often talk very fondly about the spirit of community and cooperation in Rotterdam at the time. Newcomers were well taken care of, and those who were employed contributed a portion of their earnings to a pot from which the less fortunate were supported. The Heemraadsplein square was the focal point of the Cape Verdean community, and became known as *Prasinha d'Kebród*, literally 'Square of the Broke'. In 2001, the municipality acknowledged the Cape Verdean name for the square alongside the Dutch name.[1]

The shipping industry was booming in post-war Europe, and Rotterdam was where not only Dutch but also Norwegian, British and German ships recruited their crews. In 1962, Rotterdam surpassed New York as the world's largest port, and for the remainder of the century it handled more goods than any other port in the world. The high level of activity meant that many Cape Verdeans found work soon after they arrived.

In the 1960s, the Netherlands was relatively open to immigrants. Labour migrants could easily enter in search of work without formal intermediaries. Provided they found employment and accommodation, they could eventually acquire work and residence permits. The 1970s was a much more difficult period for Cape Verdeans in the Netherlands. The world-wide recession severely affected the shipping industry, and companies started hiring Asian seafarers at lower salaries. Cape Verdean independence in 1975 also meant a loss of European citizenship and increasing difficulties with immigration regulations.

Many of the former seafarers who settled in the Rotterdam area had wives and children in Cape Verde. While working at sea, they could usually return home once a year. As late as the early 1990s, unemployed seafarers with families in Cape Verde or Portugal were still numerous in Rotterdam. The seafarers could not spend more than three months outside the Netherlands without losing their social benefits, and their lack of work made family reunification difficult (Silva 1997). Others found work on shore and managed to bring their families to the Netherlands.

In the 1970s, important links also developed between the male-dominated Cape Verdean community in the Netherlands and the almost exclusively female community in Italy (Andall 1999). There were several thousand Cape Verdean women working as domestic maids in Italy and many opted to migrate to the Netherlands in search of greater autonomy and better working conditions. As a consequence of their migration from Italy, family reunification, and increasing independent female migration from Cape Verde, women became the majority among Cape Verdean immigrants to the Netherlands beginning in the early 1970s.[2] Today the numbers of men and women are roughly equal, both among the resident population and among new immigrants.

Settlement patterns and islands of origin

Almost one-third of all Cape Verdeans in the Netherlands live in the borough of Delfshaven in central Rotterdam. This is where we find the most 'Cape Verdean' neighbourhoods of northern Europe, Schiemond,

Spangen and Bospolder, where at least 10 per cent of the residents are of Cape Verdean origin (COS 2005). Cape Verdeans, more than any other large immigrant group in the Netherlands, are surrounded by other immigrants: almost half live in areas where the majority of residents are non-Western immigrants. Today, many Cape Verdeans are choosing to move to the outskirts of Rotterdam.

Only about 15 per cent of the Cape Verdeans in the Netherlands, or about 3,000 people, live outside greater Rotterdam. There are several hundred Cape Verdeans in Amsterdam and in The Hague, and small communities are found in Zaandam just north of Amsterdam, and in the town of Delfzijl on the North Sea coast.

Mechanisms of chain migration have created links between each Cape Verdean island and specific diaspora communities (Carling 2003a). The island of origin is also an important aspect of the identity of Cape Verdeans in diaspora. Most Cape Verdeans in the Netherlands trace their origins to the northwestern islands of Santo Antão, São Vicente and São Nicolau. A recent survey of the Cape Verdean-born population in Rotterdam aged 35 or above showed that almost three-quarters were born on one of these three islands.[3]

Among the early migrants there were also significant numbers of people from Santiago. Their proportion has increased in recent years, with immigration from Cape Verde and from Cape Verdean communities in Portugal. The close identification with a particular island of origin is less pronounced in the second generation who often argue for abandoning the division by island and focusing on unity among Cape Verdeans (Bosman 1997; Strooij 2000).

The struggle for legality

Obtaining a residence permit in the Netherlands has often been a challenge for Cape Verdeans, and many have spent time as illegal immigrants. They have primarily entered on tourist visas or as seafarers and overstayed the legal limit of their sojourn. In the 1980s, it was even possible for many illegal residents to acquire a social security number and work as if they were legal residents. The black economy was also substantially larger than today, and many employers did not take the lack of a work permit too seriously. The 1990s saw a pronounced shift in policy and practice, making it more difficult to enter the Netherlands through family reunification, more difficult to live and work illegally in the country, and more difficult to acquire a residence permit after a period of illegality. As a result, there are relatively few illegally resident Cape Verdeans in the Netherlands today, perhaps just a couple of hundred people.[4] Rather than staying illegally in the Netherlands, migrants often chose to move to Luxembourg, France or Portugal, where it is easier to make a living without papers, and where the opportunities for regularisation are thought to be better.

Throughout the 1980s and the early 1990s, marriages played a very important role in sustaining the migration flow from Cape Verde to the Netherlands. Some migrants married only on paper, either with friends or relatives who wanted to help them out, or against a payment. The going rate in the early 1980s was about 2000 guilders. Taking inflation into account, this corresponds to less than 2,000 euros today. People were said to 'marry in the morning and collect their Dutch passport in the afternoon'. By the early 1990s, Dutch authorities had become acutely aware of the practice and began to make it more difficult. Among Cape Verdeans, the price for bogus marriages increased to more than 10,000 guilders (corresponding to 7,000 euros today when inflation is accounted for). Paying for marriages has apparently become a less important strategy for immigration, but 'family formation' still accounted for more than three-quarters of adult immigration from Cape Verde in the late 1990s (Statistics Netherlands 2001).

By looking at individual cases, it is evident that the 'bogus marriage' is not always such a clear-cut category. Many of the Cape Verdean women who married Dutch men have had children by these men, even if the marriage was initially conceived as a purely practical arrangement. There are also many cases of Cape Verdeans of both sexes who fetched partners from Cape Verde only to have these relationships come to an end as soon as the immigrant partners acquired their resident permits. Even if the relationship was apparently a 'genuine' one, such experiences indicate that the residence permit can be essential to the migrating partner's motivation.

Cape Verdeans in Dutch society

The Netherlands is probably the only country in the world where the Cape Verdean population is sufficiently large, and the quality of statistics sufficiently good, to make quantitative comparisons with other immigrant groups. Much of the research and public debate on immigration in the Netherlands has focused on the 'four large groups': Turks, Moroccans, Surinamese, and Antilleans.

With reference to many integration indicators, Cape Verdeans are often positioned between the Moroccans and Turks on the one hand, and the Surinamese and Antilleans on the other. One characteristic which Cape Verdeans have in common with the latter groups is the high proportion of single mothers. Among the Cape Verdeans, one in five women in their twenties is a single mother (Bijl et al. 2005). This is ten times the average for native Dutch women, but should also be compared to the situation in Cape Verde, where single parenthood is almost as common as shared parenthood: 42 per cent of children live with only one parent, usually the mother (Instituto Nacional de Estatística 2002).

In terms of employment patterns, however, the Cape Verdeans stand out from the other groups. Two-thirds of the adults have paid employment – a striking statistic that mirrors the image others have of the Dutch-Cape Verdean community (Bijl et al. 2005). This is equal to that of the native population and much higher than among most other immigrant groups. The Cape Verdeans stand out not only because many are economically active, but also because very few are self-employed or entrepreneurs. Only 2 per cent of Cape Verdeans have their own business, compared to 8 per cent among all non-Western immigrants (Grammatikas 2005). With the decline of the shipping industry and the growing number of women in the community, cleaning became an important line of work for Cape Verdeans. In the mid-1990s, a staggering 60 per cent of Cape Verdean women and 21 per cent of Cape Verdean men who were registered as unemployed had 'cleaner' as their profession (Pires 1997).

In around 1990, the local association of immigrant workers, Stichting Buitenlandse Werknemers Rijnmond, described the Cape Verdeans as 'silent migrants'.[5] This characterisation has been widely used ever since (Gemeentearchief Rotterdam 2002; Góis 2002; Mesters 1999; Strooij-Sterken 1998). To some extent, the term 'silent' reflects perceptions of successful integration. It also evokes connotations of passivity and helplessness and is often rejected by the Dutch-Cape Verdeans themselves (Naber and Veldman 1997).

The growth of the second generation

The presence of Cape Verdean seafarers in Rotterdam resulted in a number of children of Cape Verdean fathers and Dutch mothers. These were the very first of the Dutch-Cape Verdean community's second generation. The number of births gained pace in the 1970s, and, since then, the majority of children has been by two Cape Verdean-born parents. In addition, many children were brought from Cape Verde by their parents. Those who were born in the country of origin and migrated as children are often referred to as the '1.5 generation' in the migration literature. Almost one-third of the Dutch-Cape Verdean population aged 25–40 belong to this category.

Young Cape Verdeans in the Netherlands are carving out their own identity as Dutch-Cape Verdeans, which is different from their immigrant parents. Most speak a mixture of Kriolu and Dutch, but often have a better command of Dutch. Young Cape Verdeans often identify themselves as *cabo* rather than using the proper Dutch word *kaapverdiaans*. For some, this is simply understood as a shorter term with the same meaning. Many of the older migrants despise the word, however, and newcomers often see it as a term denoting 'Dutch-Cape Verdean' as opposed to 'Cape Verdean-Cape Verdean'.

While the first generation in many ways stood out as an exemplary, hard-working group, the second generation Cape Verdeans seem to share many of the problems of other non-Western immigrant populations. For instance, the proportion of first-generation migrants who depend on general welfare benefits is lower among Cape Verdeans than in the four larger immigrant groups (Bijl et al. 2005). For the second generation, however, the proportion of welfare recipients is highest among Cape Verdeans. A similar picture emerges from crime statistics. Among first-generation men, Cape Verdeans have the second lowest probability of being charged with a crime. Male descendants, by contrast, have the second highest crime rates. These observations raise questions about integration trends over time. Did the first generation have a comparatively advantageous position which they have not been successful in transferring to their children?

While available statistics point in different directions, Cape Verdeans have enjoyed a reputation as calm and co-operative in the eyes of authorities and peers from other ethnic groups (Butte 2004). The image of young Cape Verdeans took a blow in 2005, however. A group of boys aged between 16 and 20 were convicted of gang rapes and sexual abuse of several girls aged 12-15. Through the media, it became widely known that the boys called themselves 'Cabo Pimp Unit' and had operated as a group on a regular basis. The case had a particularly great impact on the Cape Verdean community because the boys had institutionalised the molestation by adopting a name, and had chosen one which explicitly identified them as Cape Verdean. In discussions on the Internet after the trials, many Cape Verdean youths expressed not only disgust over the actions, but also disappointment and frustration over the consequences for the image of Cape Verdeans. Paraphrasing the proverb 'silent waters run deep', one young man was concerned that especially now people would more easily suspect the 'silent Cape Verdean immigrants' of having dark secrets. Similar worries had been raised earlier in the year after a report by the local Labour Party suggested that more than half of Cape Verdean teenage girls in Rotterdam had been sexually abused by their fathers or stepfathers (PvdA Rotterdam 2005).

About three-quarters of Dutch-Cape Verdeans in their teens and early twenties are born in the Netherlands, and of the remainder, many left Cape Verde at an early age or were born in Portugal. Consequently, it is possible for young Dutch-Cape Verdeans to relate almost exclusively to peers with a multicultural background similar to their own. For some, the first encounter with 'Cape Verdean-Cape Verdeans' of their own age comes on holidays to Cape Verde. Stimulating the second generation's links with Cape Verde is an important aspect of the long-term diaspora policy of Cape Verde, but strengthened ethnic self-consciousness is also seen as important in an integration perspective. In Rotterdam, the Cape Verdean youth organisation CABO works to 'let Cape Verdean children get to know their roots so that they can integrate better in society' (Jongerenorganisatie CABO 2004: 9; Reekers and Lopes 2001). Newly arrived immigrants are often quite contemptuous of the young Dutch-Cape Verdeans for their lacking of or superficial 'Cape Verdeanness'. In their view, the second generation might eat *katxupa*, but their behaviour and mentality are essentially Dutch.

Dutch-Cape Verdean youth who wish to assert their Cape Verdean identity do not have easy access to 'Cape Verdean culture' as a system of values, beliefs and practices. Many turn to more accessible cultural systems with elements of 'colour' (as opposed to Dutch whiteness) and 'resistance'. These are as diverse as capoeira, reggae, hip-hop and gangsta rap. While the Cape Verdean musical tradition is rich and varied, it does not offer similarly comprehensive dimensions of ideology and lifestyle. In self-presentations on the Internet, Cape Verdean youth often use nicknames consisting of the ethnic identifier 'cabo' in combination with gangsta rap vocabulary such as 'thug', 'nigga', 'pimp' and 'bitch'. The name Cabo Pimp Unit, for instance, was inspired by the rapper 50 cents, his crew G-Unit, and his hit *P.I.M.P.*

While the term 'second generation' often evokes concerns about social problems, the emergence of a Dutch-educated Cape Verdean population also represents great potential. It has contributed to the professionalisation of Dutch-Cape Verdean organisations, increased the visibility of the community, and facilitated with Dutch authorities (Consulado-General de Cabo Verde em Roterdão 1998; Santos 2002).

Dutch-Cape Verdean transnationalism

The Dutch-Cape Verdean community has been important to Cape Verde through its political involvement and through its financial contributions (Reekers 1997). In São Vicente, one of the broadest, most imposing streets is named Avenida de Holanda, and is lined with migrants' homes. The former migrants who now collect their pensions from the Netherlands are a highly visible, well-to-do group who are admired in the local community (Åkesson 2004; Carling 2001).

When national remittance statistics were first recorded, in the late 1970s, the Netherlands accounted for more than a quarter of the transfers – more than any other country, including Portugal and the U.S. At a time when consumer goods were also hard to obtain in Cape Verde, migrants in the Netherlands were also instrumental in supplying the islands with merchandise such as television sets and video recorders (Lesourd et al. 1989). It is still common for Cape Verdeans in the Netherlands to have their garden sheds filled with consumer goods that they are planning to ship to relatives on the islands. The development of the community over the past 25 years has tended to suppress remittances flows, however. Family reunification, the transition from work at sea to living on shore, and the falling proportion of recently arrived migrants have all been contributing factors. The absolute amounts continued to rise until the turn of the century, but not the real value: in 2004, it was only a quarter of the late-1970s level. The decline was, however, mitigated by the increased transfer of social benefits from the Netherlands to Cape Verde. In 2004, these transfers were almost as large as those made by migrants.[6]

In a study of circular migration between the Netherlands and Cape Verde, Danhof (2005) found that both first- and second-generation migrants see a transnational lifestyle with circulation between the two countries as ideal. While first-generation migrants emphasised emotional ties to Cape Verde, the descendants made more explicit references to the different ways of life in the two countries. The vast majority of the pre-independence migrants came with the intention of returning. For many, this has been replaced by a desire for a transnational existence. The barriers to such a lifestyle are primarily financial. Having a house in each country and travelling regularly between the two is too expensive for most Dutch-Cape Verdeans.

It is sometimes assumed that transnationalism and integration are opposite trajectories. Given the financial demands of a transnational existence, however, it is not surprising that those who are the least integrated in Dutch society are often also among the least transnational. These people might live much of their lives within the confines of the Dutch-Cape Verdean community, but with no or little contact with Cape Verde.

Notes

[1] The street sign reads 'Heemraadsplein/Pracinha d'Quêbrod'. Upon the unveiling of the name in 2001, it was argued that the correct form should be 'Quebrôd' with the circumflex accent over the 'o'. Using the officially approved Alupec orthography, the name should be 'Kebród'.

[2] The only relevant data available are statistics on the length of stay of the current Cape Verdean population in the Netherlands. Among Cape Verdean-born residents whose most recent immigration was in 1971 or later, women are in the majority. This does not take into account differences in mortality and emigration rates between men and women, nor the influence of multiple migrations.

[3] Refers to Cape Verdean-born inhabitants in Rotterdam who have resided at least 15 years in the Netherlands. Estimated on the basis of a custom sample drawn from the municipal register of Rotterdam, on 1 April 2004, for the European research project *Immigrants and Ethnic Minorities in European Cities* (Institute for Migration and Ethnic Studies, University of Amsterdam) and unpublished population statistics from Statistics Netherlands.

[4] Engbersen et al. (2002) estimate the total number of illegal non-European residents to be in the range of 65,000 to 91,000. If the proportion of Cape Verdeans is the same among illegal residents overall as it was among those who were arrested, this indicates an illegally resident Cape Verdean population of 300-400 people.

[5] The term 'silent minority' has also been used to describe a variety of immigrant groups in the U.S., including Chinese, Japanese, Filipinos, Indians and Latinos.

[6] Calculated on the basis of statistics from Banco de Cabo Verde, Statistics Netherlands and the Sociale Verzekeringsbank (See Carling 2003b; Vuijsje 2004).

References

Åkesson, L. (2004) *Making a Life: Meanings of Migration in Cape Verde*, Ph.D. dissertation, Gothenburg: Department of Social Anthropology, University of Gothenburg.

Andall, J. (1999) 'Cape Verdean Women on the Move: "Immigration Shopping" in Italy and Europe'. *Modern Italy* 4(2): 241-257.

Bijl, R.V.; Zorlu, A.; Rijn, A.S.V.; Jennissen, R.P.W.; Blom, M. (2005) *Integratiekaart 2005*. Cahier, 2005-16. Den Haag: Wetenschappelijk Onderzoek- en Documentatiecentrum (WODC), Ministerie van Justitie.

Bosman, P. (1997) *Cabo Verde aan de Maas. Kaapverdianen in Rotterdam: Groepsidentiteit en religie*, Doctoraalscriptie maatschappij-geschiedenis, Rotterdam: Faculteit der Historische en Kunstwetenschappen, Erasmus Universiteit Rotterdam.

Butte, D. (2004) *Kaapverdiaanse jongens: minder agressief en delinquent dan ze zelf aangeven?* Rotterdam: GGD Rotterdam en omstreken.

Carling, J. (2001) *Aspiration and Ability in International Migration: Cape Verdean Experiences of Mobility and Immobility*. Dissertations and theses, 2001/5, Oslo: Centre for Development and the Environment, University of Oslo.

Carling, J. (2003a) 'Cartographies of Cape Verdean Transnationalism'. *Global Networks* 3(4): 335-341.

Carling, J. (2003b) 'Crescem ou Descem as Remessas da Holanda para Cabo Verde?' *Letras das Ilhas* 2(1): 2.

Consulado-Geral de Cabo Verde em Roterdão (1998) *Relatório de Actividades 1997*. Rotterdam: Consulate-General of Cape Verde.

COS (2005) *Buurtinformatie Rotterdam Digitaal*. Rotterdam: Centrum voor Onderzoek en Statistiek.

Danhof, K. (2005) *An Intergenerational Approach to Circular Migration Between the Netherlands and Cape Verde*. Unpublished thesis, Groningen: Faculty of Spatial Sciences, University of Groningen.

Engbersen, G.; Staring, R.; van der Leun, J.; de Boom, J.; van der Heijden, P.; Cruijff, M. (2002) *Illegale vreemdelingen in Nederland*. Rotterdam: RISBO Contractresearch BV/Erasmus Universiteit.

Gemeentearchief Rotterdam (2002) *Sporen van migratie in Rotterdam.* www.gemeentearchief.
rotterdam.nl/sporenvanmigratie.

Góis, P. (2002) *A Emigração Cabo-verdiana Para (e na) Europa e a Sua Inserção em Mercados de Trabalho Locais: Lisboa, Milão, Roterdão.* Master's dissertation, Faculdade de Economia, Universidade de Coimbra.

Grammatikas, D. (2005) 'Er is werk... aan de winkel!' *Lize-bulletin* 14(2): 7.

Instituto Nacional de Estatística (2002) *Recenseamento Geral da População e Habitação 2000.* Praia: INE.

Jongerenorganisatie CABO (2004) *Werkplan Jongerenorganisatie CABO 2005.* Rotterdam: Jongerenorganisatie CABO.

Lesourd, M.; Diehl, J. P.; Duchemin, P.; Fornesi, I. (1989) *Cap-Vert. Émigration internationale et transfert des émigrés. Rapport de phase I.* Praia: Ministério de Plano e Cooperação.

Mesters, B. (1999) 'Mensen met dromen en heimwee'. *De Volkskrant* (Amsterdam), 17 April.

Naber, P.; Veldman, F. (1997) *De stilte voorbij. Onderzoek naar de leefwereld en de maatschappelijke positie van Kaapverdiaanse jongeren in Rotterdam en zaanstad.* Jongerenorganisatie Cabo.

Pires, D.T.D.R. (1997) *Immigratie en integratie op de arbeidsmarkt: Een vergelijkende onderzoek naar de arbeidsmarktpositie van Kaapverdianen in Lissabon en Rotterdam.* Rotterdam: Faculteit der Sociale Wetenschappen, Erasmus Universiteit Rotterdam.

PvdA Rotterdam (2005) *Het stille verdriet van tienermeiden in Rotterdam.* Rotterdam: Gemeentreaadsfractie PvdA Rotterdam.

Reekers, E. (1997) *Migranten en Achterblijvers. De contacten tussen Kaapverdianen in Rotterdam en Santo Antão.* PhD thesis, Amsterdam: Department of Cultural Anthropology and Non-Western Sociology, University of Amsterdam.

Reekers, E.; Lopes, I. (2001) *Thuis: Kaapverdië of Rotterdam. Kaapverdiaanse jongeren gaan op zoek naar hun roots.* Rotterdam: Jongerenorganisatie Cabo.

Santos, Z.D. dos (2002) *Kaapverdiaanse jongeren. Op welke wijze draagt Jongerenorganisatie Cabo bij aan een positieve loopbaanontwikkeling bij mensen die actief zijn binnen de vereniging?* Unpublished thesis, Rotterdam, Hogeschool Rotterdam.

Silva, A. (1997) *Heimwee naar het eigene: de werkelijkheid achter de zoektocht van de Kaapverdianen naar de 'eigen identiteit'.* Doctoraalscriptie, Amsterdam: Faculteit der Sociaal-Culturele Wetenschappen, Vrije Universiteit Amsterdam.

Statistics Netherlands (2001) *Cape Verdean Born Persons Registered in the Central Register of non-Dutch Nationals of the Dutch Ministry of Justice.* Unpublished statistics. The Hague: Statistics Netherlands.

Strooij, H. (2000) 'Eilanden aan de Maas: De Kaapverdische gemeenschap van Rotterdam', in *Afrikanen in Nederland,* I. van Kessel and N. Tellegen (eds), Amsterdam: Koninklijk Instituut voor de Tropen, pp. 43-60.

Strooij-Sterken, H. (1998) 'Kaapverdianen. Hoe lang nog de "stille migranten" van Rotterdam?', in *Vier eeuwen migratie, bestemming Rotterdam,* P. van de Laar, T. de Nijs, J. Okkema and A. Oosthoek (eds.), Rotterdam: MondiTaal, pp. 266-281.

Vuijsje, M. (2004) 'Feesten voor het moederland', in *Stille gevers. Migranten en hun steun aan het thuisland,* J. Van der Meer (ed.), Amsterdam: De Balie, pp. 11-23.

Chapter 9
Cape Verdeans in Sweden

Lisa Åkesson

The first Cape Verdeans to permanently settle in Sweden arrived in the late 1950s.[1] They came from what was then still a famine-stricken society, and they arrived in a country characterised by a booming post-war economy, an inhospitable climate and an almost total unfamiliarity with non-European immigrants. These first pioneers were young men, they came from the islands of Boa Vista and São Vicente and they arrived in Sweden quite accidentally. Like many other young male Cape Verdeans, they had worked their way out into the world as seafarers, and when the ships on which they were hired arrived in Gothenburg, Sweden's second largest city and a major port, they decided to try their luck in the new country.

When these first migrants settled in Gothenburg they began sending for members of their families. During this period of time, labour was in great demand in Sweden, and the newly arrived easily found a relatively well-paid job. The men were generally employed in the shipping industry, while the women typically worked as cleaners or in restaurants. Those who were already established in the labour market introduced newcomers to their workplaces, which meant that a Cape Verdean presence came to characterise smaller enterprises. Cape Verdeans who came during this period of time often emphasised how they helped each other find jobs, and some of this solidarity seems to have survived into the present day. Newcomers are helped in seeking employment, and there is still a certain concentration of Cape Verdeans in some Gothenburg workplaces.

A similar pattern of mutual support can be found with regard to housing. The first arrivals lived together in cramped apartments in the centre of Gothenburg. In the mid-1960s, some moved to the newer housing estates in Biskopsgården, which is situated close to the harbour, where many of the Cape Verdean men worked. Once some had settled in Biskopsgården they helped others to find apartments there. Today, people with Cape Verdean backgrounds are found in a variety of professions and living in very different areas of town. Biskopsgården has, however, continued to function as the social centre of the community. The Cape Verdean association meetings take place in Biskopsgården, and community members talk about the area as a place where 'many' Cape Verdeans live.

In the early 1970s, Sweden was hit by the international economic recession, which adversely affected the labour market. The Gothenburg shipyards closed down and many Cape Verdean men had to look for new jobs. Another consequence of the economic crisis was that labour migration came to a halt, making it harder for Cape Verdeans and other migrants to gain residence rights in Sweden.

Since the beginning of the 1980s, family reunification and family formation has been the most common mode of immigration for Cape Verdeans. Today, about 600 people born in Cape Verde live in Sweden. To this we can add their children and grandchildren, who, to varying degrees, consider their Cape Verdean origins an important aspect of their identity. The majority of the first generation emigrated from the Barlavento islands. As noted, the Swedish Cape Verdeans are largely concentrated in Gothenburg, and the two main Cape Verdean associations are based in that city. The oldest organisation, *Associação Caboverdeana*, attracts mainly middle-aged and elderly people, while the members of *Cabo Verde IF* are generally younger.[2] This division reflects one of the most important internal differences in the Cape Verdean community; the division between 'the young' and 'the old'.

Two generations

Those labelled 'old' are those who arrived between the late 1950s and early 1970s, i.e., when Sweden was still welcoming labour migrants. Many in this group are approaching retirement or have already retired. The majority of them worked as manual labourers in Sweden. The first generation, considered a hard-working person as an ideal, especially for males. Elderly Cape Verdean men are proud to name all the places where they have worked and emphasise the demanding character of their various jobs.

The ideal of hard work is very much connected to the idea of returning to Cape Verde as a person who has made it. The primary sign of being a successful migrant is the construction of a nice and sizeable house in the homeland. This is important not only for their status as returned migrants in Cape Verde, but also for their social standing vis-à-vis the Cape Verdeans in Sweden.

Among those with a house in Cape Verde, a transnational lifestyle has become increasingly common. Retired transnationalists can live an economically independent life in Cape Verde thanks to their relatively large pensions, while also having full access to health care and other kinds of social security in Sweden. Not everyone returns, however.

Some have voluntarily renounced their contacts with Cape Verde, while others feel they cannot return because they have failed to fulfil the culturally prescribed migration trajectory of working hard, building a house and returning as someone who has made it in this life (Åkesson 2004).

For many of the older Cape Verdeans in Sweden, the question of returning, either permanently or temporarily, is vital. For a long period of time, they lived with the idea that when their working days were finally over they would return to the homeland. For some this has been the ultimate objective of all their years of working in Sweden. Many, however, have come to realise that the homeland they dreamt about is not the place they experience upon their return. The dilemma of experiencing one's sense of belonging as fractured after many years of living outside of Cape Verde was expressed by a Cape Verdean man who lived in Sweden for more than forty years:

> I feel more estranged in Cape Verde than in Sweden. Inside me, I feel that the *terra firm'* [firm land] is my home village. I have strong ties to it, but when I return there I feel alienated. When I'm in São Vicente I want to go back to my home village, but once there I want to return to São Vicente, and when I'm in São Vicente I want to go back to Sweden. Where do I feel one hundred per cent myself?

The fulfilment of the ideal migration trajectory is not the only factor that is decisive for the social status of the first generation. Differences in educational background have over the years created some tensions among the older Cape Verdeans in Sweden. In colonial Cape Verde, only a small and privileged minority attended the *liceu* (secondary school). The social boundary between those who attended the *liceu* and the rest of the population was clear-cut and decisive for most aspects of everyday life (Matos n.d.). For migrants belonging to 'the old' generation, this social division remains important. In Sweden, those with little schooling sometimes accuse their better-educated compatriots of being arrogant, while the latter sometimes accuse them of being 'jealous'.

The issue's sensitivity is heightened by the fact that educational background is linked to a number of other crucial social factors such as kinship, class and island of origin. Those who attended the *liceu* came mostly from one of the few privileged families who saw themselves as adhering to a European way of life. People in this group were often light-skinned and had kinship ties and other social links to Portugal. Before independence, in 1975, this social group was concentrated on the island of São Vicente. This concentration conferred a certain status on the inhabitants of that island, regardless of their schooling. In Sweden, those who come from São Vicente sometimes still portray themselves as more sophisticated than people from the other islands. Over the years, there have been some conflicts regarding the leadership and management of the Cape Verdean associations in Sweden. Typically, these disagreements are rooted in the social tensions that were created in the colonial past.

Despite the social differences among 'the old', 'the young' generation, i.e., those aged in their late teens to mid-thirties, is more heterogeneous. This is because there are young people of Cape Verdean descent who have lived their entire lives in Sweden, while others came as small children and some arrived as teenagers. Secondly, although some of 'the young' have dropped out of school at quite an early age, others have succeeded in completing a university education and found well-paid jobs. A third dividing factor is that people in this generation have different views on their ethnic identity. Some assert that they are first and foremost Cape Verdeans and others conceive of themselves as 'quite Swedish'. In the association of 'the young', Cape Verde IF, the balance between being 'Swedish' and 'Kriol'[3] has caused some discussions. Those who have not fulfilled their obligations towards the organisation have been criticised for being 'too Kriol', while people who have followed the rules and regulations have been accused of being 'overly Swedish'.

The young people I interviewed were all keen to discuss what it means to be a Cape Verdean in Sweden. The understandings they have about their ethnic identity, both as self-attributed and as ascribed by others, were clearly important to people in this group. Generally, however, they found it difficult to define how they manifest their Cape Verdeanness vis-à-vis the Swedish majority population, and they also tended to describe their group as quite invisible. Some explained that this invisibility was because lifestyle differences between Cape Verde and Sweden are quite small, and thus Cape Verdeans integrated relatively smoothly into Swedish society. This view was sometimes related to a desire to counteract views of Cape Verde as an 'underdeveloped' or non-European country. For instance, one man who wanted to impress upon me that his Cape Verdean childhood was perfectly 'modern' said, 'Actually, I've lived the same life as everybody in Europe. Since I was small I've had television, computer games and video games'.

Another important reason why there is little space for a conspicuous Cape Verdean identity in Swedish society is, naturally, the small size of the community. Some young people, however, thought that the public life invisibility was also related to the low level of entrepreneurial enterprise among Cape Verdean Swedes. They believe that this situation is caused by a lack of cooperation within the community. In order to start up your own enterprise, you need the help of others, but Cape Verdeans in Sweden 'only care about themselves'. What these informants hinted at was a sense of widespread individualism that has developed within the community.

There is one arena, however, where the young Cape Verdeans describe themselves as quite visible: Partying! The *Cabo Verde IF* has organised a number of '*Kriol* Parties', which have been frequented by large numbers of young people of Cape Verdean, Swedish or other ethnic backgrounds, who have enjoyed the music, the dancing and the 'tropical' atmosphere. According to my informants, Cape Verdeans know how to organise a nice party and *passá sab'* (have a good time) better than others. One of them, Rui, declared: 'Among young people, male and female, the *Kriol* parties are very popular here in Gothenburg. If you tell somebody that you are *Kriol*, yes, wow, they know.'

The good reputation Rui mentioned was also noted by others as well. Young Cape Verdean men are known to be flirty and good dancers, abilities which clearly distinguish them from the more wooden Swedish male youngsters. This is similar to stories I was told about young men of different ethnic backgrounds, such as Eritreans or Somalians, who had tried to pass as Cape Verdeans in order to make a favourable impression on the women they met. The somewhat flattering reputation of these young men is, however, not the only characteristic of Cape Verdean gender relations.

Women and men

Among the older generation, most of the men have been socialised into a gender system in which men have the right to exercise power over their female partners. Moreover, in Cape Verde masculinity is traditionally related to virility, and polygynous behaviour is a central aspect of being 'a real man' (Åkesson 2004). In Sweden, where the ideology (but not always the reality) of gender equality is pronounced, Cape Verdean men sometimes sense that they have lost some of their privileges. One man formulated this by saying that he feels that his father had the right to do many things that he himself cannot do today. Some men obviously feel threatened by the changes in power relations between women and men that they sense have taken place in Sweden. Many Cape Verdeans report that divorces are common among the first generation of immigrants, and they often attribute this to a clash between the male-dominated Cape Verdean gender system and the comparatively more equal relations between women and men in Sweden.

Males from the second generation often feel that they are also at disadvantage in Swedish society. The reason, however, is quite different.

Young female Cape Verdeans generally say that they have experienced no or little discrimination because of their status as 'immigrants' or 'blacks', while their male co-ethnics talk about such discrimination as an important and unpleasant part of their everyday lives. Discrimination seems to be especially common in the downtown nightlife scene, and many young men of Cape Verdean origin claim that they have been denied entry into a bar or discotheque. Male informants also point out the discriminatory treatment they receive in the labour market, and some discuss the more or less institutionalised racism of Swedish sports clubs. Clearly, many young Cape Verdean men share a feeling of not being treated equally by the society where they live.

Experiences of estrangement are something that Cape Verdean men share with many others. The young males categorised as non-European 'immigrants' (*invandrare*) are among the most demonised people in Swedish society. Young migrant women, on the other hand, are often stereotyped as passive victims of 'patriarchal cultures'. However, this kind of stereotyping does not affect the Cape Verdeans as much as it does women from the Middle East or other Muslim societies. By and large, Cape Verdean women seem to pass as some kind of slightly exotic being from an unknown little country.

Is there a community?

When Cape Verdeans talk about themselves as a group they often lament the influence of the individualistic Swedish lifestyle. This does not mean that people have come to totally neglect one another. Cape Verdeans in Gothenburg often point out, with a sigh or a smile, that 'everyone knows everyone else' in the group. This may be partly true, at least if 'knows' is understood to mean 'is knowledgeable about the existence of a person so and so'. With regard to more active contacts, ties of kinship and friendship keep people together, and those who live in the Biskopsgården neighbourhood meet each other regularly in public places like shops and public transport. But other than these encounters, a sense of a lost social network is widespread among the group. One woman put it like this:

> The *Kriols* in Sweden have become so lazy. At home, in Cape Verde, you socialise with other people; there is a party, there is always something. Here it's work and go home, work and go home. And sometimes you don't bother to go out, and maybe the weather prevents you as well. We have become part of this Swedish society, everything has become totally Swedish.

In Cape Verde, social intercourse is an important and time-consuming part of everyday life (Åkesson 2004). Those who have migrated often talk about the friendship and playfulness that they say characterises their personal relationships in the country of origin. The ability to joke, play, dance and generally create 'good vibrations' is praised as being typical Cape Verdean. This ability to have a good time is, however, described as more or less lost due to the influence of the Swedish individualistic lifestyle. 'In Sweden, you learn to live for yourself', one young man said. 'You lock yourself into a hole, you don't care about others'. In the right kind of environment, individuals can, however, recuperate their Cape Verdean social skills. This type of environment can also be found outside their homeland, however. During the holidays, Cape Verdean Swedes visit the larger *Kriol* communities in Rotterdam, Luxembourg and Lisbon, for instance. Here they find that they can socialise in a Cape Verdean manner. One woman had fond holiday memories:

> When we go to Holland, for instance, or Lisbon, and meet up with other *Kriols,* we go to parties, we have a really good time. You go to the beach, and all that. You have a really good time during the holidays, and then, when you're back here again you think 'Oh my God, we're back in Sweden again'.... Because in these places there's always a party, a *Kriol* party, every weekend there's a party, and here we don't have that. [...] We have adapted so much to the Swedes.

The feeling of being at home in other, larger Cape Verdean communities in Europe is something this woman shares with many others. To some, Holland and Portugal seem to feel more at 'home' than Cape Verde. When they return to Cape Verde some people experience a sense of loss and disappointment as they attempt to reconcile the reality they encounter with their memories and dreams of the homeland. This is not an issue when they visit kin and friends in Europe. Moreover, relations between people living in various areas of the diaspora are not burdened by the negotiations that take place between migrants and people in the homeland concerning the former's obligations to the latter.

The young woman quoted above also notes that 'we have adapted so much'. Does this mean that the Cape Verdean community in Sweden is slowly disintegrating, and that individuals are assimilating into Swedish society? My answer to this question is a hesitant 'no'. For instance, a core group remains active in one of the associations; they often live in Biskopsgården and first and foremost actively strive to maintain a view of themselves as Cape Verdeans. At the other end of the spectrum, however, there are those who hardly ever socialise with other

Cape Verdeans, have given up speaking Kriolu, and never return to Cape Verde. Among second-generation Cape Verdeans, the contrast between the core people and those who do not identify themselves as Cape Verdean has only increased. Many second-generation Cape Verdeans have Swedish partners, and in these mixed families the education of children becomes crucial with regard to the maintenance of a Cape Verdean identity over time. According to those I have talked to, this is a gendered issue. When the mother is of Cape Verdean origin and not the father, children often learn some Kriolu and are stimulated to maintain relations with Cape Verdean relatives in different parts of the world. This happens less often when the mother is Swedish and the father is a second-generation Cape Verdean. The notion that childrens' education is primarily the mother's responsibility is strong in Cape Verde, but in Sweden as well the mother is often seen as the primary caregiver. One effect of this is that the Cape Verdean identity in Sweden is primarily passed on by women.

In the end, however, an ethnic identity is not only self-attributed by those belonging to a specific group, it is also ascribed to them by those outside the group. Many people of Cape Verdean descent lament the fact that even if you are born in Sweden, you are inevitably considered an 'immigrant' (*invandrare*) when your looks differ from what is considered traditional 'Swedish'. Time and again, people who have lived in Sweden for 40 or 50 years – or even their entire lives – describe how they detest being asked where they come from. To them, assimilation is not an option. And therefore, because rigid distinctions based on assumptions about reified ethnic and cultural differences are still at work in Swedish society, people whose parents or grandparents long ago were born in Cape Verde have little choice. Independently of their desire, they are often considered to be 'immigrants' from a small and exotic country that few Swedes have ever heard of before. The way forward – at least for some of them – is to identify with their Cape Verdean origins.

Notes

[1] This article is based on participant observation and 15 interviews carried out among Cape Verdeans living in Sweden in 2005.

[2] IF stands for *idrottsförening*, which means sports club.

[3] The term *Kriol* is widely used as an adjective for Cape Verdean. Most Cape Verdeans in Sweden come from the Barlavento islands and thus use the form *Kriol* rather *Kriolu*.

References

Åkesson, L. (2004) *Making a life: Meanings of migration in Cape Verde.* Ph.D. thesis. Department of Social Anthropology, Gothenburg: Göteborg University.

Matos, M. (n.d.) *Contos e Factos.* Mindelo: Gráfica de Mindelo.

Section II
Migration and Transnationalism

Chapter 10
Making Waves: Cape Verdeans, Whaling and the Uses of Photography

Memory Holloway

Ships were the living means by which the points within that Atlantic world were joined. They were mobile elements that stood for the shifting spaces in between the fixed places that they connected (Gilroy 1993: 16).

'Gees' are occasionally to be encountered in our seaports, but more particularly in Nantucket and New Bedford. These 'Gees' are not the 'Gees' of Fogo... they are no longer green 'Gees'. They are sophisticated 'Gees' and hence liable to be taken for naturalized citizens badly sun burnt (Melville 1997: 348).

This chapter is based on an investigation of photographs of Cape Verdeans in the New Bedford Whaling Museum, Massachusetts.[1] The museum holds a large collection of photographs of Cape Verdeans that document them at work on whaling ships, on packets, and in cranberry bogs. These photographs give a vivid picture of the social position, the work and wages of Cape Verdeans in the late-19th and early-20th centuries.

The photographs discussed below present the viewer with an unusual set of documents that record the work and conditions aboard a whaling ship. By examining these photographs in relation to the ship log we gain written and visual evidence of the work undertaken by Cape Verdean crew members, how they were recruited and their social status; what it was like to sleep below deck when the pots of whale blubber were boiling overhead, how the ship smelled when the decks were slippery with whale oil, and what the crew members ate. The *Sunbeam*, one of the last of the whaling ships departed New Bedford in 1904 with a diverse crew that included Cape Verdeans who were habitually referred to as 'Bravas', regardless of their place of birth. Among the crew was Clifford Ashley, a young photographer of 21 from New Bedford who meticulously photographed the voyage.

Ashley's photographs and diaries while on board present a stark record of Cape Verdeans and their role in the whaling industry in Massachusetts. In August 1904, he, along with the rest of the crew, boarded the *Sunbeam*, a whaling bark that was bound for the Atlantic and the islands of Cape Verde. Joining a whaling crew had, since the 1770s, been a form of employment for the islanders, a means of escape and a path that led to emigration and the shores of New Bedford. For Ashley the voyage provided an extraordinary opportunity to experience the hunt, the hard work and the social relations of the ship's crew first hand.

Ashley took a logbook, a camera and sketching materials with which to record the journey. The results give an unusually full account of conditions on board the *Sunbeam*, along with the role that Cape Verdeans had in caulking and painting the ship in preparation for the voyage, the methods of recruiting Cape Verdeans as crew members, and their courage and desire to find employment. Ashley returned with three accounts of the voyage: a written text, photographs, and sketches. Taken together, the three give a full if contradictory account of the voyage, the current ideologies of the time, of the tasks assigned to Cape Verdeans and others.

Ashley's written text is a daily document of what he saw and heard. The photographs document the ship prior to the voyage, the labourers on land and the crew on board, and his final disembarkation at Brava which he toured for several days. The sketches done on board were later used as the basis for later paintings. Of the three records, the photographs are the least mediated by Ashley's interpretations. Although he edited and selected the scenes that he wished to record, the photographs have a transparency that is lacking in his written records in the logbook and in his drawings and the later paintings.

Figure 10.1. *The Sunbeam*
Photograph by Clifford Ashley. Courtesy of The New Bedford Whaling Museum.

On the warm evening before they sailed, Ashley put his sailor's chest on board, and after one night in steerage with the crew, made up his bunk in the captain's stateroom. That night he spent among the cox-swains, two of the five of whom were from Brava, and provided him with a powerful insight into conditions on board.

> On a clutter of chests and dunnage the boat steerers sprawled, drinking, wrangling, smoking... The floor was littered with rub-bish, the walls hung deep with clothing; squalid, congested, filthy.... The floor was wet and slippery, the air smoky and foul... Roaches scurried about the walls. A chimneyless whale-oil lamp guttered in the draft from the booby-hatch and cast a fitful light over the jumble of forms sitting on the chests beneath (Ashley 1926: 4).

There was certainly plenty of curiosity among New Englanders at that time for anything involving whaling. Ashley had managed to secure a commission from *Harper's Magazine* for two articles on whaling, and the purpose of his voyage was to experience the hunt firsthand. He was a New Bedford local who had observed the whaling industry as a child and he saw himself as a privileged observer and as an artist. The voyage was an opportunity to combine the two. He had been to art school, had studied in Boston and Pennsylvania and he had trained to be a painter and illustrator. Photography for him was not his primary medium. It was only a means to his greater purpose of illustrating the voyage through his writing and sketches. When he published his writ-ten account of the voyage in *Harper's* and later in his book *The Yankee Whaler*, he only used illustrations or reproductions of paintings. De-spite their singular existence as documents of a whaling voyage, Ashley never published the photographs and it was not until 1982 that they were published in book form by the New Bedford Whaling Museum (Hall 1982).

All three of Ashley's accounts of the journeys on the *Sunbeam* are specific written and visual records that offer us a firsthand view of the recruitment of Cape Verdeans for the voyage, their physical endurance, the tasks they were assigned on board, and their place in the ship's so-cial hierarchy.

The 1904 voyage of the *Sunbeam* was among the last of the whaling voyages. 'Now', the Captain told Ashley, 'whale oil ain't worth beans; you hunt him for bone.' (Ashley 1926: 9). Whaling had already hit its peak by the 1840s when whale oil was in great demand and had been used for lighting, as lubrication for machinery, for paraffin for candles and as a base for high-quality cosmetics. The ambergris found in the intestines of the whale was used as a basis for perfumes. But by the

Figure 10.2.   *Re-coppering the hull*
Photograph by Clifford Ashley. Courtesy of The New Bedford Whaling Museum.

turn of the 20th century, whale oil had been replaced by petroleum. The whales had begun to disappear, either because their numbers had been reduced by centuries of unregulated whaling, or because they had fled to other waters. In any case, whaling was no longer the lucrative enterprise that it had been during the mid-1800s. This shift from an economy of plenty to an economy of scarcity had a direct influence on the hiring of crews from Cape Verde. Ashley writes about the shift in hiring practices when he explains that:

> The Cape Verdes were the most fruitful source [for crews] in later years. The Brava, as the Cape Verde Islander was called, was black as an African, but had straight or nearly straight hair. Pre-

sumably he was a mixture of Moorish and African blood with a
dash of Portuguese. He was more energetic than the African
and proved an excellent whaleman. As it became more and
more difficult to secure crews, the agents became less particular.
After engaging enough whalemen to man the boats, they filled
up with anything that was available. They figured that a whaling
cruise would either make or break a man. In the latter case he
would desert at the first opportunity, and being of little account,
his place was easily filled (Ashley 1926: 108).

Ashley's description of the Cape Verdean both praises and condemns.
Although he had lived in New Bedford his entire life, had frequented
the wharves and had daily come in contact with Cape Verdeans who
had already established a community in the city, his physical description of the islanders is based on assumptions rather than a historical
knowledge of the settlement of the islands by the Portuguese in the
15th century. His praise is contradictory. On the one hand, he mentions
the excellence of the Cape Verdean as a whaler, and on the other, he
suggests that they were taken on board because no one else wanted the
job. White whalers were less willing to sign up for the voyages for several reasons. The work was dirty, the voyages boring, the hunt dangerous and most significantly, the pay was low. Whalers complained about
the food, the constant smell of vomit, bilge water and whale blubber,
and the endless days of predictable sameness. The whaling ships occa-

Figure 10.3.   *Dockside workers*
Photograph by Clifford Ashley. Courtesy of The New Bedford Whaling Museum.

Figure 10.4.   *Cape Verdean crew on board the Sunbeam*
Photograph by Clifford Ashley. Courtesy of The New Bedford Whaling Museum.

sionally returned with disappointing results, which meant that the 'lay' (the sharing of the proceeds from the sale of the oil) was hardly worth the voyage. It was more profitable to work in the textile mills on land than to take one's chances at sea.

As a result, the whaling ships were now filled up with anyone desperate enough. By the time of the *Sunbeam*'s voyage, most of the whaling crews were predominantly Cape Verdean, or Bravans, a general name by which all Cape Verdeans had come to be known in New England (Cyr 2005).

The *Sunbeam* was a well-seasoned whaler dating from 1871. By the time Ashley and the crew boarded in 1904, the ship had been around the Atlantic on five prior voyages. This was its sixth and next to last Atlantic voyage. (New Bedford Ship Registers, V. III, 162). To make the voyage safe and profitable, the ship had been dry docked, caulked, painted, recoppered and overhauled. Among the tradesmen and labourers who made the *Sunbeam* seaworthy again was a large contingent of Cape Verdeans, whose employment suggests not only knowledge of carpentry and other important skills, but an enduring presence in New Bedford.

They had probably arrived circa 1710 (Carreira 1982: 44). Whaling in Cape Verdean waters began in as early as the 1680s and some 50 years later, the Portuguese were collecting taxes on the trade in whale oil in Santo Antão, São Nicolau and Boa Vista. By the end of the 18th century, American whalers appeared in Azorean and Cape Verdean waters, and there is every reason to believe that they also recruited the islanders for the ships. Volunteering had a triple effect: it meant fleeing from the famines that had marked the 17th and 18th centuries on Cape Verde; it meant employment on a ship (though the pay was slight), and most importantly, it meant the possibility of emigration with all that followed in the way of money and goods sent back, and family brought over.

In the beginning, the recruiting of Cape Verdeans had been easy enough. By the mid-1800s, the local men were eager to avoid domestic hardships and they provided a ready labour supply (Creighton 1995: 141).

Furthermore, the ships had already been at sea for several months, and needed to replenish their food supplies. When they landed – for

Figure 10.5.   *Cape Verdean whalers putting up the mast*
Photograph by Clifford Ashley. Courtesy of The New Bedford Whaling Museum.

the most part on Brava or Fogo – they loaded up with fruit, vegetables, goat meat, and water, and the plentiful salt as well as a new crew. Most of the volunteers from the islands were 'greenhands', crewmen with no prior experience on ships. They were hired to carve up the whales, and to replace the sick, injured and deserters. They were also handy in supplying important information on how to procure local supplies and help loading the ship.

Once on board, the greenhands, many of them Cape Verdeans from Brava, were told to utilize their time prudently to 'learn the ropes'. 'You greenies', Captain Higgins of the *Sunbeam* told them a few days out of New Bedford, 'have got just a week to box the compass and learn the ropes… let every man work for the ship… if any dirty works goes on, I'll break the rascal who does it' (Ashley 1926: 5). They had to learn quickly the names of the sails in a new language, the mechanics of the whaleboats, and how to paddle with 18-foot oars. But that was not all that the Yankee whalers asked of the islanders. They wanted the Cape Verdeans to supply necessary information about their territorial waters, the currents, the winds and bays, and when and where the whales passed. All this was local knowledge that was necessary for a successful enterprise. Thus the Americans and Cape Verdeans became mutually dependent upon one another.

These exchanges would ostensibly result in friendly alliances. That, at least, is the argument that Carreira makes when he observes that between the men there was:

> A confidence which grew stronger as the years passed. It suited the crews to keep in touch with their helpers from one season to the next, particularly with the best and cleverest, and make sure of their land bases. Their helpers, for their part, battling against an impoverished environment where all aspects of life were hard, found in work on board the whaling ships a way of lessening their economic difficulties (Carreira 1982: 46).

One's status on board, however, depended on ability and race, and in new recruits these were often mutually exclusive. Despite the need for able men, race, language and a lack of skills often placed new Cape Verdean recruits on the bottom rung of the ship's social hierarchy. 'Where are you from', the captain asked the new recruits. 'Talk English?' And if the reply, in any language, was that they had learned their trade on a Portuguese captain's boat, the man was dressed down, even if in good humour. 'I wouldn't give a God dam for any man *he* [Mr. Diaz] broke in.' (Ashley 1926: 9). Of the 39 men on the *Sunbeam*, only eight were American born. The others were from various ports, including a Norwegian, St. Helena islander, Nova Scotian and a Gay Head In-

Figure 10.6.   *Crew member standing on whale's head*
Photograph by Clifford Ashley. Courtesy of The New Bedford Whaling Museum.

dian, while August, a 'Gee' from Lisbon was designated as a Cape Verdean. Augusto Azevedo was a 22-year-old from Brava, and according to
the crew list a seaman who would receive 1/175 of the proceeds of the
voyage. All of the others, meaning those of colour, were not called by
their names. 'All the rest were blacks', Ashley writes: 'profane, disso-
lute and ignorant they were, yet on the whole, as courageous and willing a lot as one could desire' (1926: 9).

Attempting to determine the origins of the crew in many instances
was difficult. Azevedo was not from Lisbon as Ashley had thought, but
from Brava. Many crew lists did not distinguish between Cape Verdeans and Azoreans, and in some cases, all of them were just listed as
Portuguese. However, the crew list of the *Sunbeam* is precise (Wing Papers 1904). Their places of birth were supplied along with their nation-
alities. There were nine from Brava, six from São Nicolau, though two
of them were listed as Americans, meaning that they had been natura-

lised and probably lived in New Bedford. Two were from Maio, and one from 'St. Jago' the English transcription of Santiago. All of the rest, other than the two naturalised crew members already mentioned, were listed as Portuguese. There was also a 17-year-old cabin boy who was listed as Portuguese but was from Faial (in the Azores archipelago).

These crews were multiracial for only one reason. They were the only ones willing to work for low wages. By the 1860s, at least one quarter of the crews was from Portuguese-speaking islands. The ship owners actively sought the Atlantic islanders to cut costs, and the locals accepted low wages and the hard work of whaling as an alternative to the struggle of making a living on the islands. Even more enticing, however, was the possibility of immigrating to the U.S. (Farr 1983: 164-5). Sometimes crew members deserted, and new recruits were found once the ship arrived in Cape Verde. A whaling ship was a moving society in which labour was exchanged for food and shelter. Industrial disputes, governance and rule enforcement were all handled by

Figure 10.7.   *Bailing the case*
Photograph by Clifford Ashley. Courtesy of The New Bedford Whaling Museum.

the officers who had dictatorial powers. If Cape Verdeans were relegated to lesser positions, this was no different from the attitudes found
on the North American shores.

Herman Melville had something to say about the perceptions of
Cape Verdean seamen when he wrote the short story 'The "Gees"' in
1854, which was later published in *Harper's*. Melville, who had also
boarded a whaling vessel in New Bedford as a way of gaining firsthand
experience, wrote of a crossbreed of Portuguese sailors known as
'Gees', a shortened version of the already derogatory Portagee, as he
makes clear in the opening sentences of his story, which is actually a
profile of a Cape Verdean seaman, and should be read as a criticism of
the racist theories of the time in which Africans were characterised as
docile, animalistic and accorded a subhuman status. Most notably, Melville is critical of the racial hierarchies proposed by Josiah Nott and
George R. Glidden in *Types of Mankind*, where humans were ranked,
with Africans at the bottom and Caucasians at the top of the hierarchy
(Lowance 2003).

Melville begins by stating that seamen have strong prejudices, and
that there is no end to their disdain when it comes to racial difference.
'They are bigots here', he says, and this should alert the reader to the
context in which Melville is writing and the characterisation of the
Cape Verdeans that follows. They are hardy, capable of working extreme hard, with a great appetite and little imagination.

> His complexion is hybrid; his hair ditto; his mouth disproportio-
> nately large as compared with his stomach; his neck short; but
> his head round, compact and betokening a solid understand-
> ing... his flesh is firm and lean. He has butter-teeth, strong, dur-
> able, square and yellow. He wears no hat. Since he is always
> wading in the surf, he wears no shoes. A kick from his hard
> heel is almost as dangerous as one from a wild zebra which
> makes him a formidable fighter (Melville 1997: 343-44).

In the mid-19th century, when Melville was writing, ship captains had
already come to prefer the Cape Verdean to the American sailor because he asked for no wages, and was willing to work for food.

> He comes for biscuit. He does not know what other wages
> mean, unless cuffs and buffets be wages, and he regularly takes
> the punches that are thrown in now and then. Only when hard
> and strenuous labor is demanded of them does a 'Gee show his
> true and noble human nature (Melville 1997: 345).

Figure 10.8.   *Cutting and mincing whale blubber*
Photograph by Clifford Ashley. Courtesy of The New Bedford Whaling Museum.

But a green 'Gee', is the greenest of green. This means that they fall overboard, are clumsy and a captain must take twice as many 'Gees' as Americans to cover what might go amiss. He is docile and uncultivated, believes whatever he is told and remembers everything. And they are among us. Ethnologists need not travel all the way to Fogo to see a 'Gee', Melville points out. For they can be found in American seaports, especially in Nantucket and New Bedford. But these are not the green 'Gees' of Fogo. 'They are sophisticated "Gees" and hence liable to be taken for naturalized citizens badly sun burnt... a stranger need have a sharp eye to know a "Gee", even if he see him' (Melville 1997: 348). For all this, there are the unbiased who insisted (Melville among them) that the 'Gee' never received his just due. For all that he had been accused of, Melville's was a reverse defence of the reliability and courage of the Cape Verdean seaman. They were hungry and that hunger made them eager to work at any cost.

By the turn of the 20th century, American sailors were prone to protest if not well treated, and thus Cape Verdeans were widely sought after. By the year 1900, the racial composition of the ships had shifted. Some crews were now entirely black, with Cape Verdeans in the majority and with a Cape Verdean Captain as well. One such ship, the *Eleanor B. Conwell*, also a whaling vessel, was encountered by the *Sunbeam* at sea and it was noted that it was entirely manned by a black crew, including a black captain. The steward, reported Ashley, was the only white man on the *Eleanor B. Conwell* and he had a melancholy tale to tell about his disagreements with the captain who gave him no molasses to cook with and no yeast for bread. 'As for butter, why the damned "Gee" eats lard on his bread and thinks a white man oughter.' The crew, Ashley reported, was wild and underfed and they mutinied a few months later.

Ashley returned from his inspection of the *Conwell* missing a jackknife but with his pockets full of gingerbread, since the cook had helped himself to the molasses while the captain was visiting aboard the *Sunbeam* (Ashley 1926: 19). Some have claimed that whaling was one of the few occupations where black men could rise to the rank of officers. But this did not mean they had the same opportunities to advance as their Yankee counterparts. Most of them attained their rank after whaling had reached its peak.

On the whole, Cape Verdeans did the dirty work, or, worse, 'women's work' as cooks or stewards. They waded knee-deep through whale blubber, and they stoked the fires for the try pots that rendered the blubber into oil. When a man was needed overboard to hook the whale, or adjust the tackle needed to lift the head on board, the Cape Verdeans were among the first to volunteer. Despite factual evidence that the pay was the same for all regardless of origin, whaling was not an equal opportunity employer. The pay structure reveals both the division of labour on the ships and the social hierarchy that placed Cape Verdeans at the bottom. A captain was paid 1/14 of the entire profits; a cook, 1/130 and a deckhand 1/190. Most of the Cape Verdeans were inexperienced deckhands, though over time some had managed to rise to the rank of ordinary seamen at 1/180 of the ship's take.

Because they were inexperienced, they were given the most difficult tasks. They hung for hours on masts reeling in the wind; they were relegated to the upper reaches of the ship where they dangled from the cross beams and spent hours on night watches. But, like the rest of the crew, they slept in their clothes, bathed in a tin basin in the morning and ate chunks of meat and potatoes while seated on a sea chest with a small pot of coffee between their knees. Their toil was unending. They repaired and manufactured sails, and remodelled the try pots in preparation for the catch. They slept in the stench and heat once the whale had been caught and the oil extracted. They also endured the occasional jibes directed at their bad English and when they failed to understand orders.

Ashley's photographic record gives a firsthand view of these physical demands and the endurance required once a whale was spotted. On Tuesday 9 September 1904, less than a month after they had left New Bedford, an enormous whale was spotted early one morning. The captain later remarked that it was one of the largest whales he had seen. The hunt began on 7 September and the ship's logbook notes that the whale rendered 80 barrels of oil. Two days later, on Tuesday 9 September, another whale was brought in, even more enormous, which rendered 100 barrels, an extremely large amount.

The work occurred in three stages: the first was the chase in small whaleboats, which included harpooning and then being towed at great speeds by the whale, and eventually bringing the whale back to the ship; the second task entailed cutting up the blubber and hoisting it

Figure 10.9.   *Ribeira Brava, São Nicolau*
Photograph by Clifford Ashley. Courtesy of The New Bedford Whaling Museum.

onto the ship, and third, boiling the blubber in large pots at high temperatures. All of these required stamina, the ability to work under pressure and with little sleep. Here Ashley describes the chase:

> One moment the decks were hushed and quiet. The next it was as if a squall had struck us... a hurricane of orders preceded a wild stampede... the boat crew [five men in four boats] swarmed down the falls and dropped catlike into their places. The boats were soon scattered. For four hours or more we tugged at the oars; our throats were parched, our hands were bleeding... the whale spouted... the rankness of it was still in our nostrils when... the huge monster breached clear of the sea and with a deafening roar... disappeared beneath the surface... just as another whale... broke water under our very bows. Tony gave a frantic lunge and the harpoon was buried to its hitches... For an instant our stem was sucked under... we shipped a barrel of water. Then we were off with the speed of an express train, the line whistled... till it smoked... and we were buffeted from side to side by oncoming waves (Ashley 1926: 11-12).

This description was only part one: thrilling, exhausting, and frightening in its magnitude. One can understand why most of the Cape Verdean whalers were under 25 years of age, since the dangers were obvious. By the evening of the hunt they had towed the whale to the ship.

Part two began early in the next morning when they began cutting and hauling the blubber onto the deck. This meant lifting a weighty mass with hooks, block and tackle, and it required someone to stand on the whale to put the hook in place. 'Who's overboard?' Gomes, the third mate from São Nicolau asked. From a dozen volunteers one was selected, as Ashley describes him, 'a big hulking negro, distinguished from the rest by a wide cotton rag he wore under his jaws to keep his hat in place.' A monkey rope was fastened about his waist and he was dripped sprawling on the slippery heaving flank of the whale. About him, innumerable sharks, gliding like shadows alongside, now and then tearing away a hunk of flesh (Ashley 1926: 15). Seven hours later, they were still hauling the meat and blubber on board.

And then came the third stage: the hot, slippery, and foul-smelling process of boiling the blubber that cooked all through the night and into the next day. Ashley again describes the oozing deck and the oily process:

> Fatty and unctuous, glistening and pearly white, the cavernous reservoir lay opened before us like some vast comb of honey,

trickling its stored up treasure over the sullied planking, turning it to purest snow. Stark naked, three negroes climbed into its tank like interior, and wallowing to their waists, with knives and scoops, half cut, half ladled the barrels of pulpy, dripping substance from its cells. With tubs, buckets and pails, an improvised bucket brigade passed the prized contents forward to the try pots, where two bronze like figures, standing in the capacious kettles, with groping fingers tore the oozing pulp to shreds. [...] Black toiling figures teemed like ants about the decks; and all made a picture the weirdness of which suggested a transcript from the nether world (Ashley 1926:18).

Black smoke belched from the stacks, while the men occasionally helped themselves to choice bits of well-fried scrap, and a pungent sickening odour of burning blubber filled the air. It was impossible to sleep with the smell of rotting flesh, the cockroaches that swarmed

Figure 10.10.   *Nova Sintra, Brava, Mayor at center*
Photograph by Clifford Ashley. Courtesy of The New Bedford Whaling Museum.

across the cabin and the 100-degree Fahrenheit heat in the sleeping quarters. Two days later, the entire process started all over again when another whale was spotted. Throughout, Cape Verdean seamen were fearless in the hunt, eager volunteers to stand on a whale amid sharks, and were energetic boilers and bailers.

Six weeks after its departure on 21 August 1904, the *Sunbeam* landed in São Nicolau and Ashley walked around the town with his camera, observing farmers who had brought sacks of grain to sell or trade. He looked up and down the street and documented the bustle of a local village where women carried parcels on their heads, and men conversed in small groups. At the end of September, Ashley travelled to Brava where he toured around the island on a donkey. He photographed the mayor and other local officials, and a policeman as well. He watched a thick fog roll in over Brava as women moved along the island roads. He shows us barrels of water outside dwellings, and the palm trees that dot the island. His photographs of the islands and its people are affectionate and curious, and he seems to have been glad to have been on a donkey instead of a whaling vessel.

By the end of 1924, however, the whaling industry had collapsed, and many of the whaling vessels were purchased by Cape Verdeans who converted them into packets that travelled across the Atlantic between Cape Verde and New England.

The links between whaling and Cape Verdean emigration stretches back to the early 18th century when the ships first landed on the islands. As Paul Gilroy has pointed out, ships crossing the Atlantic provided links between points. They were the physical embodiment of shifting spaces between the fixed places that they connected (Gilroy 1993: 16). Two hundred years of travelling back and forth has left its mark on both New England and Cape Verde, as manifested by the increased number of emigrants in New Bedford and a corresponding decrease in able-bodied men who remained behind on the islands. The whaling vessels, and later the packets, took on board those who needed to leave the islands. The packets travelled the same routes, docking at Brava, and eventually landing in New Bedford. Even now, one can walk down Union St. in New Bedford where whalers once met just before they boarded their ships. Today, in New Bedford Harbor, one can see the packet *Ernestina* moored there. This ship once brought Cape Verdean emigrants to the city well into the 20th century. Even now, one can hear Kriolu being spoken on the docks and in the streets. Whaling has long disappeared as a viable occupation, but those who first arrived here on the ships, continue to make their presence known in the city of New Bedford.

Note

[1] The chapter is dedicated to Gilman Wing.

References

Ashley, C. (1926) *The Yankee Whaler*. New York: Dover.

Busch, B.C. (1994) '*Whaling will n'er do for me'. American Whalemen in the Nineteenth Century*. Lexington, KY: University Press of Kentucky.

Carreira, A. (1982) *The People of the Cape Verde Islands: Exploitation and Emigration*. London: C. Hurst & Company (trans. by Christopher Fyfe).

Creighton, M. (1995) *Rites and Passages: The Experience of American Whaling, 1830-1870*. Cambridge: Cambridge University Press.

Cyr, P. (2005) Unpublished interview with the author. New Bedford.

Farr, J. (1983) 'A Slow Boat to Nowhere: The Multi-racial Crews of the American Whaling Industry'. *Journal of Negro History* 68(2): 159-170.

Gilroy, P. (1993) *The Black Atlantic: Modernity and Double Consciousness*. Cambridge, MA: Harvard University Press.

Hall, E. (1982) *Sperm Whaling from New Bedford: Clifford W. Ashley's Photographs of Bark Sunbeam in 1904*. New Bedford, MA: Old Dartmouth Historical Society.

Halter, M. (1993) *Between Race and Ethnicity: Cape Verdean American Immigrants, 1860-1965*. Chicago, IL: University of Illinois Press.

Karcher, C. (1980) *Shadow over the Promised Land: Slavery, Race and Violence in Melville's America*. Baton Rouge, LA: Louisiana State University Press.

Lowance, Jr., M.I. (ed.) (2003) *A House Divided: The Antebellum Slavery Debates in America, 1776-1865*. Princeton, NJ: Princeton University Press.

Melville, H. (1997 [1856]) 'The "Gees"', in *The Complete Shorter Fiction*, New York: Everyman's Library, pp. 343-48.

Wing, J. and W.R. (1904) *Crew List of the Sunbeam*, M.33.35, Box 14, Series B., sub-series 21 Folders 12-14. New Bedford, MA: New Bedford Public Library.

Chapter 11
And When the Women Leave?
Female Emigration from Boa Vista

Andréa de Souza Lobo

Introduction

I met Joana in 2002. She had been going back and forth to Italy for eight years. She came back during her vacations to see her family, her life-partner and her 17-year-old daughter who had remained behind in Boa Vista, Cape Verde, in her grandmother's care. Joana emigrated to Italy in 1994, with the help of a cousin who found her a job as a housemaid and got her *papéis* (documents) to allow her to enter the country. She left her daughter behind, still a baby at the time, living with her grandmother. The *pai de filho* (child's father), despite having remained behind on the island, and despite being close to the child, never shared any of the responsibilities of raising her. During all the years abroad, and despite the problems of a long-distance relationship, Joana and the *pai de filho* stayed together for eight years. It was around the time we met, however, that she had decided to leave him, claiming that she could no longer bear his Cape-Verdean *machista* attitudes, which often got her into fights with the *rivais* (rivals), women he courted while she was away. In addition to ending this relationship, Joana was also facing a family crisis, with her siblings and her other daughter pressuring her to take the younger daughter away with her to Italy. The grandmother was already old and growing tired of her rebellious attitude, and, besides, she wanted to live in Europe.

After some time without any news from Joana, I met her again in 2004, much to my surprise, while I was doing field work in Boa Vista. I saw right away that her situation had changed. She told me that she had managed to leave the *pai de filho* (child's father) and was in a relationship with another man (an Italian), and had succeeded in bringing her daughter to Italy, where she had been living for the past year-and-a-half. Joana was spending yet another vacation in Boa Vista, but this time for one major purpose: to start building a home for her permanent return to take care of her elderly mother, as gratitude for the years that she *aguentou* (took care of) the granddaughter. In our conversations, she once again brought up the difficulty of living together with her daughter after so many years apart, and the desire to have another child in order to fully enjoy the experience of motherhood, since Dona Maria, the grandmother had basically raised Joana's daughter and the one she calls *mama*.

> I do not have the kind of love I would like to have from her, she has that kind of love for someone else, the one who raised her, my mother. It feels like we are strangers sometimes, which is very hard (Joana).

The fundamental role of women as mothers is an important theme in many analyses of domesticity in Africa and the African diaspora communities in the Americas. Authors like Trajano Filho (1998), Dias (2000) and Smith (1995) write about what they call a fundamental relationship within the family, the mother-child relationship. The common point is that the families in the societies they studied are extremely centred on the woman, the mother being the central point around which other family relationships are established. The son or daughter finds in the mother the affection and love that gives him or her psychological support, care and protection. She is responsible for raising the child, supervising his or her schoolwork and solving household disputes, and it is generally she who passes on the essential values and customs of the society. Meanwhile, the father-husband tends to be an absent figure in the family's daily life for various reasons. In studies regarding the Creole societies of Guinea-Bissau (Trajano Filho 1998) and Cape Verde (Dias 2000) we learn that patriarchal ideology coexists with matrifocality. If, on the one hand, the woman is the anchor for affection in the family, the father, on the other hand, is the focus of authority and to whom respect and obedience are due.

A similar analysis can be found in Raymond Smith's work, which deals with the marginal role of the husband-father as its central thesis. This marginality correlates with the economic roles of the men in the broader social system so that neither their status nor their economic condition is important to the basic functioning of the domestic group and its developmental stages. In this case, the domestic group tends to be matrifocal, with the woman as mother being the central figure, while the husband-father, even when he is considered the head of the domestic group, remains a marginal figure. By which the author means that his association with other members of the group is infrequent and external to the effective bonds which keep the family united. Smith's analysis reveals a type of family system in which the men forfeit their importance as authority figures in the domestic relationships.

In comparing these theories about the place of women and men in the matrifocal family structure, I have verified and would like to stress, that female emigration from the island of Boa Vista raises interesting questions about family organisation in that society. The questions I would like to address concern the maintenance or reproduction of the family in a situation which, from an ethnocentric point of view, could be considered anomalous. What happens to family relationships in a situation in which the husband, the wife and the children are separated? What happens to matrifocality – so characteristic of this Creole society – in a situation in which the woman departs? To answer these questions, my main critical tool will be the analysis of the roles of women and men within the family in situations of female emigration and the arrangements that are made for the reproduction of this family, despite the absence of the *mulher-mãe* (woman-mother). Joana's story is an example of the path that many women in Boa Vista and their families take, revealing the characteristics of the relationships between parents and their children, between life-partners, and especially the importance of the relationship between grandparents and grandchildren, a relationship which varies in intensity and meaning when mothers emigrate.

Boa Vista and the women who leave

In order to discuss these questions, it is important to describe the social environment in which the women and their families choose to emigrate, as a means of improving the family's fortunes in Boa Vista. Throughout the year of 2004, I carried out field research among residents of Vila de Sal-Rei, on the theme of migratory flows and their influence on the transformations which have been occurring in the local family structure. Sal-Rei is the main village on the island, with a population of approximately 2,500 residents, out of a total 4,209 on the island that is split among the seven small settlements on this arid island.

Boa Vista is the third largest island but has the smallest population, and is peripheral to the national political scenario. It is appealing to Cape Verdeans because of its beautiful landscapes, its dunes and its extensive beaches. Its people are regarded by the other Cape Verdeans as pleasant and well-intentioned. The men are considered lazy, while the women are portrayed as strong women and as emigrants.

The natural landscapes are its greatest attraction, and thus Boa Vista has emerged as an important tourist destination, with much potential for further development. Over the past five years, tourism has developed by leaps and bounds, because of increased foreign investment in hotel construction, and some interest by the government in developing local business and the increased immigration of people from the other islands (as well as Senegal, Guinea-Bissau, Nigeria and other continental African countries), in search of employment and better opportunities. All this has brought with it many changes in local life.

Despite the development of tourism, which has increased employment for the general population, most people, particularly young women, still believe that the way to improve one's quality of life is linked to emigration. This desire is usually shared by the whole family, which makes the decision to emigrate more of a collective than individual process. It is a component of family strategies, in which the family plays an important role both at home and in the country of destination.

The female emigration network, especially to Italy, grew dramatically in the late 1960s, a period during which male emigration from Boa Vista to the Netherlands and Germany dropped as a consequence of tighter legal requirements. Italy was already a destination for some women from São Nicolau and São Vicente, due to the support of Capuchin priests, who sponsored single young women to work as domestics in Italy. The data I collected shows that female emigration from Boa Vista was influenced by this tendency, although it was not directly related to the Capuchin priests. The 1970s and 1980s saw accelerated female emigration from Boa Vista. These women, upon their arrival and settlement, managed to establish an assistance and support network, facilitating the emigration of other women so that they were later joined by sisters, cousins, and neighbours in a strong chain migration. More recently, women have begun seeking out their husbands and children, as a form of self-managed family re-grouping.

While at first only young women without children came to Italy, as influenced by the priests, with the increased flow and the participation of Boa Vista natives, more women managed to migrate, enabling them to eventually support not only their parents but the children they left behind in Cape Verde as well.

However, the fact that these mothers were single, i.e., not formally married, was a problem. While this was commonplace in Cape Verde, in Italy being a *mãe solteira* (single mother) could mean losing one's job and, consequently, a forced return to the homeland. For this reason, many women hid the existence of their children, and if they became pregnant they would return to Boa Vista before the employer could notice. Many of the former emigrants with whom I spoke told me that they returned because of their children or because of a pregnancy conceived during their vacations in Cape Verde, or even in Italy. Under these circumstances, there were two options, either staying on the island and renouncing Italy, or staying on the island for the duration of the pregnancy, and then leaving the child with family members after birth, and returning to work abroad.

Some of the women I met chose to remain behind on the island or they were forced to return. Those who *tiveram cabeça* (did their best) currently own their own homes and live comfortably, especially because they had left a daughter, sister, or niece behind in their homes to guarantee the maintenance of the high standard of living provided by emigration. Others (who did not remain abroad long enough to manage to capitalise) have only the memories of their days as emigrants, for they were not able to accumulate enough wealth or secure a comfortable living standard. Today, difficulties in the acquisition of entry visas and work permits have stemmed the flow of emigrants. However, despite these circumstances, a large number of women still manage to depart for Italy. Emigration plans are common among the women, and family networks are often called upon to help find the means to get them to Europe. Moreover, the presence of Italians investing in tourism has opened yet another doorway for emigration, particularly through relationships and marriage between Italians and Cape Verdean locals.

This dream is shared by the entire family, which, at home, participates in the emigration decision and helps to establish networks, secure documents and visas, and provides support and work contacts in Italy. The closer relatives generally contribute by purchasing the airline tickets and providing money to establish a foothold abroad. When there are children involved, there is a negotiation process to decide who will be responsible for them. If the maternal grandmother is still alive and in good health, she is the natural candidate for the caretaking of the children. When this is not an option, however, the mother must search for alternative candidates among her relatives, or among those of the children's father. Since child mobility is common in Boa Vista society, finding someone who *aguente* (take care of) the children is not exactly a problem, at least initially. As I intend to show, there is a solidarity network among women that helps with child rearing, and, when emigration is involved, supports the children and takes over responsibility for their needs.

Once they are living abroad and have secured steady jobs, the emigrants are expected to help the relatives by means of money transfers, parcels, clothes, shoes, household appliances, etc. Monteiro (1997: 470), in a case study carried out in Naples in the 1980s, states that women send more money home than men, about 18 per cent of their income, while men usually sent between 7 per cent and 13 per cent, depending on their salaries.

Besides sending more money, more familial continuity was also observed among the women. The author claims that these characteristics are not simply due to the fact that they usually have more stable jobs, but also more solid relationships with family members in Cape Verde.

'Men lack a solid and permanent connection to their homeland and male labour is unstable' (Monteiro 1997: 471, translation mine).

Åkesson (2004) analyzed emigration patterns in São Vicente and it corroborates with Monteiro's data regarding the connection between emigrant women and the family left behind in Cape Verde. Based on data from the Bank of Cape Verde (1990-2001), the author claims that the amounts of support sent by emigrants in Italy were high and continuous. 'Bonds between mothers and sons are central in Cape Verdean family relations, and mothers are morally bound to support children financially. Through these children and those who take care of them, emigrant women in Italy generally maintain strong and long-lasting bonds with their homeland' (Åkesson 2004: 40).

Apart from increasing income and raising the living standard of the whole family, the other main objective of the emigrants is to save enough money to eventually build a house, where she can live with the family and start a small business with monthly income in Cape Verde. Owning a house is the primary goal of these women, which eventually proves that their efforts abroad were worthwhile. The initial plan was to spend 15 to 20 years abroad and, upon achieving the dream of owning one's own house, to return to the island and rejoin the family. Whenever possible, another family member emigrates to replace them in their positions abroad.

Although this homecoming is regarded as a goal of life, I see a growing tendency of families regrouping and led by emigrant women. Over the past few years, there has been an effort on their part and a demand by family members in Cape Verde to enable young children and life partners to also emigrate to Italy.

The life partner reunion is a more subtle trend, although some, through marriage, try to procure the necessary documents for entry into Europe. Among the children of emigrants I interviewed, the majority expressed a desire to join their mothers abroad. This was the case with Joana's daughter, who had lived with her grandmother since childhood, and, at the age of fifteen, began pressuring her mother to make arrangements for her emigration. As in many other cases, the pressure also came from Joana's grandmother and siblings, who claimed that the grandmother was already older and also sick of the young daughter's *desmandos* (misbehaviour): staying out late, dating, disobedience, and daily arguments with the family. To better understand these matters, a closer look at family relationships is necessary.

Dispersed families, strong bonds

Women are the central pillars of the family, and it is their presence on the island that enables emigration of some of its members. As in Joana's story, it is common for the maternal grandmother to take on the responsibility of raising the children who are left behind on the island. Men, in general, provide no assistance for the children, and it is their mother, through her emigration abroad, who sustains the children by means of money transfers to cover the costs of food, school fees and other expenses. Besides providing for the children, they often give financial contributions or even full support to the remaining family in Boa Vista. Due to their importance in family maintenance, even from a distance, the women maintain a strong influence in family decisions and are called upon to co-operate in critical situations.

The family is not only important in the major decision to emigrate and in the infrastructure made available to the emigrant women. The family situation they leave behind in Cape Verde – children, life partner, aging parents – influences their stay in the host country and their integration into their new environments. Family crises in Boa Vista may interrupt a long-lasting migration project. I have studied the lives of former emigrants who claim they returned to Boa Vista because of a parent's illness, a life partner's request, pregnancy, problems with adolescent children, or merely homesickness. I shall now return to Joana's story, who said she was preparing to return to Cape Verde because her mother was growing old and was in need of care.

In his study focused on the Cape Verdean immigrant community in Italy, Monteiro (1997) stated that female emigration endangered the fragile monoparental family nucleus of mother and child. Emigration plays an important role in transforming and loosening the basic family structures, and, little by little, various new family structures emerge as an option to the traditional family in Cape Verdean society.

I partly agree with the author's arguments. However, the situation in Boa Vista shows that, despite a lengthy absence, emigrant women usually manage to maintain close ties with their relatives back home. Moreover, with the help of an information network among the women, in which the maternal grandmother is a central figure, the migrant woman is not only informed of the latest news, but also maintains her presence as a member of the group's daily decisions.

Many strategies are used to keep this relationship up-to-date despite the distance. Telephone communication is an effective means of maintaining this proximity to the local reality. The emigrants usually call relatives and friends on a weekly basis to get updated on what is happening on the island. The conversations are not about generic subjects, but the details of their children's, relatives' and life partners' daily lives.

In Italy, they gather in squares or in immigrant community centres on holidays to exchange information, rumours and news from the island. Emigrants note that the weekly gatherings replenish their energy for the following work week. During these moments, they try to re-enact the Boa Vista environment, in order to withstand the distance and homesickness. They report that the telephone calls and the sharing of information are fundamental to maintaining their feelings of belonging to the family and to the neighbourhood.

Another way of maintaining one's proximity is the exchange of parcels and money transfers. There is a constant flow of goods sent – and periodically received – by the emigrants. Any person travelling to or from Boa Vista usually takes dozens of parcels, souvenirs, lots of money, photographs, and letters. Moreover, emigrants use the cargo boats, which are increasingly frequent due to tourism. The boats transport furniture and appliances, barrels full of presents (food, clothes, shoes, toiletries, cosmetics, medicine, etc.), and products to be used or distributed by the emigrants when they return to Cape Verde on vacation. During the emigration years the women accumulate objects and *riquezas* (treasures) that they will keep in their homes upon their return, symbolising their emigrant status.

Another efficient means of maintaining a woman's presence in the heart of the Boa Vista community are the summer homecomings.[1] The women generally go on vacations to Boa Vista every two years. During the two-year period, they accumulate money, presents, clothes, costume jewellery, fashion accessories, take care of their looks, and send messages to stimulate expectation and speculation about on the details of their return to the island. The *chegadas* (arrivals) start in July, but rumours about who is coming, how long they are staying, and what news they will bring start as early as March. Both the emigrants and their families prepare for the *chegada* (arrival) and the months[2] when the emigrants will be immersed in their family environment. A series of social mechanisms encourages them to return during the summer, making it the most anticipated period in Boa Vista.

They take advantage of the weather and the flow of people, as well as the numerous events that are organised by the Municipality, groups of friends, the Catholic Church, and community associations, such as feasts, camps, hikes, gatherings, sports activities, festivals, and the much anticipated Municipal Feast, honouring *Santa Isabel*, matron saint of the island. All of these events make this period the one that locals most look forward to, especially because of the heightened level of expectation of who is actually returning and what they are bringing back with them to the island. The large number of activities and the number of returning emigrants define whether a summer season is good or bad. Since the homecomings occur once every two years, and are arranged among the emigrants in Italy, one year is generally good while the next is bad or *fraco* (feeble), for Boa Vista's natives. A greater return of emigrants means a more exciting time, more events, and a better summer.

However, it is not the social events alone that motivate the periodic homecomings. These moments allow the emigrants to show off how well they are doing in Italy, and the family, in turn, has the opportunity to enjoy the goods and the money brought home by the women and to show off their successful emigrant family members to others. They are evaluated by family and friends, and the verdict depends on how well they live up to the expectations. Certain rituals must be fulfilled to demonstrate that the departure *vale a pena* (was worthwhile) and justifies the family's efforts in *ajudar* (help) raising the children who remain behind and the tasks related to the acquisition of land, building of houses, power of attorney, and other necessary measures for the local investment of the capital acquired outside of the island.

The emigrant women are expected to cover the costs of remodelling their parents' homes, health care for family members and a better education for their children, who are either sent to Praia or São Vicente, or abroad for their higher education. The decisions and measures are taken by the emigrants during these homecomings, when they regain control of the family, arranging moves, renovations, making plans, taking care of the documents for parents and children, expediting decisions, etc. The woman's parents, around whom the authority of the domestic group is normally centred, allow their daughter to make a number of decisions, which, under normal circumstances, would not be left for her to make alone. This is a reflection of the privileged position the emigrants assume upon their return home.

My objective has not been to analyse conflicts. However, I cannot refrain from mentioning that the emigrants' privileged position does lead to problems, particularly with their non-emigrant siblings. These crisis situations extend beyond the domestic environment, revealing the ambiguity of the returning emigrants' situation. On the one hand, these women are encouraged to emigrate via the infrastructure that ensures their arrival and offers a wide range of privileges because they are emigrant, on the other, they are the victims of criticism and latent rivalries, which often emerge upon their return. In order to avoid superficial analyses restricted to the standard statement that Cape Verdean emigrants are status symbols, it is important to understand their position from the standpoint of the contrasting position of the women and relatives who remain behind in the community, and extend the analysis to the study of the interactions among them.

To understand the bonds between the emigrants and their relatives we must pay attention to two important types of interactions in Boa

Vista family life for the emigrant women: the relationship with their children and with their life partners. Conjugal relationships are generally unstable in Boa Vista. Partner rotation is considerable and informal unions predominate over official marriages. Within these unions, there is also a variety of situations including visitation unions, arrangements of polygymy, and de facto unions. The cases in which the couple shares a home at the start of the relationship are few and far between.

Male behaviour is another important characteristic. The Boa Vista men generally have more than one conjugal relationship simultaneously, either through another family, or through occasional relationships. It is worth noting that even though these relationships ought to be avoided and are important sources of conflict, they are also expected, and, to a certain extent, tolerated by the women.

The mother-child relationship, however, is marked by stability. Having a child is an important value for both men and women, and, amidst relationships marked by instability, the presence of children may mean a stronger conjugal bond, although it is by no means definitive. Despite being important for both, the relationship with children is different for men and women. The stronger bond is between mother and child, while the father is usually a distant figure for the child. It is important to clarify that he is not an absent figure in the scope of the family, but has a marginal role[3] and the bonds between fathers and children are marked more by attitudes of respect and distance than by manifestations of tenderness and intimacy. The question to be addressed here is what happens to these arrangements when the mother leaves.

What actually happens is that there is a strengthening of the bond between grandchild and grandmother[4] and other women (aunts, cousins, older sisters) who are members of the extended family, rather than, as some might suggest, an approximation between father and child. As previously mentioned, true teamwork is needed in child rearing, with all of the involved members taking turns at the task of *aguentar* (taking care of) the child. Although this is not exclusive to the emigrant families, the woman's central role is strengthened in these situations due to the economic factor – since the emigrant becomes the main provider for her family, her children, and even the fathers of the children – and due to the social value and the status acquired during the emigration period. Furthermore, the emigration of a female member that results in a child being left behind requires solidarity and organisation on the part of the family to fulfil the needs of the child in the absence of the mother. During this process, men lose their authority, which makes room for the grandmother. The family system organises itself in such a manner that a man's importance fades even further. Their relationships with their children, already distant, become even more relaxed, less responsible, or even occasional.

It is generally the bonds with the maternal grandmother and with the mother's family that are ultimately strengthened. Attention should be paid to the concept of proximity in this relationship: the importance of daily co-existence, of eating and sleeping together, is paramount in understanding the links that bind grandmothers and grandchildren. But what happens to the relationship with the mother? Does the mother-child link weaken? Joana, in describing her life with her daughter who now lives with her in Italy, notes a number of conflicts that arose from a relationship between two people who did not *viveram juntas* (live together) and laments the fact that she did not raise her own daughter, and therefore did not receive the love and affection a daughter gives her mother. This kind of love, according to Joana, is what her daughter has for the grandmother, whom she calls *mamã* (mommy).

Joana's account is shared by many children of emigrant mothers whom I met in Boa Vista. All regret having had to live away from their mothers and developing a closer relationship with grandmothers, aunts, or older sisters. However, at the same time they express their feelings of abandonment, they also point out that they have a profound affection for their mothers. They recognise and value not only their mothers' efforts so that they could *tenham uma vida melhor* (have a better life), but especially the concern that the mothers show, even from a distance, about being part of their lives, about being friends, and about being someone you can count on. This proximity between mother and child, which may not be intimate, is encouraged both by the maternal family in the child's daily life and by the emigrant.

Once again the grandmother has a fundamental role in mediating the mother-child relationship. The 'borrowing' of the children is a strategy for the grandmothers, both to help ensure that the mothers provide for provisions and monetary aid and to guarantee the help of the grandchildren with the household chores and routine errands.

It is, however, also necessary to look at the mediated quality of this relationship. A grandchild is not a child, but a child of a child. What I mean is that, unlike other African societies (Notermans 2004), in Boa Vista I do not see a lack of distinction between the grandparent-grandchild and the parent-child relationships. They are aware of the generation gap between the social mother and the biological mother. Although the children refer to their grandmothers as 'mothers' (calling them *mamã*), and often fail to identify a mother other than their grandmother, the latter takes all the necessary precautions to ensure that the child is aware of, maintains some contact with and has some love for the biological mother. I heard grandmothers reminding their grandchildren of their mothers on many occasions, putting the children on the phone with their mothers, and insisting that they had no ambitions of replacing the mother. After all, *mãe é quem pariu* (mother is she who bore the child).

The mother-child relationship is thus mediated at two levels: by the grandmother, who plays the central role in this process of constructing value for the mother with the children; and by means of the personal offerings, exchanges and sharing. To make up for the distance, a space that needs to be filled with symbols of proximity, mothers and children practice giving and receiving, reciprocal cognitive and emotional exchanges of material things. It is through reciprocity and the mutual feeling of sacrifice and longing that they are united. This prevents the strength of the relationship from fading. This occurs because the family bonds are maintained through showings of solidarity, sharing, and mutual assistance. Having something in common is the basis for a strong bond.

Emigration – a necessary evil

The aim of this project was to highlight one aspect of Cape Verdean emigration that is still relatively unexplored in the literature on the subject: the departure of the women.

The objective was not to compare between male and female emigration, and identify similarities and differences. Rather, through my analysis of the influence of the departure of women on the Boa Vista family context, we can point out the differences, as well as the fact that the Cape Verdean migratory phenomenon cannot be treated as a homogeneous process. There are significant differences in the relationships between emigrants and the society of origin which depend on gender and this cannot be ignored.

A crucial point, which I pointed out in the introduction and to which I would like to return, is matrifocality. Authors who address family organisation in Cape Verde stress the point that the family structure in this society tends toward the formation of matrifocal homes, in which the women are central while the men are absent or of little significance. This absence can be explained by the tenuousness of the male's economic situation (Couto 2001) and male emigration, a situation in which, despite long absences, men contribute financially and regularly and occupy the position of head of the family aggregate (Dias 2000). In both cases, it is the women who are left with the household chores and child rearing.

During the construction of my research project, and when I first read this literature, my first reaction was that my studies in Boa Vista might contradict the established theories. After all, how can one speak of matrifocality when the woman-mother is not present? The fathers would undoubtedly assume the responsibility of raising these children, and, if this were true, their absence and/or distance would be altered by the egression of the women. I soon discovered that this initial reflection was based on my cultural references of what it means to be a father and a mother in my society more than on the way Boa Vista natives see it. I hope my analysis has demonstrated that this is not how things necessarily happen and that the egression of women leads to new matrifocal arrangements, or rather to the strengthening of a matrifocal arrangement which is already important in Cape Verdean society: the grandmother-grandchild relationship and the female solidarity network.

In order to better understand my argument that even though they are separated by great distances, mothers, their children and grandmothers maintain strong bonds, and furthermore that, although nearby, the fathers and their children remain distant, I would like to raise the concept of *relatedness*.

The idea is that relationships must be seen as 'built by routine practice', more than as an imagined nature or formal existence of family bonds. New attention is thus given to the routine practices and to the concreteness of the substances shared among relatives. Blood relations are the first means to establishing a connection. Kinship is the first social order in which people find themselves and is an important determinant for the feeling of belonging. But this is not enough since there is a gap that needs to be filled by symbols of proximity: giving and receiving, mutual dependency, reciprocal exchanges of material values, knowledge and emotions (Van der Geest 2004: 54).

As I have tried to point out, kinship must be practised by using solidarity and mutual support. If this fails to happen, there is no commonality and the family bonds weaken. Therefore, it is not the physical distance that makes the mother-child and father-child bonds fade, but rather a breakdown in the forms of sharing. If, even in the emigration circumstances, mothers and their children can create and recreate relationships of interaction, care and affection through reciprocal exchanges, and, with the grandmother's mediation, build a common base, the relationship can remain strong and important to both.

I do not wish to give a homogeneous picture of this society. As I have stressed in the previous section, there are inherent conflicts to the emigration situation and there are cases in which mothers and children break the link that is maintained by reciprocity, move apart and lose each other. In order for this to not happen, both need to exercise care and vigilance. Leaving children behind in the search for employment comes at a price: being away from one's children, who in turn begin considering their grandmother (or other relative) the main source of emotional support.

What I have tried to clarify is that these women, embedded in a mutual solidarity network, work together in an attempt to keep mothers and children together. The reasons for this include the fact that the children who remain behind are strong bases which can unite the emigrant women and their families in Boa Vista. Due to the risks that family relationships centred on the women imply, there is a general feeling of ambiguity toward emigration. It is seen as a necessary evil. If, on the one hand, it is seen as a blessing, an alternative, and a solution, it also affects the relationship between these women and the relatives who remain behind, particularly the children.

Notes

[1] It is worth noting that the periodic returns are not restricted to the summer months; emigrants come and go throughout the year. The summer stands out, however, because of the large number of emigrants on the island and the activity generated by their presence in local routines.

[2] They generally stay for two or three months and this allows them to participate in the two main summer events, the Municipal Feast on 5 July and the Praia de Cruz Beach Festival in September.

[3] The domestic development cycle must be taken into account when we discuss the Boa Vista family structure. My analysis indicates that the types of domestic groups, and, consequently, the position of men and women within this system change substantially over time. In my description I am dealing with adult women and men who start a new family.

[4] The special character of the relationship between grandmothers and grandchildren in Cape Verde is not restricted to crisis or egression situations. This is an important daily relationship on the islands and should be analysed carefully in the studies on kinship and the Cape Verdean family.

References

Åkesson, L. (2004) *Making a Life: Meanings of Migration in Cape Verde*. Ph.D. thesis. Department of Social Anthropology, Gothenburg: Göteborg University.

Couto, C.F. (2001) *Estratégias Familiares de Subsistências Rurais em Santiago de Cabo Verde*. Lisbon: Instituto da Cooperação Portuguesa (Colecção Teses).

Dias, J.B. (2000) *Entre Partidas e Regressos: Tecendo Relações Familiares em Cabo Verde*. Master's dissertation, Department of Anthropology, Universidade de Brasília.

Monteiro, C.A. (1997) *Comunidade Imigrada: O Caso da Itália, Visão Sociológica*. São Vicente, CV: Gráfica do Mindelo.

Notermans, C. (2004) 'Sharing Home, Food, and Bed: Paths of Grandmotherhood in East Cameroon'. *Africa* 74(1): 6-27.

Smith, R.T. (1995) *The Matrifocal Family: Power, Pluralism, and Politics*. New York: Routledge.

Trajano Filho, W. (1998) *Domestic Rumors, Polymorphic Creoledom: The 'Creole' Society of Guinea-Bissau*. Ph.D. dissertation in anthropology, University of Pennsylvania.

Van der Geest, S. (2004) 'Grandparents and Grandchildren in Kwahu, Ghana: The Performance of Respect'. *Africa* 74(1): 47-61.

Chapter 12
Cape Verdean Tongues: Speaking of 'Nation' at Home and Abroad[1]

Márcia Rego

In the beginning, Cape Verde was part of the African continent. The Cape Verdeans were a rowdy bunch though, always buying and selling stuff, always taking disorder and making noise everywhere they went. They caused so much confusion that the rest of Africa got together and decided to separate Cape Verde from Africa by sending it far away, to the middle of the Ocean. But it wasn't long before the Cape Verdeans invented the ship and were out and about, causing a ruckus once again. The rest of Africa then decided to break Cape Verde up into ten little pieces, in the hope of keeping them apart and quiet, but they readily found a way to get together and make noise again. It was then that the Africans did the worst thing they possibly could have done – they took the rain away from Cape Verde. From then on, Cape Verdeans have scattered throughout the world, taking noise and confusion everywhere they go.

The story above, what I dub the 'myth of origin' of the Cape Verdean diaspora, was told in 1995 during a conference on 'Cape Verdeanness' – one of many events held in the nation's capital, Praia, to celebrate the twentieth anniversary of independence. It is a story about a new and unique people who were created by the 'old' world system – a system of empires and colonial rule – and who continued to spread and flourish around the world. Having been 'separated' from Africa, they are acknowledged as being of Africa, but not African, just as they are also of Portugal but hardly Portuguese. The imagery of a fluid and mobile people, ever capable of blurring boundaries and circumventing obstacles, reaffirms the widely shared belief that Cape Verdeans, while maintaining strong ties to Cape Verde, make resilient and resourceful emigrants (Åkesson 2004: 46, and chap. 20 of this volume). This 'myth' touches on themes that are recurrent in the local literature, song lyrics, and everyday conversations in Cape Verde. The first theme relates to the ambiguous relationship of Cape Verde to the rest of Africa. The second is the image of Cape Verdeans as a people in transit and, at the same time, as a difficult bunch to keep apart. And the third is the depiction of Cape Verdeans as a source of noise and confusion.

To understand the specificities of the Cape Verdean diaspora that was so playfully illustrated in the 'myth of origin', one must look not only to Cape Verde's colonial history, but also to its rich – if still brief – postcolonial history. The unique tensions that coloured Cape Verde's development as an independent nation – and that continue to permeate dialogues regarding its national culture – are echoed in heated debates about language use and language policy. By tracing the history of metalinguistic discourses surrounding Portuguese and Kriolu I hope to demonstrate how these discourses variously reflect and constitute Cape Verdean notions of 'nation' and 'national identity', within both the country and the diaspora.

Kriolu origins

The dissemination of the Portuguese language was central to the colonising project of the Portuguese, which in turn was intimately related to that of the Catholic Church. In its crusade against non-Christians, the Papacy had much to gain by associating with the expansionist project undertaken by Portugal while, simultaneously, the Catholic discourse of evangelisation offered the Portuguese Crown powerful ideological support for their maritime exploration and commercial ambitions. Thus, through a series of royal warrants and pontifical documents, Crown and Church progressively built the religious dimension of the Portuguese colonialist endeavour, making the Christianisation of non-Christians simultaneously its main purpose and justification (Santos and Soares 1995: 361-5).

The discovery of the Cape Verde Islands, still uninhabited in the 1450s, was welcomed by the Portuguese as a facilitating event for their ongoing commercial transactions with the West African Coast. The first ships sent to settle the Islands carried European men in the service of the Portuguese empire, along with men and women captured and enslaved on the coast to blaze the trails and toil in its mountains and valleys. Despite the crown's efforts to turn Cape Verde into an agrarian colony, and partly because of the archipelago's unfavourable climate, Cape Verde soon became specialised in the marketing of slaves.

The slaves transported to Cape Verde were acclimatised through a process called *ladinização*. This consisted of teaching them basic labour skills and the fundamentals of Catholicism and the Portuguese language. Because one of the justifications for slavery was the indoctrination of non-Christians and the 'saving of their souls', the African captives were kept on the islands to be thus '*ladinizados*', preferably until they were considered to be ready for baptism. By that time, they were assumed to have received enough language training to be offered to European slavers for a considerably higher price (Carreira 1983: 267). Although some authors are sceptical of the deliberate, systematic (and costly) teaching of slaves (Rougé 1995: 93), documentary evidence suggests that slaves who had been '*ladinizados*' were more desirable and thus carried higher market value (Carreira 1983: 267, Santos and Cabral 1991). Although the church directed its efforts toward teaching the African population to speak Portuguese, the resulting language, which was to become the mother tongue of Cape Verdeans in just a few generations, was Kriolu – defined by modern linguists as a Portuguese-based Creole.

The historical and political contexts surrounding the different representations of Kriolu, particularly those offered by Cape Verdeans or others directly involved in the colonisation – and decolonisation – of the islands, provide insight into the social space that Kriolu presently occupies in Cape Verdean society and, consequently, in its diaspora. In general terms, Kriolu can be said to have originated from the convergence (or clash) of two opposing movements. The first toward collaboration – between coloniser and colonised, between master and slave, between Portuguese, Cape Verdean and African slavers, between slavers and the Catholic Church. The second movement, in contrast, was geared toward differentiation, whether in the form of exclusion, resistance or subversion. Thus from its very origins, Kriolu was located, paradoxically, both within and outside of the Portuguese language.

Colonial linguistics

Early descriptions of the language spoken in Cape Verde portrayed a cacophonous hodgepodge through which the locals somehow managed to communicate, despite its lack of order or reason. Portuguese clergymen described the language as noisy, grammarless and chaotic; as a corrupted form of 'clean Portuguese' (Nogueira 1984: 13); and as a nuisance to the empire (Coelho 1967: 154). Colonial officials portrayed it as a corrosive force that ought to be eradicated, and were astonished to find colonials who, contrary to colonial logic, had adopted Kriolu for use in their own homes (Nogueira 1984: 13; Batalha 2004).

What these astonished inspectors observed was the result of the acculturation/deculturation process that accompanied the slave economy. On the one hand, efforts to mould the Africans to serve the colonial system created a population that was intimately implicated in that system through labour, familial and emotional ties, but one that remained outside of the societal power structures. Their practices could not be assimilated into the colonial model, and their language inevitably exceeded 'clean' Portuguese.

The colonials, on the other hand, having founded a society almost exclusively on slave trade, were dependent on slaves not only for their labour and their value as merchandise, but even for the very business of producing, training, and deploying other slaves. The elites were obliged to represent their authority not only *in relation to*, but also *through the medium of* slaves, and were thus extremely vulnerable to those over whom they exercised authority. In only a few generations, the population became highly miscegenated and the elites were everywhere surrounded by the 'uncivilised savages' whom they loathed but without whom they could not achieve the 'civilisation' they aspired to. No longer only their slaves, these 'savages' also became their mistresses, their sons and daughters, their trusted men and their healers. The colonial ideal became 'contaminated' by a world of informal exchanges that were inexpressible in the empire's official language. This situation of dissonance created a divide between official text and intimate orality; a split between a formal system inscribed in/by Portuguese, and an informal system that spoke Kriolu.

From ridiculous slang to romantic adventure

The late 1870s saw the first approaches to Kriolu as an entity susceptible to systematic analysis. Scholars such as Adolfo Coelho (1967) and António de Paula Brito (1967) attempted to understand the grammatical laws that governed Kriolu and tried to compare it to Portuguese. Initiatives to systematise the knowledge of Kriolu at this time were often justified as deriving from a 'patriotic' sentiment, a desire to better understand the world created by the Portuguese. Although regarded as a lesser language form, it should still to be treated as a Portuguese possession, and its knowledge by others was felt as a threat.

About eight decades later, as national liberation movements sprouted up around the globe and the international community reproached the institution of colonialism more seriously, Portugal changed, in 1951, the designation of its colonies to 'overseas provinces' and enhanced its efforts to 'Portugalise' them (Lobban 1995: 46). This is when we start to see 'scientific' studies describing Kriolu as a facet of Portugueseness, all in an attempt to assimilate it into the national culture. A study by Baltazar Lopes da Silva (1957) is considered by contemporary scholars of Kriolu to be the first serious study of the language. It may also be considered a consolidation – if only temporarily – of a new trend in the empire's approach to the language of the colony. By a subtle move in perspective, Kriolu goes from being unintelligible gibberish by which even 'whites' are inexplicably seduced and which, therefore, ought to be eradicated, to being an unavoidable given to be tamed under the auspices of science. Sanctioned by national authorities, Silva's study 'scientifically' attributes the status of 'dialect' to Kriolu, turning what had formerly been described as 'ridiculous slang' into a 'true Romantic adventure' (Silva 1984: 38). By being included as a facet of 'Portuguese-ness', Kriolu is, by the same token, hierarchically subjugated to Portuguese as an appendage; its definition forged upon its relation to a 'sovereign' language of 'civilisation'.

Only a few years after Silva's study was published, the 'Portuguese-ness' of Cape Verdeans became, more than ever before, an issue of concern for Portugal. War had broken out in Mozambique, Angola and Guinea-Bissau, and maintaining Cape Verdean loyalty was a matter of survival. According to Deirdre Meintel's description, 'tens of thousands of Portuguese troops poured into São Vicente and Santiago' (1984: 138) and generalised suspicion of 'terrorism (i.e., nationalism)' coexisted with 'official' affirmations that Cape Verde was 'more Portuguese than ever' (Meintel 1984:138).

'Portuguese', once synonymous with 'Empire' and 'Civilisation', had come, by this time, to subsume the former colonies under the sign of the modern 'Nation'. The signifier 'Kriolu' constituted a persistent problem to all claims of 'oneness', as moves to assimilate it competed with moves to place it outside of Portuguese. As Kriolu threatened to occupy the space of the written and other 'Portuguese' spaces, maintaining it as a dialect was no longer effective for its subordination; the coloniser's new strategy was thus redirected toward outright repression of Kriolu and other 'pre-modernisms' and 'Africanities'. Strict censorship measures were instituted in the press during the anti-colonial war years (1961-74), and various forms of cultural expressions were closely controlled. The use of Kriolu was banned from school grounds in 1959 and became increasingly a target for repression (Meintel 1984: 138-44), even as it became a banner for the nationalist movement that led to Cape Verdean independence, in 1975.

From the times of the 'ladinisation' of slaves to the final years of colonial rule, the Cape Verdean language complex was the subject of shifting representations by the different voices of official bodies. In the following sections, I will demonstrate the ways in which this language situation was further complicated by the imagining of a postcolonial Cape Verdean nation, even as such imaginings attempt to place Kriolu within a new kind of order.

Nationalising Kriolu

Since its independence, Cape Verde has seen the invention and demise of various national symbols and monuments, as its people have attempted to forge a befitting national identity for the nation they have imagined. Achieving an identity, however, is a contradiction in terms, for an identity proper cannot be achieved as an unproblematic product of an unproblematic process; the discussions and disagreements surrounding Cape Verdean national symbols reflect this kind of tumultuous approximation of a self-definition. James Siegel (1997) has phrased the problem as it relates to a national identity in the following way:

> My view is contrary, therefore, to the stream of current thought that sees identity as achieved, negotiated, crafted, and in other ways the product of a self [...] There, to find a lace of self-definition is to be thrown off balance unless one can be convincingly self-deceiving. Identity exists only at the price of enormous confusions and contradictions (Siegel 1997: 9).

Cape Verdean 'confusions and contradictions' regarding the search for a national identity can be said to gravitate around the following, sometimes intertwined, dichotomies: colonial subjugation vs. autonomy; Africanness vs. Europeanness; backwardness vs. progress; tradition vs. modernity. Procuring a self-definition that embraces both 'modernity' and 'tradition' is a task replete with contradictions, as is any attempt to identify with both Africa and Europe. The process by which Cape Verdeans have created (and recreated) their new national symbols reveals a state of confusion – of ideals, of loyalties – among the country's people and its leaders, as do current debates surrounding the officialisation of Kriolu.

The 1995 conference with which I began illustrates this well. The event occurred during a two-week commemoration of Cape Verdean independence, a time when Cape Verde hosted scholars from other Portuguese-speaking nations. As might be presumed, the lectures, debates and questions posed by the audience during the event were uttered in impeccable Portuguese. During informal coffee breaks and away from the microphones, however, the Cape Verdean contingent immediately engaged in Kriolu, leaving one or two authorities to entertain, in Portuguese, their non-Kriolu-speaking guests.

Despite the denomination as 'Lusophone Capital' during this period, the town also hosted the publication of books in Kriolu, recordings of oral 'literatures' (in Kriolu), and films of 'traditional' music and dances. In state-sponsored street concerts, contemporary Cape Verdean music, also in Kriolu, could be heard until late hours. A second conference I attended was a tribute to Kriolu and to the efforts of dedicated Cape Verdeans, in the country and abroad, who were struggling to standardise and 'dignify' the language. The occasion featured the book-signing of the new and most complete Kriolu grammar ever to be published, a feat considered to be a groundbreaking step toward making Kriolu appropriate for use as a national language. The author, Manuel Veiga (1995), at the time a Ph.D. candidate in linguistics at Aix-en-Provence, in France, was paid solemn homage.

Among the speakers was a young emigrant who had flown in from the U.S. especially for the occasion. A schoolteacher in Massachusetts, the young man was one of the people actively involved in promoting Kriolu amongst the immigrant community. Visibly emotional, he praised Veiga as a national hero, and proudly spoke of his own success in establishing bilingual programs (English and Kriolu) in the Boston Area. Interestingly enough, even at *this* conference, specifically dedicated to Kriolu, all the speeches and honours were delivered in Portuguese, with one exception: At one point, a local young poet in the audience announced in Kriolu that he wanted to recite a poem in honour of Veiga. He refused to speak Portuguese, he argued, because he should not have to give up his own language in his own country. His poem triggered a few smiles, a wave of silence, and a touch of uneasiness in the air – until the next speaker swiftly returned to Portuguese.

What this two-week commemoration revealed is that the search for true 'Cape Verdeanness' is not without its ambiguities. As a nation emerging out of a colonial past, 'fragments'[2] of the colony persist in the new society. The intellectual elite of fluent Portuguese speakers, itself a product of the colonial project of a Creole administrative class, is caught in debates about whether to seek greater involvement in African politics or whether Cape Verdeans should 'continue to see themselves as second-rate Europeans'.[3] The choice of which language(s) to be taught in schools is a salient issue of debate. On the one hand, Kriolu, inseparable from the language of the coloniser, is considered to be the sole means of expressing Cape Verdeanness – hence the present attempts to standardise Kriolu, and by so doing to a make a claim for its officialisation and dissemination through print. On the other hand, Portuguese is the language of a literary tradition, the one in which this nation was imagined and declared independent, and whose cultivation is seen as crucial for contact with the outside world.

These discussions are not restricted to scholarly meetings or government events, however. In plazas, bars, and people's homes, I heard heated discussions on whether Kriolu should be taught in schools and why; whether Cape Verde was really bilingual and whether it should strive to be bilingual; whether Kriolu should be officialised, and if so, whether it should share with Portuguese its new official status.

Beyond a debate over the choice of a linguistic 'code' to be adopted based on its suitability for this or that specific function, the current discussions surrounding Creole and Portuguese speak to the different positions that *português* and *crioulo* have come to occupy in the Cape Verdean imagination. While Portuguese is experienced as having the authority to formalise, legalise, repress and exclude, Kriolu has embodied the shameful, the vulgar and the primitive, as well as the impenetrably intimate, the communal, and the pleasurable. It is the language of jokes, satire, and irony (Ferreira 1985: 145), of romantic relationships and strong emotions (Meintel 1984: 149).

But despite the perceived specialisations and insufficiencies of each language, they have coexisted in complex and intertwining ways, each feeding on its interplay with the other. In Cape Verde, one does not sometimes speak Kriolu and Portuguese at other times. One speaks a Portuguese disturbed by, contested by, rescued by, or completed by Kriolu. A Portuguese disturbed by Kriolu is the legacy of the historical role of Cape Verde in the slave-trade enterprise, the colonial attempts to appropriate and assimilate Kriolu into the nation-empire, and the subsequent interruption of the Portuguese national project by a Kriolu revolution.

(Trans)nationalist linguistics: from dialect to national language

The major linguistic studies on Kriolu developed by Cape Verdeans since the 1970s followed a different course from the studies of colonial times, and can be read as efforts to construct Kriolu as part of 'Cape Verdeanness'. While former representations of Kriolu stressed hierarchy, dependence, and subjugation to Portuguese, more recent discourses describe Kriolu as sufficient and independent, and call for its unity throughout the archipelago as well as its protection from Portuguese.

In a 1978 article entitled *Crioulo ou Língua Caboverdiana?* (Kriolu or Cape Verdean Language?), Veiga provides a clue to the course that his own and other linguistic studies on Kriolu were to follow. His defence of the Cape Verdean language is based on a purported superiority of orality over written expression. Although constituting one of the greatest realisations of the human spirit, Veiga contends, writing should not constitute the main criterion for defining a language, because it is but a function of speech. Although arguing against the notion that Kriolu is a mutilated or degenerate form of Portuguese, he portrays it as lacking and needing development. The time has come, Veiga claims, to 'begin a structuring of our language at the lexical, phonetic and syntactic levels' (Veiga 1978: 5).

In 1979, another significant work on Kriolu was written by Donaldo Macedo, a member of the Cape Verdean immigrant community in the U.S. The title of Macedo's dissertation points to an important change in perspective from previous works: 'A Linguistic Approach to the Cape Verdean *Language* (emphasis added), not a *dialect*, and not *Creole*. He claims his dissertation represents the realisation of a personal goal, and hopes his efforts will 'give [his] people a better understanding of [...] the vehicle by which they express their innermost feelings' (Macedo 1979: v).

Macedo's work is an argument against the notion that pidgins (from which Creoles are thought to develop) are the result of a drastic simplification of the 'upper language' (in most cases, a designation of European languages) when in contact with one or more vernaculars regarded as 'lower languages' (as in languages spoken by slaves or colonised peoples). He defends the subtle, yet profoundly, different view that pidgins result from the contact between two or more groups that, for whatever reason, have 'to coexist in a delineated geographical area' (Macedo 1979: 20).

These distinct perspectives on pidginisation have been the subject of much controversy and carry important ideological implications. The 'simplification' view is based on the premise that European languages are more complex than African (and other 'indigenous') languages and, as such, require of its speakers a refined intellect. Defenders of the simplification thesis regarding Kriolu have based their arguments on the presumed less-than-refined intellect of the Africans taken to Cape Verde as slaves, and the racist view that they were incapable of abstract thought. The birth of Kriolu has thus been attributed to the 'practical spirit of the Negroes' by Lopes (1967: 408), and even to their 'rudimentary mentality' by Almada (1961: 23).

Through a comparative analysis, Macedo claims to have disproved the simplification theory, as well as offered support for an additional, yet related, conclusion: that Kriolu is *not* a dialect of Portuguese. Its structure is so dramatically different from that of Portuguese, he contends, that by Silva's (and others') own criteria, 'Portuguese can more easily be considered a dialect of Spanish than Cape Verdean Creole a dialect of Portuguese' (Macedo 1979: 75).

What also permeates recent studies is a concern with the country's 'national unity'. Veiga (1978, 1990), for instance, concludes that although Kriolu may vary superficially from one island to another, its 'deep structure' is the same throughout the archipelago, constituting one single 'national language'. Veiga further argues that a profound knowledge of Kriolu would not only serve to preserve Cape Verdean culture, but also to facilitate people's apprehension of Portuguese, which, however foreign, is still a useful and necessary legacy of coloni-

alism. He contends that '[e]xplicit and scientific knowledge of both languages will make us determine the boundaries of each of them and,
thus, the *structural interferences* will be fewer and our performances less
distorted' (1990: 12, emphasis added).

When Cape Verde was effectively established as a nation-state, it in-
herited the language of hierarchy and dependent subjugation, although
its colonisers were no longer physically there. The colonial 'fragments'
persisted, via Portuguese, into the nationalist project. This is illustrated
in the nationalists' attitudes toward Kriolu. Despite their efforts to 'dignify' and free Kriolu from its colonial representations, these same nationalists often depict it as a so-called 'immature' language, lacking the
vocabulary to serve a modern nation. On the one hand, they defend the
use of Kriolu in schools, for only through Kriolu will Cape Verdeans effectively learn and be able to express themselves. More importantly,
only Kriolu will enable Cape Verdeans to participate in a nation that is
truly theirs. Portuguese, however, is seen as more suitable for the offi-
cialdom of the state apparatus, especially for its diplomatic and other
international affairs. Hence the efforts to 'dignify' Kriolu – which is to
say 'develop' and 'modernise' it, by 'elevating' it to the status of Portuguese. But Kriolu seems to resist being officialised: it is perceived as
noisy and disorderly; it is 'mixed' and of unclear origin; it varies from
one island to another; it is non-written, emotional, and above all, informal and subversive.

These more recent metalinguistic discourses speak to a new and dif-
ferently positioned attempt to 'reduce'[4] Kriolu, to mold it to serve a nationalist project. Attributing unity to Kriolu through standardisation
and homogenisation of its varieties, circumscribing it to the authority
of grammar books, ascribing a code to it, and imposing boundaries to
divorce it from Portuguese are efforts to control a language which has
always resisted and exceeded formal treatment. The tension fuelling
these debates, then, lies in the attempt to formalise precisely that
which is informal *par excellence*, and has historically occupied the
spaces of the unofficial. Its association with the familiar and intimate,
along with its recognition as subversive and revolutionary, confirm the
place of Kriolu as a language of commentary on the official. How then
is one to understand the nationalist project to officialise it?

The new move to describe and classify Kriolu, now with the explicit
objective of 'elevating' its status, is part of the project to establish Kriolu as the foundation of a Cape Verdean national identity. Slavoj Žižek
(1990: 31) has argued that 'national identification' consists of a relationship shared by the members of a given community 'toward the Nation
qua Thing' or 'towards Enjoyment incarnated'. Not determinable in
concrete terms, the 'Nation-Thing' is only visible through the unique
way a community 'organizes its enjoyment through national myths'

(Žižek 1990: 52-3). However abstract and elusive, the Nation-Thing is perceived as uniquely 'ours' and inaccessible to 'others.'

Viewed from Žižek's perspective, the nationalist representation of Kriolu is an expression of the Cape Verdean Nation-Thing: the language through which Cape Verdeans gain access to that which is uniquely theirs, or, in Žižek's terms, the Cape Verdean 'enjoyment.' The need to protect Kriolu from Portuguese contamination can be understood as an obsession with the control and possession of the Cape Verdean Thing. The fear of the 'theft of enjoyment' as articulated by Žižek embodies the paradox that although we conceive the national Thing as accessible only to 'ourselves,' we feel the 'other' as a menace to it (1990: 54). Another paradox is that, in ascribing the theft of enjoyment to the 'other,' what is concealed is an original lack, or 'the traumatic fact that *we never possessed what was originally stolen from us*' (Žižek 1990: 54, emphasis added). The threat of contamination by Portuguese could thus be read as concealing (or revealing) the lack of unity, separateness, and integrity of Kriolu.

Indeed, I have argued, Kriolu and Portuguese can hardly be referred to as two separate codes, given that Kriolu lies simultaneously inside and outside of Portuguese. Born as a displacement from, or an 'undermining' of, Portuguese, Kriolu also served as an intermediary tool for the objectives of the Portuguese empire. Centuries later, Kriolu appears as the language of the revolution, of opposition to colonial rule. But all the while Kriolu has drawn from Portuguese, transformed it and informed it.

The interplay of language(s) in Cape Verde seems to escape all attempts at describing and controlling it, including recent efforts to establish a new order to the language situation in the country. This 'new order' implies a paradigm shift: Kriolu, which has historically occupied a place of symbiotic opposition to the official, is now expected to be independent and sufficient – indeed to *voice* the official – while catalysing a shared sense of belonging.

Characterising Kriolu as part of the Cape Verdean 'essence' says something about the Cape Verdean 'Thing' as defined by Žižek: perhaps it says that part of the Cape Verdean enjoyment is in its very displacement from Portuguese – in its ability to subvert and reinvent it. Perhaps it is this inventiveness one wishes to protect when warding off Portuguese. Could this explain, paradoxically, the resistance by part of the country's elite to officialising Kriolu? In other words, is this playfulness and irreverence also what one wishes to preserve by keeping Kriolu out of the realm of formal discipline? Or is it simply that the officialisation of Kriolu threatens the privileged position of the bilingual elite?

Kriolu Babel

As is widely known, Cape Verde has historically depended on massive emigration for the survival of its population, two-thirds of which are now scattered about in Senegal, the U.S. and several European countries. Aside from the harsh arid climate that has always hindered its economic development, the Cape Verdean nation is now faced with the reality of the European Common Market and the tightening of borders around the 'First World'. At the same time, the country gains more access to outside information through its improved telecommunications system, not only facilitating contact with the diasporic communities, but also the importation of foreign discourses and imagery. Since 1997, an increasing number of Cape Verdean residents have gained access to the Internet, and Praia now has its cyber cafés around the main plaza. The pull toward globalisation coexists in a tense relation with both the 'colonial' and the 'national' modes, further complicating the issue of Cape Verdean identity.

I have mentioned the efforts of Cape Verdeans to establish bilingual (Creole-English) schools in Massachusetts and to promote Kriolu among the immigrant community. The individuals who head these efforts are in contact with linguists and educators in Cape Verde and are very much engaged in 'national' language debates. These, as well as many other Cape Verdean emigrants, can be considered 'transmigrants' in the sense that Basch et al. (1994) define the term, i.e., as immigrants who 'take actions, make decisions, and develop subjectivities and identities embedded in networks of relationship that connect them simultaneously to two or more nation-states' (1994: 7). Of course, some are more 'transmigrant' than others, as their effective participation in these networks varies in kind and degree.

For the emigrant who never returns home, or even for their descendants, the imagining of a homeland in the middle of the Atlantic Ocean is an important part of maintaining a Cape Verdean identity. Even four generations later, many see themselves as somehow displaced, as they cluster and reconstruct communities around this 'remembered or imagined homeland' (Gupta and Ferguson 1992: 11). Back 'home', in turn, the nation is imagined as escaping the boundaries of the islands to encompass its many 'brothers of the diaspora' living in distant lands, estimated to constitute approximately twice the population of all the Cape Verde islands combined. Basch et al. suggest that by imagining emigrants as 'loyal citizens of their ancestral nation-state' (1994: 3), the nation calls for their participation in the nation-building process. In the case of Cape Verde, the imagining of 'loyal citizens' involves a peculiar twist: since many of its emigrants are older than the nation-state itself, this may mean inventing or nurturing loyalties that exist outside of and prior to the independence *per se*. This indicates a need for a concept of 'nation' that is, in fact, separate from the notion of 'state'. Whatever the specific practices and ideas of the 'national' maintaining these transnational ties, the fact is that nearly 40 per cent of the Cape Verdean national budget consists of remittances from fellow Cape Verdeans living abroad (another essential 48 per cent comes from other sources of international aid).[5] Added to these official figures are the incalculable remittances made outside of the legal channels and the imported merchandise that escape customs controls.

Much of the literature on globalisation postulates that, in one way or another, the transnational tendencies of today's world tend to 'undermine', 'corrode', or somehow 'subvert' the modern nation-state. A common premise of this perspective is not only that 'national' and 'transnational' processes exist in opposition, but that nation-states are rigid monoliths and, therefore, inherently evil; transnational processes are positioned as fluid and transcendental and, therefore, not only benign, but desirable.

While it is not within the scope of this work to rebut the dichotomous opposition between globalisation and nation-states, my objective in referring to this discussion is to offer the Cape Verdean case as a counterexample; as indeed indicative of an opposing trend. The spanning of boundaries, physical or otherwise, is far from corroding the Cape Verdean nation; it is, in many ways, crucial to the country's very existence. Cape Verde's situation of deprivation and poverty does not allow it to be a self-sustaining and autonomous nation. However, this has not precluded it from imagining itself as an independent nation moving towards a utopian future. Forever reminded of a fundamental lack by its very name (*Green* Cape), Cape Verde imagined itself as independent from its colonisers, but also unavoidably related to many other peoples and nations.

For the Cape Verdeans in the diaspora – that is, those who have established residence within the physical boundaries of other nation-states – the Portuguese language occupies a social space distinct from that which it occupies in Cape Verde. Aside from those occupying official posts or those living in Portugal, most other emigrants have the English, French, Dutch, or Italian languages occupying the legal and formal spaces that Portuguese occupies in Cape Verde. Their participation as citizens of a *state* is realised through other languages of bureaucracy and other hierarchical discursive practices. Their participation in a shared *nation* of Cape Verdeans, however, in this nation that spans boundaries and provides a sense of belonging to a homeland, can only be done through the horizontal dimension of social relations; through the malleability of Kriolu. In turn, Kriolu constantly incorporates both vocabulary and imagery from the languages of its many host countries, continuously reshaping itself in the process. In its mingling with other tongues, Kriolu confirms its ability to adapt and to move through unofficial channels, variously translating facets of a Cape Verdean 'national identity.'

In closing, I refer once again to the myth of origin of the Cape Verdean diaspora – which is simultaneously a myth about Kriolu and the people who speak it. The myth tells of the uncertain and mixed origin of Cape Verdeans ('they caused much confusion'), their ambiguous identification with Africa ('the rest of Africa sent them far away'), their transnational tendencies ('they invented the ship, and were out and about'), their ability to bend rules and their expression of a shared sense of belonging ('they found a way to get together again'). We can perhaps conclude that Kriolu is the 'noise' mentioned in the myth – it is the noise that defines Cape Verdeans, that sets them apart from the rest, that brings them together and keeps them together ('taking noise and confusion wherever they go') through banishment, hardship and exile.

Notes

[1] Research for this essay was funded by the Conselho Nacional de Desenvolvimento Cientifico e Tecnológico (CNPq), Brazil, and by the Department of Anthropology at University of California, San Diego. A Mellon Fellows Grant through the Duke University Writing Program funded presentation of this research at the International Conference on Cape Verdean Migration and Diaspora in April 2005, at the Centro de Estudos de Antropologia Social, ISCTE, in Lisbon. All translations are mine. I wish to thank Tamera Marko, Michael Petit, Michele Strano and an anonymous reviewer for their valuable input.

[2] The term 'fragment' here refers to the work of Chatterjee (1993), in which he examines the role of 'anticolonial' nationalist elites in imagining the postcolonial nation.

[3] Personal communication by the Minister of Culture, at a roundtable about 'Cape Verdeanness'.

[4] The choice of 'reduction' here was inspired in Rafael's (1993) use of it in describing the Spaniards' project of translation and conversion in the Philippines – part of which was the 'reduction' of the Tagalog language through grammatical analysis and phoneticisation.

[5] According to 1988 statistics in Foy (1988: 111).

References

Åkesson, L. (2004) *Making a Life: Meanings of Migration in Cape Verde.* Ph.D. thesis. Department of Social Anthropology, Gothenburg: Göteborg University.

Almada, M.D. de O. (1961) *Cabo Verde: Contribuição para o Estudo do Dialecto Falado no Seu Arquipélago.* Lisbon: Junta de Investigações do Ultramar, Centro de Estudos Políticos e Sociais.

Basch, L.; Schiller, N.G. and Blanc, C.S. (1994) *Nations Unbound: Transnational Projects, Post-colonial Predicaments and Deterritorialized Nations-States*. Amsterdam: Gordon and Breach.

Batalha, L. (2004) 'The Politics of Cape Verdean Creole', in *Los Criollos de Base Iberica*, M. Fernández, M. Fernández-Ferreiro, N.V. Veiga (eds.), Madrid and Frankfurt: Ibero Americana and Vervuert (Lingüística Iberoamericana, vol. 24), pp. 101-109.

Brito, A. de P. (1967) 'Dialectos Crioulos-Portugueses', in *Estudos Linguísticos Crioulos*, J. Morais-Barbosa, (org.), Lisbon: Academia Internacional da Cultura Portuguesa, pp. 329-430.

Carreira, A. (1983 [1972]) *Cabo Verde: Formação e Extinção de Uma Sociedade Escravocrata, 1460-1878*. Mem Martins, PT: Europam.

Chatterjee, P. (1993) *The Nation and its Fragments: Colonial and Postcolonial Histories*. Princeton, NJ: Princeton University Press.

Coelho, A. (1967) 'Os Dialectos Românicos ou Neo-Latinos na África, Asia e América', in *Estudos Linguísticos Crioulos*, J. Morais Barbosa (org.), Lisbon: Academia Internacional de Cultura Portuguesa, pp. 1-108.

Ferreira, M. (1985) *A Aventura Crioula*. Lisbon: Plátano Editora.

Foy, C. (1988) *Cape Verde: Politics, Economics and Society*. London and New York: Pinter Publishers.

Gupta, A.; Ferguson, J. (1992) 'Beyond "Culture": Space, Identity and the Politics of Difference'. *Cultural Anthropology* 7(1): 6-23.

Lobban, R.A. (1995) *Cape Verde: Crioulo Colony to Independent Nation*. Boulder, CO: Westview Press.

Lopes, E.C. (1967) 'Dialectos Crioulos e Etnografia Crioula', in *Estudos Linguísticos Crioulos*, J. Morais-Barbosa (org.), Lisbon: Academia Internacional da Cultura Portuguesa, pp. 405-447.

Macedo, D.P. (1979) *A Linguistic Approach to the Capeverdean Language*, unpublished dissertation, Boston, MA: University School of Education.

Meintel, D. (1984) *Race, Culture, and Portuguese Colonialism in Cabo Verde*. Syracuse, NY: Maxwell School of Citizenship and Public Affairs, Syracuse University.

Nogueira, R. de Sá (1984) 'Prólogo', in *O Dialecto Crioulo de Cabo Verde*, B.L. da Silva, Lisbon: Imprensa Nacional Casa de Moeda, pp. 7-25.

Rafael, V. (1993) *Contracting Colonialism: Translation and Christian Conversion in Tagalog Society under Early Spanish Rule*. Durham and London: Duke University Press.

Rougé, J.L. (1986) 'Uma Hipótese sobre a Formação do Crioulo da Guiné e da Casamansa'. *Soronda* 2: 28-49.

Santos, E.M.S.; Soares, M.J. (1995) 'Igreja, Missionação e Sociedade', in *História Geral de Cabo Verde*, L. de Albuquerque and M.E.M. Santos (orgs.), Lisbon and Praia: IICT-INAC, vol. II, pp. 359-508.

Santos, E.M.S.; Cabral, I. (1991) 'O Nascer de uma Sociedade Através do Morador-Armador', in *História Geral de CaboVerde*, L. de Albuquerque and M.E.M. Santos (orgs.), Lisbon and Praia: IICT-INAC, vol. I, pp. 371-428.

Siegel, J. (1997) *Fetish, Recognition, Revolution*. Princeton NJ: Princeton University Press.

Silva, B.L. da (1984 [1957]) *O Dialecto Crioulo de Cabo Verde: Surto e Expansão*. Lisbon: Imprensa Nacional-Casa da Moeda.

Veiga, M. (1978) 'Crioulo ou Língua Caboverdiana?' *Voz di Povo*, Feb. 13, pp. 5-6.

Veiga, M. (1990) 'Prefácio', in *O Crioulo da Ilha de São Nicolau de Cabo Verde*, E.A Cardoso (ed.), Praia: Instituto Caboverdiano do Livro, pp. 11-13.

Veiga, M. (1995) *Introdução à Gramática do Crioulo*. Praia: Instituto Caboverdiano do Livro e do Disco.

Žižek, S. (1990) 'Eastern Europe's Republics of Gilead'. *New Left Review* I/183: 50-62.

Chapter 13
Cape Verdean Transnationalism on the Internet

Sónia Melo

Introduction

Cape Verdean migration and its transnational activities are most likely unknown to the majority of researchers that work in those fields of study. Being a small country, the importance of the transnational phenomena to the country and its people is not well known. Although scattered around the world, many Cape Verdeans keep active links with their place of origin. In the last decade, the Internet has become another means and another space through which Cape Verdeans can maintain easier, closer and more frequent contact with their families, friends and business partners.

Transnational practices have been defined as 'occupations and activities that require regular and sustained social contact over time across national borders for their implementation' (Portes et al. 1999: 219) and they have been considered in terms of different scales, usually described as transnationalism from above and transnationalism from below. The first has been conceptualised in relation to multinationals, corporate affairs, the state or civil society institutions (Sklair 2001; Sassen 2002, 2004). On the other hand, transnationalism from below has focused on the individual level or on groups of migrants and their activities in both receiving and sending countries (Smith and Guarnizo 1998; Rouse 1995; Smith 2000). Within this last category research has concentrated in two different ends – the highly skilled (Dobson et al. 2001; Vertovec 2002) and the less-skilled workers (Anderson 2001).

Internet use by migrant communities has recently become a topic of study. Researchers have focused on how those communities maintain active links through cyberspace for a different number of reasons: finding jobs, maintaining their sense of identity and belonging to a certain group or nationality, or keeping active solidarity ties and political links with the place of origin (e.g., Mitra 2000; Stubbs 1999; Yang 2003; Ong 2003; Georgiou 2006; Bernal 2006; Benítez 2006). This chapter will take Cape Verdean transnationalism on the whole as a crucial factor that accounts for both Internet growth in Cape Verde and the development of different online activities among Cape Verdeans.

During my ethnographic research on the islands of Cape Verde, it became clear that migration played a key role in Cape Verdean society. Connections between local Cape Verdeans and Cape Verdean migrants are very frequent and both groups engage in a variety of activities. Migrants send money home to help in the establishment of businesses. They also actively participate in the organisation of cultural and religious festivities, vote in general elections in Cape Verde, find jobs for their relatives, and visit Cape Verde during their summer holidays. In the same way, the ability of Cape Verdean migrants to keep active ties with the place of origin is deeply linked to the construction of a Cape Verdean cyberspace. In fact, much of what one finds online today has been created by or because of migrants living outside the archipelago.

I will consider the following aspects: how the country's long history of migration and the links that Cape Verdean migrants have maintained with the place of origin have made Internet use in Cape Verde grow; how Cape Verdean transnational practices are the driving force not only for online communication in Cape Verde, but also contribute significantly to the making of specific online sites. Moreover, I will look at how and why of all Cape Verdean migrant groups those in the U.S. have been the most active in fostering the Cape Verdean networking space and communication via the Internet. In addressing these questions, I will draw on offline ethnographic materials – interviews, field notes – and materials collected online on Internet sites and web pages related to Cape Verde or Cape Verdeans. The offline data has been collected in both Cape Verde and Massachusetts.

The Internet and migration

The introduction of the Internet in Cape Verde dates from the late 1990s. Compared to the situation in mainland Africa, Cape Verde has a large concentration of phone landlines – 15.1 per one hundred inhabitants in 2002 (PNUD 2004). This has aided the proliferation of online connections. Nevertheless, most of the phone connections as well as the Internet access points are located in the two main cities of Praia and Mindelo. This situation reflects the general technological urban/rural divide in the country. With few exceptions, most Internet connections are concentrated in urban locations in which students and the middle and upper classes account for the majority of the users.

Because phone calls are extremely expensive in Cape Verde (PNUD 2004), the population is increasingly turning to the Internet to maintain their emotional and business ties. The Internet itself is not at all cheap for the average Cape Verdean; an hour of Internet use can cost up to 2.50 euros, while wages are often below 100 euros a month. For

those who can afford it and have the necessary skills, however, the Internet is increasingly replacing the phone as a means of maintaining
those links because it offers more communication alternatives, such as
emailing or chat rooms.

The number of Cape Verdeans living outside the archipelago out-
numbers those living on the islands (Carling 2003). A large percentage
of the archipelago's income stems from migrants' remittances as well
as foreign aid. Being able to communicate with people abroad is essential. Because of this, the Internet has increasingly become an important
channel of communication between members of families, friends,
business partners, academics, journalists and community leaders that
share the same status – being apart from each other. This reality reflects the embeddedness of the Internet in the context of Cape Verdean
experience of migration, demonstrating that, just as Miller and Slater
observe, 'Internet media [are] continuous with and embedded in other
social spaces, that they happen within mundane social structures and
relations that they may transform but that they cannot escape into a
self-enclosed cyberian apartness' (2000: 5). The use of the Internet by
Cape Verdeans reflects Cape Verdeans' daily life experiences and Cape
Verde's context as a place where migration is a central phenomenon.

New media: online radio stations and newspapers

Talking about the concept of 'bridgespace', Adams and Ghose (2003:
420) make a strong point when they note that bridgespaces do not create links between people. Links are created by people – but people's actions require channels, and these channels may be static structures like
roads, or dynamic systems like airline flight schedules or the Internet.
In the Cape Verdean case, the Internet has definitely served as a channel through which people have managed to keep links and communication working between those who have stayed on the islands and
those who have left. To illustrate this I will draw on the examples of
the online radio stations and online newspapers that came into existence in the archipelago. Most of the radio stations that now transmit
online have done so with the aim of reaching the Cape Verdean migrant audience. As the director of one radio station views it,

> the Internet is just like having another medium. We would like
> to be closer to Cape Verdeans who live abroad.... We also want
> the radio station to be modern; we want to be at the forefront of
> what is happening (Radio station director I, Praia).

The words of this informant are echoed in the interviews with other people involved in the same business. The Internet becomes an additional relatively cheap communication medium with incredible scope. It goes far beyond what the radio waves of these stations can ever reach, as their transmission range is sometimes local or, at the very most, national. Having an online transmission enables these radio stations to be accessed wherever there is a PC with an Internet connection. It allows the transnational in the sense of both 'moving through spaces and across lines' (Ong 1999: 4) that metaphorically represent continents and nation-states borders. The potential audience is beyond the national scope and will be further augmented once the number of Cape Verdeans with an Internet connection increases substantially, which is more likely if they live in Europe or the U.S.

Cape Verdean migrants want to be informed and want news from their homeland. They have often pressured media people they know back in Cape Verde to set up an online page or site. These sites allow the nourishing of cultural ties from a distance and, at the same time, it permits migrants to actively contribute to something back home. Moreover, as stated by the informant above, there is the general feeling that by creating that need migrants are also pushing the country towards development and modernity. Slater has also discussed this particular aspect of the modernising effect of the Internet in relation to the study of Internet use in Trinidad where 'the Internet was largely perceived as a modern means to be *more* modern' (Slater 2003: 146). People engage the technology in order to catch up with modernity, which is perceived to be happening at its highest levels beyond the frontiers of Cape Verde. By demanding current updates on what is happening in the country via the Internet, local Cape Verdeans believe that migrants are also pushing Cape Verde towards the future, with the development model of Western industrialised societies in mind. The satisfaction of the migrants' needs has thus a double meaning in Cape Verde: it keeps businesses running and secures jobs while, at the same time, it forces people to catch up with the latest developments in the so-called 'first world' from which migrants bring material novelties and new needs.

The world beyond Cape Verde is thought to provide the tools for people to use technology and services not yet available in their country. Migrants are considered the mediators between two worlds: the world of development and modernisation (usually equated with Europe and the U.S.) where they make a living, and this other world on the fringes of development to which Cape Verde, as a spatial and economic location, is thought to belong to. Migrant intervention is called upon to help solve their daily problems, some of which are resolved with online shopping.

> In our first year, our web page was free, but after that we had to pay. That was a problem. Not a money problem – the cost was only US $50 per year – but I couldn't pay because we do not have credit cards in Cape Verde. I had to ask a friend. I sent him all the details and he paid for it with his credit card. That's how we've been operating of late (radio station director 2, Praia).

Much of what people cannot get in Cape Verde (as online shopping with credit cards points out) is provided by the help of Cape Verdean migrants who have access to goods and services. When web pages and sites of the various online newspapers and radio stations fail, migrants are not only the first to enquire about the problem, but also the first to whom people in Cape Verde turn to for assistance. In some cases, migrants will send money to maintain the systems, or provide valuable help to keep the operation running. To a certain extent, by pressuring Cape Verdeans to keep their web pages updated, migrants can check up on how their donations are spent. Migrants have become more demanding and regard the service provided to them by the online media as something to which they are now entitled.

> The Cape Verdean nation is scattered around the world. It is very expensive to send newspapers to everybody and Cape Verdeans are always worried about their country. A Cape Verdean in the U.S. will be worried about his brother, his father, his mother. He will send them money. He wants to know about his homeland. That is why we have decided to produce an online version of our newspaper (newspaper director, Praia).

Migrant remittances not only provide income to families back in Cape Verde but also provide a vital boost to the country's economy. The government of Cape Verde considers these cash flows essential for the country as foreign aid now tends to be channelled to other, poorer countries (Carling 2004). Similarly, the desire of migrants to keep up with the new back in Cape Verde is stimulating development of ICTs and Internet technology enterprises in particular. By using cyberspace Cape Verdean migrants 'develop and maintain numerous economic, political, social and cultural links in more than one nation' (Mitchell 2000: 853). The fact that most migrants have family members in Cape Verde and maintain active emotional ties with their homeland has triggered increased economic and political ties. The Internet is facilitating those ties because of its instantaneous and direct nature. Distant places suddenly come together online without undue mediation. For Cape Verdeans with access to this technology, communication between the capital city of Praia and places like Ribeira Grande (Santo Antão), which is far from the capital and can only be reached by boat connection via yet another island (São Vicente), is as effortless as with any other place such as Boston located on an entirely different continent.

But the important factor here is that migration has always played an important role in the family and economic lives of Cape Verdeans. Thus there have always been forms of communication between Cape Verdeans on the islands and emigrants in places like Boston or Lisbon. The use of the Internet has simply intensified already important relationships. Not having changed anything on its own, the Internet has nevertheless amplified existing forces with transformative potential (Agre 2002). By maintaining communication networks more actively via cyberspace, Cape Verdean migrants have further stimulated the creation of a diasporic public sphere in order to allow 'conversations between those who move and those who stay' (Appadurai 1998: 22), but also between the various migrant communities scattered across the globe. Cape Verdean migrants living in the U.S. have been at the forefront of this project, which I will demonstrate in the next section.

Local politics, global reach?

Many web sites and personal web pages related to Cape Verde have been set up and are maintained by members of migrant communities. One finds sites based in the Netherlands, Portugal and the U.S. Although there are also Cape Verdeans living in Senegal, São Tomé or Angola, up until now they have not been active in setting up web sites. The most active Cape Verdean migrant online communities are in the U.S. and Europe. This illustrates an important aspect of the world digital divide and how it is reproduced among migrant groups. Of all the Cape Verdean migrant groups, those living in the U.S. are the most active in producing web sites and web pages and are also responsible for the maintenance of some of the most sophisticated and most up-to-date sites related to Cape Verde. Although the Cape Verdean communities in Europe are very involved in the affairs of Cape Verde – they visit the country more often than their American counterparts and they also contribute a considerable amount of money (Carling 2003, 2004) – they do not seem to be as involved in the development of web sites. This situation reflects such issues as access to the technology, local politics and community power, which I will now discuss.

Some of the first Cape Verdean online initiatives came from emigrants living in the Boston area, where a sizeable population of Cape Verdeans live. The reason, according to one informant, is that Internet use first developed in the U.S., where technology is comparatively cheaper. Thus the Cape Verdeans in the U.S. were the first to actually have access to the technology before any of the other Cape Verdean communities. An example of this early development is 'The Cape Verdeans in Cyberspace' initiative, which was founded in 1995. The project was started by a number of Cape Verdean academics and professionals who, according to one member, 'wanted to create a forum, a virtual arena where everything that is Cape Verdean in nature, of interest to Cape Verde or people with an interest in Cape Verdean matters would have a space; a big arena where multidirectional dialogue could happen'.

From the start, this was a project integrated into other initiatives generated by the same group of people: conferences, cultural and social activities, the creation of a newspaper and a radio station. According to some of these people, the Internet was just another medium available for the dissemination of their ideas and initiatives. Their community empowerment notions stemmed from the internal U.S. politics. In the 1980s, the Cape Verdean community wanted to initiate strategies of acquiring further political and social visibility very much in the same way that various other ethnic minorities in the U.S. had. As an ethnic group, Cape Verdeans also wanted to differentiate themselves from African-American or the Lusophone groups. As one informant pointed out,

> we are close to the Portuguese, but we are different people! We eat differently, we dance differently, we feel differently! There are not many of us in America, but in Boston there are 80,000 of us and in New England 400,000! Local politicians have started noticing us as a potential voting bloc (Cape Verdean-American journalist).

This informant reveals the dynamics of the internal politics of U.S. society. Since its inception as a nation, the U.S. has been built on different ethnicities and religions. Moreover, there has always been an important racial dimension to North American society that has dominated much of U.S. political life. Since the 1960s, the Black Power movement has challenged racial practices and prejudices within society. This was followed later by Latinos, Asian Americans, Native Americans and other racially and ethnically based movements who made their way into the political process. In the 1970s, racial minorities in the U.S. were encouraged to organise along interest-group lines, in pursuit of greater political power and allocation of public resources. These racial minorities have also pressed their demands for recognition and equality. As Omi and Winant note: 'racial movements come into being as the result of political projects, political interventions led by intellectuals' (1994: 86). They point out that intellectuals are, in the Gramscian sense, 'social actors whose position and training permits them to express the worldviews, ideas, and sense of social identity of various social actors. Priests, teachers, artists, and entertainers fit this definition' (1994: 193).

In the Cape Verdean case, the organisation of their political project in the U.S. has also been in the hands of Cape Verdean intellectuals. To confirm this, one can return to the example of the 'Cape Verdeans in Cyberspace' initiative, which was founded at the Dartmouth College and produced by professionals and academics. This was envisaged as a forum where different initiatives related to Cape Verde could have visibility online. In the 1990s, the organisation had already amassed more than 300 Cape Verdean academics and professionals from different areas. Borrowing the words of the Cape Verdean journalist quoted above, this was during a time when Cape Verdeans were no longer solely the people working the factories; they were also people who organised conferences and various cultural and social activities in the streets of Boston.

The empowerment of the Cape Verdean community within American internal politics has, therefore, stimulated the creation of a Cape Verdean cyberspace. The online space created by Cape Verdeans living in the U.S. stimulated the growth of a local project into a larger project that connects the entire diasporic Cape Verdean nation.

The global Cape Verdean nation

I would now like to focus on two different sites produced by Cape Verdean migrants. I chose these two in particular because they are visited by considerable numbers of people everyday; the sites are updated regularly and seem to involve a considerable amount of people who maintain them. The first is Cabonet (www.cabonet.org) and the second is Caboverdeonline (www.caboverdeonline.com). These two sites connect and reach out to Cape Verdean migrants and capitalise on the notion of a Cape Verdean diaspora. The diaspora has been discussed as a different type of transnationalism because it implies 'a vision and remembrance of a lost or an imagined homeland still to be established' (Faist 1999: 46). The two Internet sites not only encourage the idea of Cape Verde as the homeland of all Cape Verdeans everywhere, but also encourage Cape Verdean migrant groups to create a nation that reaches beyond the borders of Cape Verde itself.

The two sites are similar in nature. Both have a cultural, social, news dissemination and political character. The first web site, cabonet, is totally in English and advertises gatherings, parties, social and cultural events, but it also deals with the main news from various Cape Ver-

dean communities. There is news about the carnival organised by the
Cape Verdean community in Angola right next to news of a major drug
arrest at the international airport of Sal in Cape Verde, and a social
event for Cape Verdeans living in the Netherlands. Both local news
items related to the Cape Verdean diaspora and local news items related to Cape Verde itself appear on this site in a non-hierarchical manner. The same happens with the Caboverdeonline site, which has a
clear mission statement about contributing to the promotion of a 'global Cape Verde' and the distribution of information to the Cape Verdean global community, utilising 21st-century media to link a virtual
community in meeting places like the *praças* in Cape Verde. This site
is bilingual – Portuguese and English – to reach those migrants who
cannot read English. News items in English about Cape Verdean community issues in the U.S. are placed next to items in Portuguese about
Cape Verdean football. This site also has a variety of advertising banners: real estate companies in Cape Verde and their housing development projects, in a clear effort to migrants to invest in real estate in
Cape Verde; other banners advertise U.S. banks with their special mort-
gage rates, which are only of interest to emigrants in the U.S. These
businesses are located on two different continents but appear on the
same site as if they belonged to the same reality. Distance has been dis-
carded and more than one local context is brought together at the same
online site because these migrants maintain 'occupations and activities
that require regular and sustained social contact over time across national borders' (Portes et al. 1999: 219).

Both sites also promote diverse political initiatives and gatherings
aimed at empowering Cape Verdeans where they live. Caboverdeonline
in particular organises initiatives to provide information related to migrants and their living and working conditions and promotes places of
contact and discussion forums about issues related to Cape Verde and
its economic, social and political situations. The site also hosts fund
raising and charity initiatives to support social projects both in the U.S.
and in Cape Verde.

Although only Caboverdeonline includes content in Portuguese, both
sites have a goal of reaching the 'global Cape Verdean Nation'. Both
have the aim of being a hub, a central node in the network that brings
together the Cape Verdean diaspora spread out across various continents. This way of thinking and acting echoes Massey's definition of
place as a point of intersection in different networks.

> Instead [...] of thinking of places as areas with boundaries
> around, they can be imagined as articulated moments in net-
> works of social relations and understandings, but where a large
> proportion of those relations, experiences and understandings

are constructed on a far larger scale than what we happen to define for that moment as the place itself, whether that be a street,
or a region or even a continent (Massey 1994: 154).

Cape Verde as a place has become an online network constructed of
those different relations between migrants living in very different contexts with very different relationships to the homeland. The two sites
aim to create a community of affinity based on a common ancestry,
place of birth and/or family ties in Cape Verde. Moreover, they also
share the experience of migration. The Cape Verdean nation emerges
not as a geographical but as a symbolic place to which one has a variety
of ties. The Cape Verde depicted on both sites is, then, not just the actual place off the West African coast, but a place that is part of an imagined geography: a network that links the different places of the Cape
Verdean diaspora and Cape Verde itself simultaneously and at the
same level. It is a network of people, of various events and festivities
built upon another network made up of fibre optics and computers.
Those who maintain these sites are attempting to build a 'global Cape
Verde' that though rooted in different geographical locations, connects
and communicates beyond the constraints of physical geography. The
classic relationship between state, nation and territory as Basch et al.
(1994) have demonstrated is being challenged. In this case, through
the use of Internet technologies and the networks set up by Cape Verdean migrants. The aim of both cabonet and caboverdeonline is to capitalise on the shared 'Cape Verdeanness' and migration experience to
produce forms of political and social action.

Conclusion

When one looks at the Cape Verde-related web sites, one cannot avoid
observing that many of the online initiatives reflect the context of Cape
Verde as a country marked by the experience of migration. Migration
has been the driving force in the development of a Cape Verdean Internet presence, both internally and externally. Internally, the need to
communicate with the Cape Verdean diaspora has led local actors to establish sites and web pages, allowing information and communication
flows from Cape Verde to travel well beyond their national and territorial boundaries. Externally, members of the Cape Verdean diaspora have
been trying to create a space for Cape Verdean matters that transcends
geographical and political borders. Above all, it has been other Cape
Verdean migrant groups, especially the Cape Verdeans living in the U.
S. who have played a prominent role in the creation of a cybercommu-
nity among Cape Verdean migrants. One of the reasons for this devel-

opment is the social capital (Bourdieu 1980) that the community has acquired within the local American political struggle for more recognition. These efforts have also encouraged the same actors to construct an online 'imagined community of action' (Law 2003) among diasporic Cape Verdeans and Cape Verdeans living in Cape Verde. This state of affairs places migrants at the heart of the development of the Cape Verdean online presence. Moreover, bearing in mind the Internet sites considered in this chapter, their use of the Internet is promoting the intersection of more than one public sphere: the Cape Verdean community politics in the U.S., the various other migrant communities around the world and Cape Verde itself. Where they intersect we see the creation of a transnational sphere that moves the Cape Verdean nation beyond its geographical and political borders.

References

Adams, P.C.; Ghose, R. (2003) 'India.com: The Construction of a Space in Between'. *Progress in Human Geography* 27(4): 414-437.

Agre, P. (2002) 'Real-Time Politics: The Internet and the Political Process'. *The Information Society* 18(5): 311-331.

Anderson B. (2001) 'Different Roots in Common Ground: Transnationalism and Migrant Domestic Workers in London'. *Journal of Ethnic and Migration Studies* 27(4):673-683.

Appadurai, A. (1998) *Modernity at Large – Cultural Dimensions of Globalization*. Minneapolis: University of Minnesota Press.

Basch, L., Schiller, N.G.; Blanc, C.S. (1994) *Nations Unbound: Transnational Projects, Postcolonial Predicaments, and Deterritorialized Nation-States*. Amsterdam: Gordon and Breach.

Benítez, J.L. (2006) 'Transnational Dimensions of the Digital Divide among Salvadoran Immigrants in the Washington DC Metropolitan Area'. *Global Networks* 6(2): 181-199.

Bernal, V. (2006) 'Diaspora, Cyberspace and Political Imagination: The Eritrean Diaspora Online'. *Global Networks* 6(2): 161-179.

Bourdieu, P. (1980) 'Le Capital Social'. *Actes de la Recherche en Sciences Sociales* 31: 2-3.

Carling, J. (2003) 'Cartographies of Cape Verdean Transnationalism'. *Global Networks* 3(4): 335-341.

Carling, J. (2004) 'Emigration, Return and Development in Cape Verde: The Impact of Closing Borders'. *Population, Space and Place* 10(4): 113-132.

Dobson, J.; Mclaughlan, G.; Salt, J. (2001) *International Migration and the United Kingdom: Recent Trends*. RDS, Occasional Paper 75, Home Office.

Faist, T. (1999) 'Developing Transnational Social Spaces: The Turkish-German Example', in *Migration and Transnational Social Spaces*, L. Pires (ed.), Aldershot: Ashgate, pp 36-72.

Georgiou, M. (2006) 'Diasporic Communities On Line: A Bottom Up Experience of Transnationalism', in *The Ideology of the Internet: Concepts, Policies, Uses*, K. Sarikakis and D. Thussu (eds.), New York: Hampton Press, pp. 131-145.

Law, L. (2003) 'Transnational Cyberpublics: New Political Spaces for Labour Migrants in Asia'. *Ethnic and Racial Studies* 26(2): 234-252.

Massey, D. (1994) *Space, Place and Gender*. Minneapolis, MN: University of Minnesota Press.

Miller, D.; Slater, D. (2000) *The Internet – An Ethnographic Approach*. Oxford: Berg.

Mitchell, K. (2000) 'Transnationalism', in *The Dictionary of Human Geography*, R.J. Johnston, D. Gregory, G. Pratt, M.J. Watts (eds.), Oxford: Blackwell, pp. 853-55.

Mitra, A. (2000) 'Virtual Commonality: Looking for India on the Internet', in *The Cybercultures Reader*, D. Bell and B. Kennedy (eds.), London: Routledge, pp. 676-695.

Omi, M.; Winant, H. (1994) *Racial Formation in the United States*. New York: Routledge.

Ong, A. (1999) *Flexible Citizenship – The Cultural Logics of Transnationality*. Durham, NC: Duke University Press.

Ong, A. (2003) 'Cyberpublics and Diaspora Politics among Transnational Chinese'. *Interventions* 5(1): 82-100.

PNUD (2004) *Relatório Sobre o Desenvolvimento Humano em Cabo Verde (RDHCV): as Novas Tecnologias de Informação e Comunicação e a Transformação de Cabo Verde*, Praia: PNUD.

Portes, A.; Guarnizo, L.E.; Landolt, P. (1999) 'The Study of Transnationalism: Pitfalls and Promise of an Emergent Research Field'. *Ethnic and Racial Studies* 22(2): 219-237.

Rouse, R. (1995) 'Questions of Identity: Personhood and Collectivity in Transnational Migration to the United States'. *Critique of Anthropology* 15(4): 351-380.

Sassen, S. (2002) 'Global Cities and Diasporic Networks: Microsites in Global Civil Society', in *Global Civil Society Yearbook 2002*, M. Glasius, H.K. Anheier, M. Kaldor (eds.), Oxford: Oxford University Press, pp. 217-240.

Sassen, S. (2004) 'Local Actors in Global Politics'. *Current Sociology* 52(4): 649-670.

Sklair, L. (2001) *The Transnational Capitalist Class*. London: Blackwell.

Slater, D. (2003) 'Modernity Under Construction: Building the Internet in Trinidad', in *Modernity and Technology*, T.J. Misa, P. Brey, A. Feenberg (eds.), Cambridge, MA: MIT Press, pp. 139-160.

Smith, P.; Guarnizo, L.E. (eds.) (1998) *Transnationalism From Below*. New Brunswick, NJ: Michael Peter and Transaction Publishers.

Smith, R.C. (2000) 'How Durable and New is Transitional Life? Historical Retrieval through Local Comparison'. *Diaspora* 9(2):203-235.

Stubbs, P. (1999) 'Virtual Diaspora: Imagining Croatia On-line'. *Sociological Research Online* 4 (2).

Vertovec, S. (2002) 'Transnational Networks and Skilled Labour Migration'. Paper presented at the conference Ladenburger Diskurs Migration Gottlieb Daimler-und Karl Benz-Stiftung, Ladenburg, 14-15 February.

Yang, G. (2003) 'The Internet and the rise of a transnational Chinese Cultural Sphere'. *Media, Culture & Society* 25(4): 469-490.

Chapter 14
Images of Emigration in Cape Verdean Music

Juliana Braz Dias

Emigration and music are two distinctive features of the Cape Verdean people. The context of emigration has been a fundamental factor in the construction of the Cape Verdean way of life. Similarly, Cape Verdean identity has been shaped by the idea, which is assumed by the archipelago's natives, that there is an inherent musicality among them. My aim in this work is to present the interplay between these two domains, and the role music plays in making this continuous and powerful emigration flux possible for Cape Verdeans.

Emigration directly involves a great number of Cape Verdeans. As described in chapter 1, Cape Verdeans in diaspora probably outnumber those in the homeland. But we should not limit our analysis to the numerical proportions of the phenomenon. Cape Verdean emigration is significant not only for the number of people it affects, but also for the type of influence it exerts on their lives. In short, it is ingrained into Cape Verdean society.

When many Cape Verdeans first left their homeland in the 1960s, they were part of a much larger migratory movement. At that time, the economically powerful nations opened their borders to workers from other parts of the world, leading to the establishment of an intense flux of people from the peripheries to the core of the world's economy. Like many other countries, Cape Verde joined this new global configuration, offering inexpensive labour to the U.S. and various European nations. However, what matters when studying Cape Verdean emigration, is to realise that this was just part of a much more extensive history. Unlike other countries that became emigrant nations over the past few decades, Cape Verde has been an emigrant nation for centuries. Some scholars suggest that Cape Verdean emigration has its origins in the late 17th and early 18th centuries, even if large-scale emigration can only be proven to have developed in the 19th century (Carreira 1983).

Emigration determines individual and family projects; interferes with the country's socio-political organisation; is an essential aspect of Cape Verdean national economy; and, above all, it has been completely assimilated into Cape Verdean culture. We see the formation, among Cape Verdeans, of what we could call a 'culture of emigration' (see

Åkesson 2004, and chap. 20 of this book). Among the natives of Cape Verde, being an emigrant to foreign lands became a positive trait.

With emigration tightly woven into their socio-cultural history, Cape Verdeans have sought ways to make it all socially possible. They have constructed a series of mechanisms that allows for the maintenance of links between migrants and non-migrants, and provides for the existence of Cape Verdean society beyond the archipelago's geographical borders. The continuity of this society in time and space depends on various practices shared among the emigrants – practices that preserve the emigrants' ties with their homeland.

My objective here is to characterise the music produced by Cape Verdeans as fundamental to the construction of the ties that unify this diasporic society. Music is one of the main forms of communication that connects the various Cape Verdean communities throughout the world.

Music – both in everyday situations and rituals – is very present in the lives of Cape Verdeans. Its significance is evident among the inhabitants of Cape Verde, in the communities of the diaspora, as well as in the relations established between those who leave and those who remain behind in Cape Verde. As I will show, music fulfils various functions in the context of migration.

Cape Verdean music has had a strong role in the process of construction and reconstruction of social identities. It is an essential tool in the formation of the idea (and feeling) of what it means to be Cape Verdean, and aids in the adaptation of Cape Verdeans to foreign lands, as well as in their re-adaptation when they return to the homeland.

The musical domain has also shown its importance as a means of preserving the Cape Verdean memory. It constructs an arena of discourse parallel to that of the establishment; it remains open to constructions that originate in various sectors of the Cape Verdean society. Music has allowed the Cape Verdeans to contradict, reaffirm or simply complement the official history of the country – including the history of its multiple emigration streams.

Moreover, Cape Verdean music has been especially powerful in the construction of representations of emigration, as I intend to show in the following. The ideas and values produced and disseminated through music have played an important role in how Cape Verdean individuals orient themselves after they have decided to leave their homeland.

Musical production in global networks

In order to examine the ways in which music has become a venue for establishing relationships that bridge Cape Verdean communities throughout the world, we should start by pointing out the forms of production and distribution of Cape Verdean music. Even with a brief glance at these systems of production we can get some indication of how music engages and links Cape Verdeans together in different parts of the globe.

The tradition of migration and the lack of a music industry in Cape Verde have meant that a major part of Cape Verdean musical production is concentrated in the host countries, especially the Netherlands, France, Portugal and the U.S.

As we have seen, a great number of Cape Verdeans ultimately decide to leave their home country with the purpose of making a better living. Many of them viewing music as a significant form of cultural expression and as a fundamental part of what it means to be Cape Verdean, and so many of these emigrants enter the music world in their attempts to create new lives in their host country. Many may have already aspired to a career in music while still in Cape Verde, and decided to leave the archipelago precisely to search for a level of professionalism and better opportunities for career development abroad.

In the new host country, Cape Verdeans strive for professional success and to produce recordings. The most viable way to gain access to this market is via record companies owned by Cape Verdeans. Beyond the borders of the archipelago, Cape Verdean musicians produce a lot of recordings. The musical universe that opens up for them abroad depends on their level of success and often includes performance tours and contracts to play in nightclubs.

Performances in large venues and small gigs in nightclubs or restaurants usually attract significant Cape Verdean emigrant audiences, who express their longing for the music of their homeland at these events. With the increased international popularity of Cape Verdean music, audiences also include emigrants from other countries of Lusophone Africa, as well as nationals in Portugal, France, and the Netherlands, and so many others who have become interested in Cape Verdean 'culture' in their own countries.[1]

Like Cape Verdean emigrants in general, musicians make the effort to return to the homeland as often as possible. During their visits they perform and promote the music they have produced abroad. The music establishes a dialogue between those who departed and those who remained behind, which preserves the links that unite them.

Even more significant than the travels in which the musicians engage are the paths of their product, the merchandise, mainly the recordings of Cape Verdean music, which enter an elaborate network that links the various communities of Cape Verdeans throughout the world. Especially important in this realm has been the role played by the recording company Sons D'África (Sounds of Africa). With its headquarters in Damaia, in the suburbs of Lisbon, Portugal, where there is a large concentration of Cape Verdeans and emigrants from other Lusophone African countries, Sons D'África functions both as a record producer and record store that specialises in Cape Verdean music.[2] The owner is Cape Verdean, and many of the label's projects reveal his emotional ties with the islands, as he continues his efforts to preserve the Cape Verdean musical tradition. But Sons D'África's role is much broader than this. It has had a significant influence on the formation and maintenance of a musical community across national borders. It has branches in various countries, including Cape Verde, and reaches a significantly large world audience. It has also been crucial in the establishment of communications between emigrants otherwise dispersed throughout the world.

The network that Sons D'África has created is powerful enough to take Sema Lopi, a musician from the countryside of the island of Santiago to audiences in the Netherlands, for example. It has also stimulated musical production of Cape Verdean emigrants in Portugal, who reach audiences in faraway places like Maputo, Mozambique.

The study of these networks could be considerably extended if we analysed the role of radio stations, which are indispensable in the maintenance of links between Cape Verdeans all over the world.[3] However, the example of Sons D'África is sufficient in illustrating the extent to which music stimulates the flow of information.

Cape Verdean music is also disseminated among the archipelago's communities by less formal means. The increased access and affordability of recording technology has meant that more and more individuals independently produce and market their own music. It is fairly common for Cape Verdean emigrants who are not professional musicians to save up enough money to fulfil their dream and record their own CD. They often then send their recordings to Cape Verde, to promote them in their small home communities. And, of course, their music serves as an aspect of emigrant history lived abroad.

Two important points are worth noting. First, it is important to recognise the originality of these transnational processes that are not linked in any particular way to a large-scale industry. Parallel to the official productions of multinational music companies, we see the informal trading of small musical productions and individual CDs, which effectively links various parts of the globe together and promotes an alternative world configuration. Second, I would like to emphasise the implications of this musical flux in the strengthening of relations that helps maintain the existence of this transnational society. The songs that travel such long distances take with them ideas, feelings, practices, values, and experiences of the Cape Verdeans who live abroad and who can, therefore, share their experiences with those who have remained in the homeland. The distance is minimised and the links between migrants and non-migrants are further strengthened, allowing for the existence of a society that is not bound by the borders of the archipelago.

In what follows, I turn to the content of some of these songs in search of the images that are transported along with this flux of information. I also search for the meanings of these songs in terms of emigration imagery among Cape Verdeans.[4]

Cape Verdean music has developed into a great number of distinct musical genres, which acquire particular characteristics on each island of the archipelago, as well as in the communities of the diaspora. The scope of any analysis of such a vast domain would be enormous. Therefore, I will limit my analysis to two genres of Cape Verdean music: *mornas* and *coladeiras*. These two musical styles have frequently brought up issues related to emigration.

Emigration in *mornas*

Morna was originally closely linked to the musical experiences of the inhabitants of the Cape Verdean islands of Brava, Boavista, and São Vicente. However, a primary feature of the *morna* as frequently noted by Cape Verdeans is that it later spread across the entire archipelago and out to the communities of the diaspora. Today it is generally identified with the Cape Verdean population as a whole.

The *morna* was traditionally performed by a string ensemble and vocalists. The lyrics are sung almost exclusively in Creole. There are nonetheless, some *mornas* that are composed in Portuguese. *Morna* lyrics deal with emotional themes such as love, emigration, the suffering caused by separation, *sôdáde*,[5] the bonds with the homeland and the cruel destiny of Cape Verde and its people.

The other musical genre I shall describe is known as *coladeira*. Its instrumentation is almost identical to that of *morna*. But the style of its lyrics gives *coladeira* one of its main distinctive features. In contrast to *mornas*, *coladeiras* are more critical, and are often very humorous sarcastic and irreverent, and they usually focus on the behaviour of certain individuals and everyday situations.

Mornas and *coladeiras* thus form a very special pair. The two styles often appear on the same recordings. Cape Verdean musicians tend to use both styles equally. But there is a unique aspect to this peaceful coexistence: *coladeira* defines itself, to a large extent, in its opposition to *morna*. The *morna* is considered by Cape Verdeans as a song that emphasises lyricism, especially in its outpourings of love, sadness, sorrow, and the entire range of melancholic feelings. The *coladeira*, on the other hand, is more about mocking, joking, and playfulness. It is jocose, satirical, and derisive. While the *morna* expresses resignation and conformity, the *coladeira* represents protest and sharp criticism. Each is suited to the expression of a particular kind of message. The verses clearly reveal this contrast in the way the two styles approach the issue of emigration.

Despite these contrasts, the relationship between *mornas* and *coladeiras* is not one of mere distinction. Together they form a pair of opposites that actually complement one another. This too can be perceived in the lyrics of the songs. As we shall see in what follows, an analysis of the ways each of these two styles address emigration can reveal the distinguishing characteristics that mark the relationship between the two musical genres.

A large proportion of the many *mornas* that have been composed over the past century focus on emigration. In fact, *morna* has proven to be the best musical genre to address this issue. The lyrics deal with the dreams of those who want to emigrate, the expectations of those who leave, the experience of parting and bidding farewell to beloved ones, the pain felt in leaving the homeland, the longing felt by those who are away and their hopes of returning home.

The lyrics of the late Fernando Quejas, a Cape Verdean composer who lived in Portugal for most of his life, exemplify an image of emigration that is typical for *mornas*.

Côrrêdor di Fundo	Long-distance runner
Si bo distino, caboverdeano,	If your destiny, Cape Verdean
é di embarcâ pâ ês mundo fóra,	Is to sail away
caminho di mar câ tem lonjura,	Nothing is too far at sea
é um desafio, um aventura!	It is a challenge, an adventure!
'Stréla polar mantê bo fulgôr	North star, keep your twinkle
lumia-l caminho pâ rumo certo,	Illuminate his way with the right bearings
'tê êl encontrâ q'êl paraíso,	Until he finds the paradise that
mêrêcêdor!	He deserves!
Si bo distino é côrrê mundo,	If your destiny is to cover distances
bo, emigrante, é côrrêdor di fundo,	You, emigrant, are a long-distance runner
na pista más comprido d'um oceano!	On the longest track of an ocean!
Côraçon, câ bo arrebentâ,	Heart, do not break
aguentâ, divagarinho,	Take it all, slowly
q'ê pâ-l pôdê gôsâ sabura	So that he can enjoy the wonders
q'ês mundo tem!	That this world has!

(Fernando Quejas)

The message is explicitly directed towards Cape Verdean emigrants. The *morna* places them at the center and gradually turns them into heroes. They are 'long-distance runners', capable of facing the challenges of the longest of all tracks – the ocean. The author also recognises the hardships that the emigrant must tolerate. He acknowledges the pain of parting and asks the emigrant's heart to remain strong enough to endure that sadness. He also asks the North Star to guide the traveller. But, at the same time, the author addresses emigration in an overall positive way. The act of emigrating is constructed – from beginning to end – as something desirable. Emigration is an adventure and the outside world, awaiting the emigrant, is seen as a paradise, a world of delights to be enjoyed.

I would further like to note that it is neither the primary function of the cited lyrics to offer an elaborate picture of the emigrant's experience, nor to point out the hardships that the emigrant endures abroad. The lyrics are, above all, the construction of an image about emigration where it becomes an ideal, a goal in life. It is precisely this kind of construction that encourages a great number of Cape Verdeans to emigrate.

Cape Verdean society possesses a very peculiar characteristic in that it needs emigration to supply its material, structural and cultural reproduction.[6]

A series of socio-economic factors encourage Cape Verdeans to emigrate. But there is also an important cultural force that feeds this phenomenon. It is the overvaluation and idealisation of the act of emigrating, which is constructed as a mostly positive experience. The *morna* has a strong role in this construction and in the consolidation of emigration into a value.

Emigration is not only turned into an ideal, but emerges as the very 'fate' of Cape Verdeans. This construction is evident in Quejas' lyrics, and is frequently present in other *mornas*, as we can see in the following excerpts from a song by the composer B. Léza:

Distino d'omi
Oli'm na meio di mar
Ta sigui nha distino
Na caminho d'América

[...]

Bai Terra-longe
É distino di omi
Distino sem nome
Qui nô tem qui cumpri

[...]

(B. Léza)

A man's destiny
I am here in the middle of the sea
Following my destiny
On my way to America

[...]

Going to the Far-Away Land
Is a man's destiny
Destiny without a name
That we must fulfil

[...]

In these lyrics, the author speaks for the emigrant himself. He refers to the emigrant's obligation to fulfil a predetermined destiny. Moreover, he equates emigration with the concept of masculinity. To be a man is to take the journey to the 'far-away land'. I highlight how this notion of the inevitability and the acceptance of emigration as a destiny for Cape Verdean men constitute new mechanisms in the process of providing incentives to the harsh reality of actually leaving.

The moment of departure and the overall pain involved in the experience of emigrating is the main theme of various *mornas*. Among them, one that has become a classic of Cape Verdean music is the *Morna de Despedida* (Morna of Farewell), by Eugénio Tavares:

Morna de Despedida	**Morna of Farewell**
Hora de bai,	Departure time,
Hora de dor,	Time of pain,
Ja'n q'ré	I wish that
Pa el ca manchê!	Daylight would never come
De cada bez	Each time
Que 'n ta lembrâ,	That I remember her
Ma'n q'ré	I prefer
Ficâ 'n morrê!	To stay and die!
Hora de bai,	Departure time,
Hora de dor!	Time of pain,
Amor,	Love,
Dixa'n chorâ!	Let me cry!
Corpo catibo,	Captive body,
Bá bo que é escrabo!	You go, since you are a slave!
Ó alma bibo,	Oh living soul,
Quem que al lebabo?	Who shall take you?
Se bem é doce,	Although the arrival is sweet,
Bai é maguado;	The departure is sour;
Mas, se ca bado,	But those who won't leave
Ca ta birado!	Cannot return
Se no morrê	If we die
Na despedida,	In saying good-bye
Nhor Des na volta	God, upon our return,
Ta dano bida.	Will give us life.
[...]	[...]

(Eugénio Tavares)

The above lyrics reflect the dilemma of many Cape Verdeans who must decide whether to leave or stay. This is a recurring theme in Cape Verdean culture which is especially explored by the members of the literary movement known as Claridade (see Batalha 2004: 77-81). Prior to the Claridade movement, Eugénio Tavares handled this subject of mixed emotions with much ingenuity: the dread of departure, the desire to stay, yearning to emigrate in order to return some day, wanting to belong to the group who have already undergone this experience.

The act of leaving is painful, but that particular type of suffering is valued in Cape Verdean culture, and is rewarded upon the emigrants' return. Homecoming is their moment of glory – not only because they rejoin their families and friends but because it puts an end to the distance and pain, and especially because it marks the beginning of a new period: the time to enjoy the perks acquired abroad. Cape Verdeans acquire distinction and prestige through emigration that can only be fully enjoyed upon their return. Here too, *mornas* play a fundamental role by helping construct the concept of return as a value. As noted above, it encourages Cape Verdeans to leave, turning the painful departure into precisely the other side of the coin for those who want to harvest the fruits of the much valued return. Departure and return, death and life: one does not exist without the other.

Besides the pain of leaving, another feeling that is highly valued in Cape Verdean culture is *sôdáde*. This emotion is also portrayed in *mornas* as an inevitable and indispensable part of the experience of emigrating.

Sôdáde

Sôdade ê cheio d'espinho
El ta picâ na alma
Ca tem ninhum carinho
Que ta liviá'l sê dor

Odjo ta f'câ raso d'água
Quand'el ta bem mansinho
Coraçom cheio de mágua
Ta ficâ paradinho

Sôdáde ê sofrimento
De odjâ quem nô querê
Na flor de pensamento
Sem nô podê tocá'l

Sôdáde ê um corrente
Que ta prendê nôs alma
Quem desprendê'l contente
Nunca mais ta tem calma

(Félix Monteiro)

Sôdáde

Sôdáde is covered with thorns
It pierces the soul
And no treat
Will alleviate its pain

Tears come to the eyes
When it slowly comes
The heart, full of sorrow,
Remains still

Sôdáde is the pain
Of seeing the one we love
With the mind's eye
Not being able to touch her

Sôdáde is a chain
That binds our soul
He who unties it
Will never find peace

Sôdáde is described throughout Félix Monteiro's *morna* as the source of much pain. It is a thorn; it is suffering. However, in the last verse, the author also shows that *sôdáde* is the necessary link, the tie with the

past, the homeland, and loved ones. It is indispensable in the maintenance of the emigrant's hope of return and feeling of belonging. It
shows that the emigrant is still part of the world he/she left behind.
Without *sôdáde*, past experiences lose their meaning.

Many other *mornas* show this same pattern. The songs not only
praise *sôdáde* as a noble feeling, but also trigger the feeling of *sôdáde* in
those who listen to these songs.

By adopting themes that are so close to the experience of the emigrants, *mornas* turn into a privileged communication channel among
those directly involved in emigration. They prove to be quite effective
in orienting the practices of those who decide to emigrate, as well as of
those who have already emigrated.

Another point I wish to highlight is the recurring presence of the
sea in *mornas* lyrics. The following verses reveal how this symbolic appropriation of the sea takes place:

Oh Mar!

Oh mar! Oh mar! Oh mar!
Bô levá nha kretxeu
Dixá-me kantá-bo ês morna baixinho
Pa bô flá-me
Komu el dixá-me mi só

Oh mar! El dixá-me ta txorá
Sem um konsolansa
Pel ka skesê di mim
Pamó na el N tem speransa

Oh mar! Trazê-me sê resposta
Na bô onda azul kôr di séu
Bem flá-me kuzê kel flá-bo
Pam ka txorá más
Mágoa di sodade

Oh Sea!

Oh sea! Oh sea! Oh sea!
You took my love
Let me sing this *morna* softly
So that you tell me
How she left me lonely

Oh sea! She left me crying
Without consolation
Tell her not to forget me
Because I put my hopes in her

Oh sea! Bring me her reply
On your celestial-blue waves
Come tell me what she told you
So that I no longer cry
Tears of *sôdáde*

(Euclides Tavares)

The ocean is a symbol that evokes one of the most remarkable characteristics of Cape Verdean society: insularity. The sea isolates every island, as well as the archipelago as a whole. But it also serves as a link
between Cape Verde and the rest of the world. It fuels the dreams of
those who think of emigrating. It is the path that takes to the 'far-away
land', and allows Cape Verdean society to maintain its outward gaze.

As we have seen in the above-cited lyrics, the sea also serves as a
mediator. Not only does it cause separations, taking Cape Verde's children away, but it also acts as a link between those who have left and
those who have stayed. The ocean is personified in many compositions
as a messenger in a dialogue with the author of the *mornas*. The sea is

portrayed as an important means of communication between those who have emigrated and those who have remained in Cape Verde – actually one of the main characteristics of the music itself. Both the sea and the music serve as mediators between the various Cape Verdean societies spread throughout the archipelago and the diaspora.

Emigration in *coladeiras*

As indicated above, *coladeiras* and *mornas* form a pair of opposites, with a sharp contrast in their treatment of important issues in Cape Verdean life. As in *mornas*, emigration is a recurring theme in *coladeiras*. But the *coladeiras* introduce revolution into the musical discourse on emigration.

Whereas *mornas* construct emigration as a world of adventure and delights and voice the pains of lovers, mothers, and children who have been separated by the ocean, the *coladeiras* focus on the difficulties that emigrants face in their host countries; they point out the harsh realities of life abroad; they talk about working hard, and about the problems between themselves and the native population and even among Cape Verdeans in the diaspora communities themselves; and, mainly, they talk about the delusions faced by the Cape Verdean emigrants who do not end up finding everything they had dreamed of once they are abroad. The *coladeira* below deals with this latter topic.

Bran Bran d'Imigraçon
Es bran bran di imigrason
Dja da-me kabu di nha bida
N kóri mundo ku iluzon
N inkontra diziluzon
Ma na fundo ê kel mê
Nha distino ka muda

Nhôs dixa-me ku nha funko
Nha miséria tambê
Nha grogo pan bebe
Nha kankan pan txera

Emigration Mess
This emigration mess
Has ruined my life
I ran around the world with an illusion
And only found sorrow
At the end it is all the same
My fate has not changed

Leave me with my *funco*[7]
And with my misery too
With my *grogo*[8] to drink
And my snuff to inhale

(Pedro Rodrigues)

In contrast to what we have seen previously when analysing *mornas*, emigration here is seen not as a solution, but as the problem. The 'faraway land' is transformed from a paradise into a confusing world full of disappointments. The long-hoped-for changes have not occurred and the song's protagonist prefers to abandon his dreams and return to his Cape Verdean ways. He prefers the hard life, a life of 'misery', but with attributes which at least make him feel at home: the old *funco*, the *gro-go* and the snuff.

The problems faced by the emigrants in the *coladeiras*, no longer concentrates on their feelings (in the pain of *sôdáde*), but more on the everyday situations encountered in their new lives.

Vida dur' ê ná Merca	**Tough life is that in America**
Vida dure ê na Merca ke tem	Tough life is what you find in America
Ma tambê gente ta ganhá bem	But people there earn good money
Tem trabói pa tude kem ke parsê	There are jobs for all those who show up
Ka ganhá dólar ê sô kem ka krê	You'll go without earning dollars only if you don't want to
Gastá-l tambê nem ka mestê dizê	But spending them, too, don't even mention it!
Ke vaidade mora li tambê	Because pride also lives there.
De óne a óne gente oiá um amdjer	Year after year, one sees a woman
Ta pasá na rua ta dá-me um raiva	Passing by and making me mad
Tempe ka tem nem pa dá dôs dêde	There is no time for even a small chat
Ke tude óra ta tem ki fazê	Because there is always something to do
Nem ke ês krê ma ês ka podê	Even if they want it, they can't
Ke everyday tude gente ê busy	Because everyday everyone is busy

(Frank Cavaquinho)

This *coladeira* shows, in contrast to the *mornas*, a greater relationship to the realities experienced by the emigrant. The 'far-away land' is no longer a paradise and becomes a place where life is all but easy. The author recognises the advantages of life in the U. S.: there is always work and the pay is good. But the song's protagonist reveals all the strangeness of this new context, which is so unfamiliar to him. Excessive consumerism surprises him, and represents a risk to the money he has saved. The lack of time for socialising also frustrates the emigrant, and he quickly learns he has to adjust to a new lifestyle where time is money.

Many *coladeiras* were composed by emigrants and are directed at a Cape Verdean audience living in the diaspora. It was with this in mind that Manuel D'Novas (himself an emigrant in the Netherlands) wrote the following song:

Holanda ê d'Holandês	**Holland belongs to the Dutch**
Amdjor bô txá de falá snêra	You better stop talking foolishness
Holanda ê ka de bósa	Holland is not yours
Holanda ê de Juliana	Holland is Juliana's
Holanda ê de Holandês	Holland is for the Dutchmen
E bô ê kabeverdian	And you are a Cape Verdean
Ka bô txá nada konfundibe	Don't let anything confuse you
Kordá, bô spiá	Wake up, watch out

Kemá ês podê petóbe pa bem nadóde	Because they can send you back swimming
E txegá ke lime na dente	And you'll get home with seaweed in your teeth
Bebê bô pils	Drink your pilsner beer
Bafá-l ê ke txorresgue	Have biscuits for a snack
Sempre ta lembrá kemá kriol bô ê	Always keeping in mind that you are Creole
Bazá bô pófe sempre na respeite	Smoke your pot always with respect
'Téka dizi' na Roterdam	Take it easy in Roterdam
Pamó mundo tem mute volta	Because the world turns
E nunka nô sabê	And we will never know
Futuro de kriol ê um bokóde komplikóde	Why the future of the Creoles is so complicated
E kriol já ta kansóde	The Creoles are tired
De güentá balonse	From this unruly people's rocking
Dêss pove descomandóde	
Manhã ka bô dizê ke N ka vizóbe	Tomorrow, don't tell me I didn't warn you
Konde bô parsê ke roska montóde	When you show up unbalanced
Ta katá grogue, ta pedi lifitim	Searching for grogue, asking for cigarette butts
Ta dá pa dôde na macaquice	Acting crazy

(Manuel D'Novas)

This song criticises the behaviour of some Cape Verdeans who live in the Netherlands, and warns these emigrants of the consequences of their actions. Manuel D'Novas has composed numerous *coladeiras* and even some *mornas* on the theme of emigration. In this particular song, he exhorts Cape Verdean emigrants to not forget that they are, above all, Creoles (that is, natives of Cape Verde). He reminds them that they are in the Netherlands, but also that they do not really belong there; that at any moment they may need to return home; that their true home is Cape Verde. He tells them to always keep some of their old Cape Verdean habits, even while they adopt new Dutch ways – for example, when he tells them to go ahead and have *krakeling* (biscuits) for a snack, or a Dutch beer. This song enforces the discourse regarding the construction of a Cape Verdean nation, emphasising the importance of maintaining the nation even in the diaspora.

A curious detail worth noting is that the two latter *coladeiras* include some foreign words in their lyrics, which reflects the multilingual experience of the Cape Verdean emigrants in their new environments.

Conclusion

The selection of *mornas* and *coladeiras* presented here reveal how these two Cape Verdean musical genres complement one another in the construction of emigration imagery. Advantages and disadvantages, dreams and disillusionment, inexpressible feelings and concrete situations are all combined to account for a very complex experience – one that Cape Verdean emigrants experience from the moment they decide to emigrate, until their return to the homeland, often years later.

More than contradictory ideas and values, *mornas* and *coladeiras* reveal the complexity of the emigration phenomenon and help Cape Verdeans deal with it. The songwriters often address these individuals directly, guiding them in this endeavour. Moreover, these songs play a fundamental role as they serve as a channel of communication for the members of this highly dispersed society. Without this mediator, the emigrants' experiences abroad would remain a very vague reality for the Cape Verdeans who remain behind. But the sharing of these experiences through music allows them to be reunited.

My analysis deals exclusively with the discourses produced by *mornas* and *coladeiras*. Other issues would certainly arise in the analysis of other genres of Cape Verdean music. *Zouk*, for example – a style that has become enormously popular among younger listeners – shows great potential for contributing to this discussion (see chapter 16). Although *zouk* does not always explicitly address emigration, its very emergence occurred in the context of emigration. Further research on its lyrical content and contributions to the maintenance of Cape Verdean transnational society would therefore be valuable.

Notes

[1] Cape Verdean music has attracted a larger audience not only because of the stronger relations between Cape Verdeans and the local population in their host countries. Its inclusion into the genre known as 'World Music' was another decisive factor for international recognition. Recently, Cape Verdean singer Cesária Évora won the *Grammy* award in the World Music category, which drew the attention of a greater international audience to her work.

[2] The CDs sold by Sons D'África are mostly recordings by Cape Verdean artists. They encompass various styles of Cape Verdean music, such as *morna*, *coladeira*, *funaná*, and the so-called Cape Verdean *zouk*. But the stores include a much wider range of musical styles, including music from the rest of Lusophone Africa, as well as Brazilian music, reggae, and rap, etc.

[3] I would particularly like to highlight the role of *RDP África*, a Portuguese radio station that serves the populations of Lusophone Africa and African immigrants in Portugal in particular. Its musical broadcasts often feature Cape Verdean music.

[4] The lyrics to be analyzed have been reproduced from Monteiro (1988), Quejas (1998), Rodrigues and Lobo (1996) and Tavares (1969). All translations are by the author.

[5] It is a widely held belief among Portuguese speakers that *saudade* is a word that has no equivalent in any other language, except for Portuguese-derived languages, such as Kriolu, where one finds the corresponding concept *sôdáde*. It can be taken to mean a feeling of longing for something, someone or somewhere. A rough equivalent would be 'homesick-

ness', but it should be noted that *sôdáde* can be felt of any place, time, person, or event, and need not be restricted solely to home and family.

[6] The significance of emigration for social reproduction in Cape Verde is described and analysed in depth by the author elsewhere (Dias 2000).

[7] A rudimentary type of housing, with stone walls and a thatched roof.

[8] An alcoholic beverage derived from sugar cane.

References

Batalha, L. (2004) *The Cape Verdean Diaspora in Portugal: Colonial Subjects in a Postcolonial World*. Lanham, MD: Lexington Books.

Carreira, A. (1983 [1977]) *Cabo Verde: Migrações nas Ilhas de Cabo Verde*. Praia: Instituto Caboverdiano do Livro.

Dias, J.B. (2000) *Entre Partidas e Regressos: Tecendo Relações Familiares em Cabo Verde*. Brasília: Universidade de Brasília (unpublished Master's dissertation).

Monteiro, J.F. (ed.) (1988) *56 Mornas de Cabo Verde*. Mindelo: Gráfica do Mindelo.

Quejas, F. (1998) *Andante Cantabile: Fernando Quejas, Uma Vida de Mornas*. Lisbon: [author's edition].

Rodrigues, M.; Lobo, I. (1996) *A Morna na Literatura Tradicional: Fonte para o Estudo Histórico-literário e a Sua Repercussão na Sociedade*. Praia: Instituto Caboverdiano do Livro e do Disco.

Tavares, E. (1969) *Mornas: Cantigas Crioulas*. Luanda: Liga dos Amigos de Cabo Verde.

Chapter 15
Cape Verdean Migration, Music Recordings and Performance

Rui Cidra

Introduction

This work explores the cultural impact of migration and the international music industry on the production of Cape Verdean popular music.[1] By examining the nature of the social networks that have been established between Cape Verde and Portugal with regard to music and dance from the first half of the 20th century onwards, I will endeavour: a) to describe the development of a transnational realm of musical production that brings together musicians, performers, public, recording companies and producers of musical events who live in Cape Verde and in different countries of the Cape Verdean diaspora or else who travel regularly between the two; b) to examine expressive dynamics connected to the history of Cape Verdean migration to Portugal and transnational processes of musical production and commodification. I approach these questions by addressing the musical practices of migrants living in Portugal and musicians living in Cape Verde but travelling abroad when touring or recording. I will consider different kinds of spatial mobility implicit in musical production. Although these movements are connected with the lives of emigrants, they cannot be understood using only traditional definitions of migration, and should instead be seen within the framework of the transnationalism triggered by popular music and its commercialisation.

Ethnomusicological literature on the expressive culture of people in movement, be it in the context of migration from rural to urban areas or emigration, has pointed to a relationship between social dynamics, as a result of settling in new places, and transformation processes in the performance of music, poetry and dance. Originally directed at questions of musical change and an examination based on the comparison of moments prior to and after migrations (Stokes 2001), recent literature has a wider range of interests that generally point to less essentialist forms of conceiving musical practices of mobile populations and acknowledge the range of complex relations between those who have migrated or travel regularly and those who have stayed at home.

I seek to address the set of dialogues, trajectories and transnational practices mobilised in the production of Cape Verdean musical expressions. Cape Verdean popular music has been created historically on a transnational scale, developing simultaneously in different interconnected places. The cultural dynamics that cross its history are intertwined with the fact of migration and have involved links between musical life on the islands and outside them. The relations between migrants and the people who remained on the islands have had effects at different periods of time on the forms of sound organisation, poetic themes and different dimensions of musical performance and production.

The impact of people's mobility on Cape Verdean music first manifests itself in relation to the movement of people coming from outside Cape Verde to live in the territory, to visit or pass through the islands during long Atlantic voyages. Cape Verde has been an intense 'contact zone' (Pratt 1992) in the Atlantic throughout modernity, and its multiple forms of expressive culture have developed from dialogues between cultural expressions brought from the outside world by slaves, sailors, colonial officers, colonists, missionaries and other travellers. The cultural reality shaped by these movements alludes to the transnational space that Paul Gilroy called 'the Black Atlantic' (Gilroy 1993).

Simultaneously, migrants in different parts of the world have maintained strong ties to the expressive culture of Cape Verde, recreating and transforming genres, taking with them musical instruments, repertoires and, in general, their expressive practices. Musical performances among relatives, friends and community members or in public entertainment spaces have played an important role in forms of sociability, processes of identification and memory configuration. Migrants who settled in different migrant communities built musical production networks that enabled migrant and non-migrant musicians to record their music. Until recently, all recordings of Cape Verdean music were made entirely outside the country. Some of the leading figures in the development of Cape Verdean music genres were, or are, migrants (Manuel d'Novas, Tazinho, Bana, Titina, Voz de Cabo Verde, Paulino Vieira, Djonsa Lopi, Armando Tito, Jorge Humberto and Tito Paris, to mention a few).

The migrants' return to Cape Verde meant the introduction of foreign musical genres, in the form of records or musical practices, which interacted with local musical expressions. Successive generations of migrants were also responsible for introducing musical instruments, records, radios, turntables, sound equipment and other technology essential to the reproduction of sound and musical performances. The impact of emigration on Cape Verdean society even widened the poetic output of existing genres, especially in producing one of their main themes, that of *saudade* (*sodade* ou *sodadi*, in Kriolu), and in the various comments they make about the experience of emigration in repertoires of different epochs. The complexity of relations and mutual influences has made it impossible to separate the music that is produced in Cape Verde both conceptually and in absolute terms from what is produced outside the islands. This contribution aims to gain an understanding of the formation process of a musical production realm closely connected to migration and travelling practices or a 'travelling culture', to use James Clifford's term (1997), by examining ways of maintaining, innovating and creating music in a context characterised by different types of spatial mobility and moorings.

I would like to propose a diachronic analysis of the production of Cape Verdean music in Portugal, in the 20th century, divided into three periods: the colonial period which brought musicians and dancers from Cape Verde over to Portugal to perform in events organised by the *Estado Novo* as part of its cultural policy; the structuring of a community of labour migrants to Portugal and a new communitarian organisation of musical performance in a period starting a few years before Cape Verde gained its independence, in 1975, and throughout the 1990s; a period that stretches from the early 1990s to the present and in which Cape Verdean music reached beyond the restricted bounds of communitarian networks and changed significantly as to its production, visibility and commercialisation.

I would like to distinguish two generic social contexts where music and dance performance seem to have different values for those who take part in it – as musicians, performers or members of the public. On the one hand, musical performance in the community networks of family, friends and neighbours, and, on the other, the professional circuit aimed at concert performances and recording. These two contexts involve different ways of reinterpreting the musical heritage of Cape Verde, different ways of travelling with music, poetry and dance. I will look at examples of musicians from different islands who have been involved both as interpreters and songwriters in music such as the *morna*, *coladeira*, *mazurca* and *solos de violão*, which are widespread throughout Cape Verde, as well as the *batuko* and *funaná*, which are performed by the people from the island of Santiago.

The colonial period

Portuguese state policy influenced the way Cape Verdean music and dance was shown to the general public during the *Estado Novo*, which meant they were mainly performed within the restricted relations that existed between Portugal and its colonies. The first musicians to perform in Portugal did so in events aimed at demonstrating to the Portuguese metropolitan population and the international community the political authority and cultural diversity of the Portuguese colonial empire. A musical group led by the guitarist Luís Rendall and a group of *cantaderas* (women singers) from the island of Boavista, which included the noted Cape Verdean singer, Maria Bárbara, formed to take part in the Portuguese Colonial Exhibition in Porto, in 1934. In 1940, the Mindelo-born songwriter and singer, B. Leza (Francisco Xavier da Cruz) and his accompanying musicians, represented Cape Verde in the Portuguese World Exhibition in Lisbon. B. Leza remained in Portugal for about four years singing at family gatherings, with friends and in several variety shows in Lisbon theatres. During his stay in Portugal, he wrote some of his best known compositions, in particular the *morna* 'Ondas Sagradas do Tejo'.

Cape Verdean music, especially the *morna*, had been known mainly in Lisbon through the literary works of travel writers (of 'colonial literature') or Cape Verdean intellectuals. Metropolitan politicians and intellectuals connected to the colonies before and during these exhibitions were aware of Cape Verdean music through musical scores and harmonisations for piano such as those by J.B. Alfama (1910) along the lines of those made for traditional Portuguese music since the end of the 19th century, through general essays about life in Cape Verde that featured its music, through two pioneering works on expressive culture written by Eugénio Tavares (1932) and Pedro Monteiro Cardoso (1933), as well as through the first editions of the cultural magazine *Claridade*.

Cape Verdean performances at these exhibitions together with literary works on Cape Verdean cultural expressions led to Cape Verdean music being played on the radio and recorded in the 1940s and 1950s. It became established as a form of Portuguese popular radio music (known as *música ligeira* from the French *musique légère*) from one of the 'overseas provinces'. In the late 1940s, Cape Verdean students in Portugal, like Fernando Quejas and Marino Silva, with prior musical experience on Cape Verde radio, were accepted as singers for the national radio station Emissora Nacional. Initially hired to sing Brazilian songs, a repertoire they were familiar with from their days in Cape Verde, and also French *musique légère*, which they learned about at the radio station, they were mainly responsible for introducing *mornas* and later *coladeiras* into the repertoire of the radio's orchestra (known as the *orquestra ligeira*). Songs written by composers and poets like Eugénio Tavares and B. Leza were performed at *Serões para Trabalhadores* (a workers' evening entertainment program) and over twenty recordings were made between 1953 and 1972. Little known in Portugal, there were no written or recorded versions of these musical genres. Fernando Quejas and Marino Silva gave the conductors at the radio stations directions that respected the melodies, rhythms and harmonies of the musical compositions and, more generally, of Cape Verdean genres. The songs suggested were subjected to the compositional and interpretative conventions of the popular radio music of the time.

Throughout the 1940s, Emissora Nacional advanced their plan to create and broadcast Portuguese erudite and popular music. Melodies and rhythms that were considered representative of Portuguese folklore were subjected to standard composition and arrangement processes by musical directors and composers connected to the radio station. In the case of *música ligeira*, this process was extended to the writing of lyrics. In the 1950s and 1960s, with the implementation of a new political rhetoric about Portuguese colonies that accentuated miscegenation as an original characteristic of Portuguese expansion and as demonstration of national unity, Cape Verdean music suited the national radio network's politics.

Given its affinities with Portuguese music – concerning its vocal and instrumental styles, melodic contours, harmonies and instrumentation – Cape Verdean musical and poetic genres, especially *morna*, could generally be perceived as Portuguese *música ligeira* with its familiar sounds to listeners in Portugal and overseas. At the same time, it presented distinctive cultural traits that could account for a political image of ethnographic diversity and conviviality within the empire. The plan to present *mornas* and *coladeiras* as Portuguese radio popular music involved, in the first recordings, translating the lyrics from Kriolu to Portuguese, a practice later abandoned.

With the increasing international opposition to Portuguese colonialism, music performances from the colonies were integrated into a political strategy to reinforce Portuguese sovereignty over those territories. As part of this political campaign, musicians were brought from the colonies for touring in Portugal. Among them were Conjunto de Cabo Verde, formed after a visit to Cape Verde by the Overseas Minister Adriano Moreira in 1962, and subsequently brought to Portugal to tour as a 'folklore' group from the overseas provinces. Amândio Cabral's work was also influenced by the Portuguese state propaganda apparatus. As a well-known performer of *serenatas* and *tocatinas* in Mindelo he sang for Emissora Nacional between 1960 and 1962. In the year the colonial war broke out, he was requisitioned by the Ministry of Overseas to perform for the Portuguese military in Angola and Mozambique.

At the same time as Cape Verdean music was being recorded and appearing in events organised by the *Emissora Nacional*, and the *Estado Novo* in general, it was also shared in networks of kin and friends in the Cape Verdean community in Lisbon. Parties at private homes brought together Cape Verdeans who played musical instruments and had strong emotional ties with the repertoires of their homeland. Music, poetry and dance were the main link to the islands in these contexts of sociability. The parties were attended by students and people with jobs in the civil service, industry and transport, especially maritime navigation. The mobility of Cape Verdean musicians with seafaring jobs, who lived mostly in Rotterdam but had kinship ties in Lisbon, allowed them to join these Cape Verdean parties in Portugal during their short stopovers.

The recordings that were made throughout the 1950s and 1960s in Portugal were widely distributed in Cape Verde and within the Cape Verdean diaspora communities. This contributed towards the establishment of a popular repertoire of *mornas, coladeiras* and guitar solos that had hitherto been mainly orally transmitted through informal learning processes between musicians. Until then, the existing records had been produced in the U.S. in the early 20th century and belonged to collections of music illustrating different national or ethnic groups that made up American society. Migrants, most of them seafarers, had records made independently in the 1930s and 1940s in South America (Brazil and Argentina) or else recordings were made on the island of São Vicente, in broadcast studios, and then pressed on vinyl in the Netherlands thanks to a family of shopkeepers.

Along with records that fell under the control of the *Estado Novo*'s cultural policy, the Netherlands in the 1960s emerged as an important centre for Cape Verdean music and records involving migrant musicians (such as Tazinho) or else university students (Humbertona), political activists and enterprising migrants. Djunga di Biluca, a migrant in Rotterdam, set up a small record company that was first called Edições Casa Silva and later Morabeza Records. This enabled vinyl recordings of musicians in transit or those settled in the Netherlands and Belgium, such as the acoustic guitar players Tazinho and Humbertona, and above all, the group of migrants known as *Voz de Cabo Verde* and their soloists, Luís Morais and Morgadinho. Casa Silva was also connected to the 'anti-colonial struggle' and PAIGC propaganda activities. With these political leanings, it published recorded poems of Cape Verdean writers and intellectuals and political speeches by party leaders, as well as the *Angola 72* LP by the Angolan singer Bonga, who was then exiled in the Netherlands, and who was backed by Humbertona and the Angolan Mário Rui Silva. Records with political content were put into sleeves belonging to other records and transported covertly to African countries by Cape Verdean and Angolan sailors.

Formed in Rotterdam, in 1965, by musicians whose musical experience developed in São Vicente and Dakar, the career of the *Voz de Cabo Verde* group had a considerable impact. The group had a repertoire of Latin-American dance music versions that were very popular internationally (genres such as the *merengue, bolero, cumbia, salsa*, etc.) and played in various clubs in the Netherlands and Belgium. At the same time, they recorded a large number of *mornas* and *coladeiras* in vocalised or instrumental versions (featuring two of their instrumentalists: Luís Morais on the clarinet and Morgadinho on the trumpet) that were disseminated throughout Cape Verde and the diaspora community. The group played a decisive role in establishing an instrumental group structure (including bass, electric guitar, keyboard and drums) consisting of electronic musical instruments and making Caribbean and Latin American music popular in Cape Verde.

The years of Cape Verde national independence

At the end of the 1960s, the Portuguese government encouraged Cape Verdean immigration in order to compensate for the loss of Portuguese labour power through emigration to Europe and North America, and deployment to the colonial wars. This resulted in the development of a new community of Cape Verdean migrant workers in Portugal (see chap. 5). Bana, one of the singers connected to *Voz de Cabo Verde*, settled in Portugal in the early 1970s, and went on to play an active role in shaping public performances of Cape Verdean music in Portugal. He opened a bar-restaurant-disco called Novo Mundo in the heart of Lisbon (later successively renamed Monte Cara, Bana, and Enclave). It served Cape Verdean food along with Cape Verdean, Brazilian and Latin American music. In order to be able to have musical performances there on a daily basis, as well as to record with a company he set up (also named Monte Cara), Bana encouraged young musicians starting up in Mindelo to come to Lisbon and develop their careers as musicians. Musicians who at different periods between the 1970s and 1990s became Monte Cara's core instrumentalists – Armando Tito, Paulino Vieira, Tito Paris, Toi Vieira, Vaiss, among others – went on to play essential roles in the development of Cape Verdean and African music in Portugal. They played dance music in clubs and were instrumentalists, arrangers and musical producers in recordings of Cape Verdeans, mostly singers (living in Portugal, other communities or in Cape Verde), as well as interpreters from other Portuguese-speaking African countries that, like Cape Verde, did not have their own recording apparatus or record companies.

Bana's entrepreneurial activity took into account the centrality of music in the leisure practices and identities of the Cape Verdeans at a time when availability was scarce: public venues where the growing labour migrant community could listen and dance to Cape Verdean music; and music recordings available for their consumption, in the diaspora and the homeland. Unlike other migrants, migration for musicians was exclusively related to performance schedules. They made up a realm of Cape Verdean music that was structured to produce and to perform in Portugal and other Cape Verdean diaspora communities, especially migrant associations in Europe (France, the Netherlands, Luxembourg, and Switzerland) and the U.S. (Boston and San Francisco). In the 1980s, and increasingly in the 1990s, some musicians established solo careers or became 'mobile' musicians, which allowed them to back up various Cape Verdean and African singers who lived in Portugal and were included in the Portuguese market categories of 'PALOP music' or 'African music'. Cape Verdean groups likewise included instrumentalists from other African countries, mainly Angolans and Mozambicans, with musical instruments not played by Cape Verdeans living in Portugal.

Paulino Vieira was the most active musician in Portugal throughout the 1970s-90s as a multi-instrumentalist, arranger and musical producer. Born into a family of musicians from the island of São Nicolau, he developed his musical training during his childhood and adolescence in the Salesian school of Mindelo. He migrated to Lisbon, in 1973, in order to play as an accompanying musician for the singer Bana in a renewed *Voz de Cabo Verde* group. Initially in charge of the musical direction of the group, he later also became responsible for the musical arrangements and production of about one hundred records of African popular music. His multifaceted musical talent and creativity led to a growing number of musicians from Cape Verde wanting to record with him in Lisbon.

In the years following independence, musical expression networks established by professional musicians and businessmen who had migrated to Portugal, France and the Netherlands opened up new possibilities for musicians on the islands to record their records. In most cases, they paid travel expenses, recording sessions (studio rental, contracts with musicians living in these countries) and records. They asked for time off or interrupted the normal course of their lives in Cape Verde in order to make records outside the country and distribute them. Some records were often commercially distributed by migrant businessmen dedicated to record publishing who were rather unscrupulous with regard to agreements reached with musicians and payment of copyright dues, a question that remains unsettled within Cape Verde's legal framework to this very day. Musicians who lived in Cape Verde and migrant musicians in Portugal who kept up their musical practices in their social lives considered the recording of an LP or EP as soloists as a vital means of achieving symbolic capital. For migrants, making a record was really a major sign of success.

The growth of a Cape Verdean community in Portugal, in the period following independence, did not only reflect in the shaping of a circuit of professional musicians and a record market for Cape Verdeans living in the various diaspora communities or in Cape Verde itself, as it also meant that expressive practices intensified and diversified in informal contexts of musical experience. Migrants from the different Cape Verdean islands took along their musical instruments on their migrations or bought them in Portugal, maintaining the practice of genres and repertoires specific to every different island within their own families and communities. A considerable number of *batukaderas* and *tocadores* of *funaná* from the island of Santiago emerged in the early 1970s, in Lisbon. Unlike the music and performances in public entertainment spaces usually associated with migrants from the *Barlavento* islands (São Vicente, Santo Antão and São Nicolau), *batuko* and *funaná* evolved in neighbourhoods, get togethers, cafés, associations, festive occasions and ceremonies, such as baptisms and first communions, as well as events often organised during election campaigns by local councils.

Funaná and *batuko* poetry created by migrant performers in Portugal spoke of the harshness of migrant life. *Batuko* groups brought together women from neighbourhoods such as Fontaínhas, 6 de Maio (Damaia), Cova da Moura (Buraca) or Marianas (Carcavelos). Their repertoire was about their experiences, such as getting visas in order to emigrate, legalising their situation in Portugal, working at wholesale fish markets, commerce or private homes, and about how family life had to be structured because of migration. In *funaná*, *gaita* (button diatonic accordion) players such as Djonsa Lopi, Julinho da Concertina, Beja Branka, Katuta, Daniel and Jovelino di Paulo, Marujo Gomes, Tchota Soares, Mulato Ferreira, and *ferro* (metal rod) players such as Florzinho or Flor di Mundo, Ntonito Sanches, concentrated on poetic improvisations that dealt with leaving the 'homeland' and the destructuralisation of personal social relations evoked through the naming of places, people and events in their lives. Migrants from the island of Santiago who made records in Portugal in the early 1980s, such as Blyck di Tchuchi, Norberto Tavares, António Sanches, or the groups Sol d'África and Túlipa Negra joined in a general shift towards the highlighting of the cultural genres of Santiago in the period following independence, involving themselves in the transition from traditional rural music towards popular music as sanctioned by the record industry or commercial networks.

Cape Verde music in the world music market

In the first half of the 1990s, Cesária Évora's international popularity and Cape Verdean music's subsequent arrival on the world music scene meant changes in the way Cape Verdean music was produced, mediated and received. The Cape Verdean migrant, businessman and mentor of Lusafrica Publishing, José da Silva, planned Cesária's career from Paris and with the help of musicians who lived in Cape Verde, the U.S. and Portugal. After some experiments in promoting the singer backed mainly by electronic music influenced by contemporary African and French Caribbean *zouk* genres, José da Silva decided to restructure her career around representations of the 'past', 'tradition' and 'authenticity'. Together with the musicians and the singer herself, he selected *mornas* and *coladeiras* written by some of Cape Verde's most celebrated songwriters of the 20th century (B. Leza, Eugénio Tavares, Frank Cavaquinho, Ti Goy and Manuel d'Novas, among others). This placed the style in which she interpreted these songs within the setting of acoustic stringed instruments (guitars, *cavaquinho* and guitar) and keyboard (piano) – nowadays amplified for theatre performances – and in the manner of informal *tocatinas* and 'Cape Verdean evenings'. The musical mood was a return to when Cesária was a well-known singer in Mindelo during the 1940-60s period, and could be heard singing in events related to the city's port activities.

Cesária's popularity opened up a new market for Cape Verdean music, and determined differences between commercialisation of music for Cape Verdeans proper and music aimed at a world market. These differences lie in every facet of production and mediation, from creating a musical style, designing a CD sleeve and constructing the artists' image. The marketing conditions of the international market pointed to the representation of cultural differences and local identities underpinned by history and the past.

With Cape Verdean music now on the map of the international record industry, there was a growing interest in Cape Verdean music by record producers, musical events promoters and the European public. The artistic careers of Tito Paris, Bau, Lura, Tcheka (Lusafrica), Hermínia, Voginha, Vasco Martins, Simentera (Mélodie) and Celina Pereira (Piranha Music) were linked to record companies in Paris, the international capital of world music, and Berlin (in the case of Piranha Music) as well as European tours mostly aimed at a non-Cape Verdean audience in theatres, and world music and jazz festivals. The increased mobility of musicians and music production agents, which had been established through marketing networks developed by the migrant community since independence, was now being influenced by transnational processes that determined how the record industry was to operate. Musicians who were developing their own creative processes in Cape Verde or Portugal would meet in Paris to record and ultimately become part of the international concert circuit.

Of the Cape Verdean musicians living in Portugal, Tito Paris was the best known internationally in the 1990s and Lusafrica Publishing's second large investment (1994). His image as a musician suggested less the past and 'nostalgia', so characteristic of the aesthetics of world music (Erlmann 1993), than contemporary popular dance music in which he used a variety of wind, percussion, strings and keyboard instrumentation. The way his career evolved exemplifies some of the transnational processes that informed Cape Verdean music from the second half of the 1990s onwards and the public changes in Cape Verdean music in Portugal. His records were produced in Paris and he regularly promoted his work in Europe, Cape Verde and other Portuguese-speaking African countries in general. He created a musical style based on the available resources he found in the Portuguese musical milieu where he worked. He created a repertoire of *mornas* and *coladeiras* written by him or other Cape Verdean songwriters, with instrumental arrangements showing the influence of jazz, Latin-American and Brazilian music on his musical education, in a dialogue with Portuguese musicians from different musical areas (mostly jazz and erudite music) and professional Cape Verdean musicians.

Conclusions

Cape Verdean migration to different parts of the world throughout the 20th century became a hotbed for new musical experiences to develop within migrant communities. These social and cultural experiences were linked to the musical practice of the islands through the circulation of records, migrant musicians returning home and bringing with them influences they had acquired abroad, and through a set of relationships wrought between migrants and the local population with respect to records and musical performance. These relationships helped in the establishment of a transnational realm of musical production that developed throughout the 20th century.

The musical practice that evolved with migration included informal and everyday levels of music and dance performance – migrants who took expressive cultural practices with them, which in turn were essential to their experiences, their identities and survival as individuals – and levels of musical practice as formalised by state policies (during the colonial era) or strategies to set up networks of musical expression (from the years before independence to the present): public venues for musical performances; record production structures; musical circuits linked to the enterprising endeavours of migrant associations in different parts of the Cape Verdean diaspora and, from the 1990s onwards, concerts organised within international record industry networks, especially in the European, Asian and American world music markets. This set of expressive dynamics across the Cape Verdean diaspora is closely connected to the fact that, in the absence of a record industry in Cape Verde, all marketing of musical products in the 20th century had to go through recording, record production and performance outside Cape Verde.

Cape Verdean musicians who migrated to Portugal after independence gave priority to recording a repertoire of *mornas* and *coladeiras* seen as central to Cape Verdean musical memory and which had not yet been recorded in its entirety. Later, the work of professional musicians, mostly of those with careers as solo interpreters and songwriters, was clearly associated with the creation of new repertoires and musical innovation within the musical and poetic genres of Cape Verde. The adoption of new musical production technology, the influence of various musical styles and genres, very often acquired in conversation with African and Portuguese musicians with backgrounds in rock, erudite music or jazz, but mainly with fellow Cape Verdean musicians living in the diaspora, generated in the 1980s-90s new musical directions in the work of musicians such as Paulino Vieira, Dany Silva, Tito Paris, and more recently Vaiss or Humberto Ramos, for instance. The influence of other music performances resulted in their integrating stylistic traits into compositions, the creation of instrumental arrangements and styles of instrumental interpretation, in a process of permanent renewal of Creole artistic practices.

The influence of different expressive cultures on the practices of Cape Verdean musicians marked the different epochs in the history of Cape Verdean music in the 20th century and cannot be perceived as exclusive to music as interpreted outside the islands. Rather it describes the complex geographies in which Cape Verdean popular music is produced. The impact of Brazilian music for a considerable part of the first half of the 20th century, of Caribbean and Latin American musical genres in the second half, of rock, zouk, reggae or jazz since the 1970s stems from the activity of migrants and other travellers who, during the course of their lives, crossed Cape Verde.

An example of Cape Verdean cultural cosmopolitanism can be seen in the work of the guitar player and composer Luís Rendall. His connection to Portugal went hand in hand with a number of changes that Cape Verdean music performances underwent in Portugal. Luís Rendall had taken part in the Porto Colonial Exhibition (1934) and toured with the Conjunto de Cabo Verde about thirty years later. He divided his time between Cape Verde and Portugal, throughout the 1970s and

1980s, where he enjoyed the benefits of Cape Verdean transnational networks, but his compositional and interpretative skills remained based on his musical experiences as a young man in Cape Verde. Although a well-travelled man, his cosmopolitanism was rooted in the Cape Verde of the 1920s-30s when he came into contact with ship crews, mainly Brazilian sailors, with whom he learned the vast repertoire of *chorinhos, baiões,* sambas, foxtrots and waltzes. In Portugal, he was chiefly interested in recording his compositions, sometimes with his own money, and also took part in *tocatinas* and get-togethers with friends.

This sense of cosmopolitanism has in recent years assumed new configurations by increased contacts with musicians from outside the Cape Verdean community, Cape Verdean music's incorporation into the world music market and its contact with a new public, as well as the musicians' exposure to a range of cultural and musical types disseminated on a global scale through the popular culture industry. This has sparked the construction of individual musical universes made up of a variety of references that in the case of respected musicians has its focus on Cape Verdean popular music.

The combination of musical languages in Cape Verdean music, which musicians often speak of as 'fusion' and upheld in discourses of Creole identity, is the subject of artistic reflection and the result of a new awareness that musicians acquire in their work, moved by a desire to innovate the musical structure of Cape Verdean genres and create individual artistic profiles in a global market that prizes local, individual and more unusual languages that blend with familiar and recognisable elements.

Musicians living in Portugal are clearly intent on using other musical languages to renew the Cape Verdean repertoire. This is the case of the pianist, arranger and composer Humberto Ramos and the guitar players and composers Vaiss and Hernani Almeida. Their own individual leanings include using their training in erudite music and jazz to discover new harmonic and melodic possibilities for renewing the musical structures of Cape Verdean genres.

Musical performance, along with the professional milieu of musicians, plays a significant role in the social gatherings of musicians, friends and fellow Cape Verdeans in homes, cultural associations and other public spaces, such as cafés and restaurants, of the Cape Verdean diaspora in Portugal. Musical practice in these performative contexts results from a relationship established with music and dance that organises social life and leisure activities. Music, poetry and dance become special links with the country of origin as significant ways of ensuring survival and emotional and intellectual 'well-being' within a migrant context.

In these performative contexts, it is very important to play a repertoire that both instrumentalists and public can share. The experience of interpretation and listening for the interpreters and listeners triggers individual and collective processes of imagination and of proximity to Cape Verde, of configuration of memory and experience of identities.

Note

[1] I would like to thank Leonor Losa for revising the text, Francisco Sequeira at the Sonoteca da Rádio de Cabo Verde, Estúdios do Mindelo, for some of the information that I display here about the history of recording Cape Verde.

References

Alfama, J.B. (1910) *Canções Crioulas e Músicas Populares de Cabo Verde*. Lisbon: Imprensa Comercial.

Cardoso, P. (1983-1933) *Folclore Caboverdiano*. Paris: Solidariedade Caboverdiana.

Clifford, J. (1997) *Routes: Travel and Translation in the Late Twentieth Century*. Cambridge, MA: Harvard University Press.

Erlmann, V. (1993) 'The Politics and Aesthetics of Transnational Musics'. *The World of Music* 35(2): 3-15.

Ferreira, M. (ed.) (1986) *Claridade: Revista de Arte e Letras*. Linda-a-Velha, PT: África Literatura Arte e Cultura.

Gilroy, P. (1993) *The Black Atlantic: Modernity and Double Consciousness*. Cambridge, MA: Harvard University Press.

Pratt, M.L. (1992) *Imperial Eyes: Travel Writing and Transculturation*. London: Routledge.

Stokes, M. (2001) 'Ethnomusicology: IV. Contemporary Theoretical Issues', in *New Grove Dictionary of Music and Musicians*, S. Sadie and J. Tyrrell (eds.), Oxford: Oxford University Press, pp. 386-395.

Tavares, E. (1969/1932) *Mornas: Cantigas Crioulas*. Luanda: Edição da Liga dos Amigos de Cabo Verde.

Discography

AAVV (1964) Mornas de Cabo Verde. Sabine Largame. Solo de violão. Quem bô é. Solo de violão. Edição da Casa Silva: Roterdão [EP].

AAVV (1964) Mornas de Cabo Verde. Oriondina. Solo de violão. Ganha poco vive bem, Quem tem ódio. Edição da Casa Silva: Roterdão [EP].

AAVV (1999) Cap-Vert un Archipel de Musiques. Ocora Radio France: Ocora C 560 146/47.

Bonga (1997/1972) Angola 72. Lusafrica/ Morabeza Records [CD/LP].

Conjunto Cabo Verde (1962) Conjunto de Cabo Verde. Faze'mperte. Samcente. Intentaçon de Carnaval. Junior. Alvorada, Rádio Triunfo: Porto [EP].

Conjunto de Cabo Verde (1962) Conjunto de Cabo Verde. Folclore de Cabo Verde. Minduca. Cinturão tem Mel. Estanhadinha. Doutor Albertino. Rapsódia [EP].

Rendall, L. (1980) Uma Tarde em Lisboa/Lumy. Edição Voz de Cabo Verde/ author's editon: Lisbon [Single].

Rendall, L.(1980) Cabo Verde e o Seu Grande Compositor Luís Rendall. Voz de Cabo Verde, author's edition: Lisbon [LP].

Rendall, L. (1988) Luís Rendall. Memórias de Um Violão. Associação de Amizade Portugal-Cabo Verde [LP e Cassete].

Sol d'África (1980) África é, author's edition/Tini das Neves.

Sol d'África (1981) Trapiche, author's edition/Tini das Neves.

Tavares, N. (s.d.) Vôlta Pâ Fonti. Série Sodad. Sons d'África Edições.

Titina (1965) Titina, Mornas. Finta. Distino di Home. Mama Na Bôde. Tanha. Alvorada, Rádio Triunfo [EP].

Titina (1966) Titina, Acompanhada pelo Conjunto de Marino Silva. Aviadora. Funha. Firvura. Sabine Largame. Alvorada, Rádio Triunfo [EP].

Vieira, P. (1979) São Silvestre/Ano Novo. Discos Monte Cara [Single].

Vieira, P. (1982) M'Cria Ser Poeta. Discos Monte Cara [LP].

Vieira, P. (1996) Nha Primero Lar. Lusafrica.

Vieira, P. (2003) Paulino Vieira na Sua Aprendizagem, author's edition.

Chapter 16
Diasporic Networks, Political Change, and the Growth of Cabo-Zouk Music

JoAnne Hoffman

On any given weekend, if you stepped into a discothèque in the capital city of Praia, or the port city of Mindelo, or the diaspora communities of Brockton, Rotterdam, Paris, and Lisbon, you would undoubtedly hear the strains of *cabo-zouk*[1], a music which combines driving Antillean *zouk* rhythms and romantic lyrics in Cape Verdean Kriolu. Coinciding with a dramatic change in government in the early 1990s, *cabo-zouk* has continued to gain in popularity, to a point where today it dominates the airwaves, nightclubs, and stages of Cape Verdean communities throughout the world. Despite its widespread popularity, there are many who decry its hegemonic influence on Cape Verdean youths. Critics repeatedly question the authenticity of this music, and fear that it will erode the knowledge of Cape Verde's traditional music, and ultimately its cultural identity. Its existence seems to lie in direct opposition to already established genres of music and results from the overlapping of local and global historical, musical, and political processes.

Antillean origins

Cabo-zouk is a modern, highly technical, urban dance music initially produced by Cape Verdeans living in the Rotterdam diaspora. Its rhythm and much of its technical, instrumental, and vocal styles were unabashedly appropriated from the Antillean music known as *zouk*, which developed in the French West Indies in the mid-1980s, but quickly swept the international music scene, especially Europe, the Caribbean, and Africa. *Zouk*'s acknowledged originator is the group Kassav, which consciously set out to create a 'rhythmically complex, technically flawless music with an international sound' that could be unquestionably identified with the Antilles; the lyrics are in the vernacular language, a Creole understood and used daily by most; but repressed, denigrated, and associated with the lower classes of the Antilles (Guilbault 1993: 22).

Early development of *cabo-zouk*

In the late 1980s, *zouk* took over the discothèques of Europe; Cape Verdeans first came into contact with this music in Paris and the Netherlands. Despite the language difference, Cape Verdeans were deeply affected by this music, and in relatively short order, the appropriation
process began in the Cape Verdean communities of Rotterdam and
Paris when musicians began composing *zouk* with Kriolu lyrics.
Although innovations to existing genres had previously come from the
diaspora, a completely new Cape Verdean genre emanating *from* a diaspora community clearly stretches the existing boundaries of permitted
musical innovation.[2] Despite *cabo-zouk's* popularity with the younger
generation, it would first be ignored, and later, when commented on,
would draw the unremitting ire of many intellectuals, musicians, and
those of an older generation.

By many accounts, the groundwork for this new phenomenon from
the Cape Verdean side was laid by the pop group, Cabo Verde Show,
created in Dakar, in 1977, by Cape Verdean immigrants, Manu Lima
and Luís da Silva. Although their music was, in many ways, more complex rhythmically and stylistically than the *cabo-zouk* that would follow,
Cabo Verde Show's influence on the new generation in the Netherlands is clear in that it changed and increased the role of the synthesi-
ser and, while singing in Kriolu, consciously incorporated foreign
rhythms, including *zouk*.

Although criticisms of the new music were heard from its inception,
Cabo Verde Show appeared at a time when Cape Verdean youths were
ready for this new, modern sound. In 2001, when asked about his
group's legacy, Manu Lima pointed out, 'in that time, many people
who heard us play said 'this isn't Cape Verdean music, it is Caribbean',
but none of the criticisms stopped our concept of the music [...] record
after record contained themes that became true anthems for Cape Verdean youths as much in the islands themselves as in the diaspora' (Fortes 2001: 14, my translation). This group, known for its musical innovations and lively stage persona, moved its base to Paris, but they often
performed in the Netherlands as well, where they intersected with
Cape Verdeans who would later record and perform *cabo-zouk*.

Rotterdam and the Dutch groups

Starting in the late 1980s, Rotterdam became the epicentre of a flood
of new musical activity in the Cape Verdean community. Livity, formed
in 1987, was the first successful group of the new style, but many
others would follow, including Gil and the Perfects formed by Gil Se-

medo in 1991, who was the first 'superstar' of the Dutch groups. *Cabo-zouk* did indeed play an important role in their popularity, but many critics of the Dutch groups often ignore the fact that, from the beginning, *funaná*, and even straight-ahead *coladeira* were present on many of these recordings, as well as music with other foreign influences, such as American R&B, Zairean *soukous*, Jamaican *reggae*, and, most recently, Angolan *kuduro*. In addition, the Dutch groups interjected English lyrics into their Kriolu as well, indicating not only their assimilation into Dutch society, where almost everyone speaks English, but a desire to be included in a world-wide youth culture where English is often the *lingua franca*. In many ways, this notion of inclusion in a wider youth culture disconnects *cabo-zouk* from a geographical centring on the islands themselves and thus give it its unique Cape Verdean identity (Gilroy 1993a: 5). Undoubtedly, this geographical separation was made possible by new technologies of communication, and makes critics of the music uncomfortable, precisely because it could make Cape Verde, if not a residual, at least an arbitrary point of identification (Gilroy 1993a: 2).

In 1990, Splash! was formed, initially serving as a studio band for individual singers who wanted to record *cabo-zouk* and other modern dance styles. Due to the prohibitive cost of touring with a band, *cabo-zouk* is generally performed to recorded music in clubs throughout Europe, Africa, and in Cape Verde. Although this makes it financially possible to reach the disparate, and relatively small, transnational Cape Verdean communities, the intrinsic reason for this performance practice lies in the fact that because of the sophisticated technical equipment required neither Antillean nor Cape Verdean *zouk* lend themselves to live performance (Benoit 1993: 53). The recorded back-up created by an essentially small group of musicians living in the Netherlands provides a homogenous, identifiable sound. Splash! also tours as a complete band, often accompanying performers not directly associated with them, thus maintaining this stylistic consistency even in live performance. Given the Cape Verdean tradition of impromptu musical gatherings, this frequent lack of live instruments is a particularly contentious one for critics of the new sound. In response, most performers proudly point out that they do not lip synch – this version of 'playback' merely allows for live vocals with prerecorded instrumental parts.

Cabo-zouk recordings are generally made in the Netherlands, but due to the technical complexities of the music and the important role sound engineers play in the production of the *cabo-zouk* sound, mixing is often done in Paris by engineers who have extensive experience with the Antillean *zouk* sound. A small group of financiers and producers have expanded musical distribution networks simultaneously with international touring schedules, as the groups not only tour the Cape Verdean communities in the Netherlands, France, Luxembourg, Italy, Portugal, the U.S., and, of course, Cape Verde, but also the other former colonies of Portugal in Africa, and Senegal, which has a substantial Cape Verdean population. Because of logistics and copyright law restrictions, the rights to distribute are sold locally within separate countries. Performers make their living solely on concert tickets, which makes frequent touring imperative for survival (Romer p.c.).

Zouk is just as popular in the archipelago as in the European diaspora. When the Antillean group Kassav, performed in Varzea Stadium in Praia on the evening of 1 July 1991, it was one of the 'biggest spectacle[s] of music, dance and lights' (Lopes 1991: 9) Cape Verde had ever seen. To be competitive, it is essential for the Dutch groups to tour Cape Verde regularly – a group has to be liked on the islands first before it can be successful elsewhere. 'If they like you here [in Cape Verde], don't worry. They will like you everywhere' (Moreira p.c.). Thus it is clear that this music was not imposed on the archipelago, as is generally the case, success within the islands precipitated sales in the world-wide Lusophone market, but not always the other way around. It should be noted that audiences, at least in the city of Praia, are not naïve listeners who blithely accept any group from the diaspora. In fact, if performers from the Netherlands were sub-standard, Cape Verdeans were not shy in voicing their disapproval.

In the 1990s, groups and individual performers associated with *cabo-zouk* and other modern dance styles began to appear, with varying degrees of success and quality, in the other diaspora communities, but the Netherlands remained the base of the strongest, most successful performers. One of the most striking changes was in the number of female *cabo-zouk* performers, who had previously been relegated to the lesser choral parts. A large number of them were based in the U. S., but the most successful female performer came, not surprisingly, from Rotterdam.

Suzanna Lubrano's 2002 release, *Tudo pa bo* [All for you], won the Kora All-African Music Award for Best Female Artist in 2003. Given the frenzy over Cesária Évora's international success, it is difficult to conceive that Cape Verdeans would not be pleased to have one of their own perform on a live, televised program seen in 75 countries with 600 million viewers, much less be honoured with the highest award. But the Cape Verdean government, in a clear demonstration of its disdain for *cabo-zouk,* gave her absolutely no financial support or initially even any acknowledgement (Reis 2003b, 2003c). More than two weeks after the awards, the Cape Verdean government finally surrendered to popular pressure (and potential political capital) and honoured her in Praia (Reis 2003b, 2003c).

Family resemblances

To the dismay of critics, *cabo-zouk* has had continued popular support for more than a decade and is in no danger of disappearing any time soon. It has resonated strongly with an entire generation of Cape Verdeans throughout the world. One of the main critiques of this music is that it is simply not Cape Verdean – it belongs to another culture. On the surface this is difficult to argue with in that it does not fall easily into the existing musical genres of Cape Verde. But musically, despite the claims of its many detractors, *zouk*'s strongest identifiable feature, its rhythm, is not very different from that of the *coladeira*. The initial idea was not to create a new music, but to play off the popularity of Antillean *zouk* by combining it with *coladeira*, to create what was called *cola-zouk* (Lopes p.c.). Although the name did not stick, literally every performer, composer or arranger I spoke with stated that, in their view, the rhythm of the *coladeira* was very close to that of *zouk*. It is possible to take another view of the music and see it as simply the latest development, albeit with a different name, of music that Cape Verdeans already knew well. Many would agree with one performer who said, '*cabo-zouk* is 'our' *coladeira*' (Neto p.c.). And, indeed, the rhythms are similar.

Creole connections

Like *cabo-zouk*, Antillean *zouk* is a Creole music from a Creole culture that has similar historical and cultural roots to Cape Verde. Paul Gilroy (1993b, *passim*) posits the existence of a web of cultural, historical and musical connections among the former colonies in the Atlantic with slave, plantation, and colonial histories. Although it is geographically part of Africa, Cape Verde's history and culture make it part of that web, and, more specifically, it relates to *zouk* from the French Antilles, islands composed of Creole peoples, with a colonial past and African roots, who use a Creole vernacular, and also have an official European language (Guilbault 1993: 6).

When examining the roots of Antillean *zouk* one can see that all of its musical predecessors were themselves Creole music and related to each other in 'complicated networks of similarities, in both overall and specific details, and to varying degrees' (Guilbault 1993: 48). Guilbault uses the term 'family resemblance' to describe how the predecessors of the music are related to each other and, ultimately, to *zouk* itself. This 'family resemblance' that was consciously exploited by the founders of Kassav in creating *zouk* was, for Cape Verdean musicians, their own as well. They related very strongly to the music not simply because of the similar rhythms, but similar colonial pasts, including slavery, Catholicism, language, and complicated issues of race. When Kassav arrived in Cape Verde, in 1991, they were enthusiastically welcomed not only because of their music, but also their success as Afro-Caribbean musicians with similar Creole roots. Cape Verdeans indeed saw and heard that 'family resemblance' in their music.

Another important aspect tied to the music itself, and shared by both *zouk* and *cabo-zouk,* is that the accompanying dance is performed by couples dancing in close proximity. Although other music, where men and women dance without touching, such as reggae or rap are enjoyed, the close proximity promoted by dancing to *cabo-zouk* is an important part of the social life between men and women, and no music without this feature would have been adopted so completely by Cape Verdean youths.

The hybridised nature and technical complexity of *cabo-zouk* gives it an urbanised, contemporary sound which resonates strongly with increased numbers of urban Cape Verdeans both in Cape Verde and in the diaspora. In a striking change in the years since Cape Verdean independence, large numbers of people have relocated to cities, so that more than half the population is now urban. These high levels of urbanisation are relatively new in Cape Verde, and for those emigrants who moved directly from rural areas to foreign cities, it must have been especially jarring, but the experience is one shared by an entire generation. An even more telling statistic, relating to this music and its popularity, is that almost half of the population of the archipelago is under 18 years of age, of whom a large percentage listen to *cabo-zouk.*

Generation and diaspora

Cabo-zouk is the music of a specific generation of Cape Verdeans – those who came of age since independence. The experience of *cabo-zouk* as something new, separate from their parents' music, unites Cape Verdean youths (*jovens*) throughout the world. This is, perhaps, a generational rebellion that Cape Verde has never experienced. The crushing poverty, recurring droughts, and continuous oppression, only further intensified by the struggle for liberation from Portuguese colonialism, gave little room for intergenerational musical squabbles. Prior to independence, previous generations of Cape Verdeans both in the diaspora and in Cape Verde used their music as a symbol of an identity that separated them from Portugal. On a visible level, the *morna* and *coladeira* served to combat what Fanon called 'the cultural estrangement so characteristic of the colonial epoch' (1994: 37), and on a more hidden level, *funaná* and other repressed genres worked in opposition to the 'negation of the historical process' spoken of by Cabral (1994: 55). *Cabo-zouk* was created by the first generation to have little or no memory of a Cape Verde that was not free of Portuguese colonialism. This is not to say that Cape Verde has thrown off the effects of 500 years of colonisation and colonialism in 30 years, but simply to acknowledge that music plays a different role in an independent nation than in an occupied one. To the consternation of many, slightly more than a generation after independence, *cabo-zouk* has chosen to ignore the cultural obligations filled by earlier genres and has taken a different path.

Cabo-zouk is, clearly, popular music, which 'seems to lend itself to syncretisation and cross-fertilisation – especially because it is relatively unconstrained by the generic rules that fetter traditional or elite genres' (Gross 1994 et al.: 28). In addition to being a popular dance music with few pretensions, the fact that *cabo-zouk* is based in Rotterdam seems to have given it further liberties of musical style and language. The musical acceptance of the necessary heterogeneity and diversity as experienced by Cape Verdean musicians in the Netherlands allowed them to expand the boundaries of their music, to a degree that critics question whether it is, indeed, Cape Verdean at all (Gross 1994 et al.: 11). But despite its location in the diaspora, political events at home did play a part in its creation.

Political and economic change in Cape Verde

In 1991, Cape Verde had a peaceful, but radical, change in government, from the socialist Afrocentred policies of the founding party, PAICV, to the pro-capitalist Eurocentred policies of Movimento para a Democracia (MpD). There was no substantial violence associated with this change, but bad feelings on both sides ran rather deep and continue to the present day (the PAICV is currently back in power). The MpD wanted to distance itself from the identity and beliefs of the PAICV so much that it actually changed the nation's flag, national anthem, and the constitution to reflect its own ideologies, which included a multiparty state. Although Cape Verdeans had clearly indicated at the polls that they were ready for something new, this political change reverberated strongly throughout the culture, and must have been quite tumultuous for both residents of Cape Verde and the diaspora communities.

After independence, the PAICV ambitiously adopted the ideology of its founder, Amílcar Cabral, who saw culture, both national and popular, as a fundamental part of independence and recovery from colonialism. The PAICV's view was that given the limited size of the market for Cape Verdean music, governmental support to 'facilitate the lives and activities of artists' (*Voz di Povo* 1990: 7) was necessary, and should be substantial. In distancing itself from the old regime, the MpD also had to leave behind the musical groups associated with that regime, literally every existing group in Cape Verde. Thus *cabo-zouk* and the new modern sound from the Netherlands thrived, in part, because of the chaos and lack of support for the arts after the change in government, while the MpD set its priorities and chose its friends.[3] Additionally, the MpD espoused the belief that music, like everything else, should be governed, at least somewhat, by the free market. But after most of the state funding dried up, there was a clear lacuna in Cape Verdean music.

Not surprisingly, music that was relatively new, and therefore had no association with the old regime and was based outside the country, and the political polemic, would step in. *Cabo-zouk* had no history with regard to Portuguese oppression, independence, and island or political differences within Cape Verde. This music would also have to, in essence, support itself, unlike any music that had preceded it, and thus be not only a cultural, but a commercial success. *Cabo-zouk* and the new modern dance music appeared to be exactly what the MpD had wanted, albeit, not exactly where the party wanted it – the aesthetics were not defined by the state, the function of the musicians was not defined by the state, and it was a relative commercial success.

In Cape Verde, the problem of linking music to the open market lay in the fact that there was no tradition of professional musicians or commercial music. Historically, no matter what the level of expertise, music was, even for the best musicians, a sideline to their real professions, which supported them financially. Even wealthier musicians needed assistance to record or tour (*Voz di Povo* 1990: 7). Although it has always been difficult for poor musicians, the sudden cut in funding added to an already difficult situation and resulted in a decline in recordings and tours, except for musicians with substantial financial resources. The existence of popular music had not been based on record or concert ticket sales, because, in the past, the foundation of Cape Verdean music had been cultural, not commercial, and there is a strong belief that music could be one or the other, but not both (Mascarenhas 1992: 5). The fact that *cabo-zouk* had to be commercial leaves it open to criticism; for example, the accusation that it has 'no artistic or cultural goal' or that its creators 'have the audacity to call it Cape Verdean music. It is pop music with Crioulo' (Reis 2003a). The musicians who make this music certainly have a knowledge of, and on occasion a preference for, other genres of music, but *cabo-zouk* is what sells among Cape Verdean youths.

Language

This music cuts against the grain of traditional music in other ways as well. In the past, musical genres were clearly associated with a specific part of the archipelago – *morna* and *coladeira* most recently with the *Barlavento* (Windward) islands, but found throughout the archipelago; and *funaná* with the *badiu*[4] of the island of Santiago. Despite the fact that Cape Verdean emigration to the Netherlands was primarily from the *Barlavento* islands (Batalha 2004: 17), members of these groups are a mix of *badiu* and *sampadjudo* musicians. Whatever the island affiliation of the composer, lyrics tend to be written in a *badiu* Kriolu that is softened, rather than accented, by the style of the music. Thus, the music can be performed 'authentically' and, perhaps more importantly, heard with the same emotional connection, by Cape Verdean youth from any part of the archipelago or diaspora communities.

Cabo-zouk is most often performed in Kriolu, which, in the past, has clearly served as a marker of Cape Verdean identity in and of itself. Language is especially important for those in the diaspora, as it may be their only daily link back to their culture. Manuel da Luz Gonçalves, of the Cape Verdean Creole Institute states, 'Kriolu is the medium for sharing feelings of brotherhood, hospitality, and nostalgia, which are nurtured by this umbilical cord to the mother country. Kriolu is part of our identity, our way of knowing' (Gonçalves 2004: 6). In the case of *cabo-zouk*, however, its Kriolu lyrics are not enough to silence critics who question its authenticity, perhaps because of its lack of even a cursory nod to existing nomenclature.

Critiques

The intense dislike of this music must be placed in the historical context of the continuing discussion about what it means to be Cape Verdean. To a degree that cannot be understood from the outside, it is a ubiquitous topic of Cape Verdean discussion and in the print media; and more than the plastic or literary arts, music is seen as the crux of Cape Verdean identity, a source of pride in their language and culture. With the growing popularity of *cabo-zouk* in the early 1990s, an increasing number of articles appeared espousing the view that Cape Verdean culture is somehow being sold out. There is a particular worry about in the youth of the Dutch diaspora who have 'lost touch' with what it means to be Cape Verdean, which contrasts with a less antagonistic worry about the cultural connections of youths in other diaspora communities.

There may be some legitimacy to the complaint that *cabo-zouk*'s performers know little about Cape Verdean culture and music. Suzanna Lubrano left Santiago when she was four years old and for most of her life spoke primarily Dutch, only learning Kriolu at age 18 when she started singing with the Cape Verdean groups (Romer p.c.). Roger Moreira was raised in Guinea-Bissau by a Senegalese mother and identified himself as an 'African' and felt that Cape Verde was, indeed, 'different' from his home (Moreira p.c.). Several other well-known musicians were either born in the Netherlands or emigrated there as young children, leaving them little first-hand knowledge of the islands. On the other hand, an equal number of musicians spent their childhood and adolescence on the islands and have much stronger roots and a more extensive knowledge of the traditional repertoire.

Clearly, the musicians involved in *cabo-zouk* have varying amounts of temporal and geographic connection to the islands, which is not unusual for musical groups formed in diaspora communities. Each one of them, however, was and is part of an active Cape Verdean community in Rotterdam. If they themselves do not have clear memories of the islands themselves, their parents surely have and they undoubtedly heard Cape Verdean music and Kriolu spoken in their homes. At the same time, Dutch-Cape Verdeans think of themselves and position themselves in a conscious way as part of a larger world, perhaps in a way no Cape Verdean emigrants have done before. On the one hand, they seem to be proud Dutch citizens, and on the other hand, they are very tied to the islands, if not physically, then musically. Despite their physical location, they make their livelihood from their Cape Verdean identity.

Why the Netherlands?

An issue that seems perhaps incongruous is why the musical center for *cabo-zouk* would occur in the Netherlands, rather than in another larger and more established diaspora community. The reasons are complicated, and possibly in part, serendipitous (the gathering of young musicians in one community), but do have an historical precedent. Despite the fact that it was (and is) a relatively new and small diaspora community, before *cabo-zouk* it has twice served as a location for the recording of Cape Verdean popular music styles that were considered revolutionary and influential. In 1967, the group Voz de Cabo Verde, known for electrifying both the *morna* and *coladeira*, formed and recorded in the Netherlands, bringing a new modern sound to a country on the cusp of independence. Post-independence, Bulimundo recorded their groundbreaking electrified version of *funaná*, which became associated with the euphoria and empowerment of independence. Unlike the *cabo-zouk* performers, however, both of these groups were clearly rooted and identified as living on the islands themselves, and were modernising genres identified as Cape Verdean. This recording history helped to create *cabo-zouk* in that Cape Verdean musicians as well as studios and impresarios already familiar with the music were located here.

There was also a general belief among the musicians I interviewed that 'everyone is welcome in the Netherlands' and that the Dutch were much less conservative than the Portuguese or the French. Additionally, some felt there were fewer problems here than in other Cape Verdean diaspora communities, and that the community itself was more open to change. At first blush this appeared to be a reflection of the Dutch ideals of tolerance in social and cultural matters, but, in reality, this has, unfortunately, not filtered down to daily life for most Cape Verdean immigrants in the Netherlands, where economically they may be only marginally better off than in other diaspora communities.[5] These marginally improved circumstances may be due to housing assistance given across class lines in the Netherlands, which, unlike France and Portugal, makes it more difficult to completely separate and marginalise immigrants.

Despite the reality and apparent contradictions of Dutch tolerance toward immigrants, *cabo-zouk* musicians genuinely believe that their own integration into Dutch society fosters an atmosphere of greater musical creativity and freedom than in other, particularly European, diaspora communities. When *cabo-zouk* musicians talk about the Netherlands being more open and less conservative, they are not only referring to the Dutch, but also specifically to the Cape Verdean music scene in the Netherlands. Despite the fact that the Netherlands may not be a racial paradise, it appears to afford Cape Verdean musicians more options with regard to musical creativity, especially with regard to modern dance music.

Portugal and France

On the other hand, Cape Verdeans in Portugal, especially the descendants of less-skilled immigrants from the interior of Santiago who came looking for working in the 1960s and 1970s, often live isolated from Portuguese society, cohabiting with other African immigrants (many from Portugal's former colonies), gypsies, and other poor Portuguese, in segregated, run-down neighbourhoods, far from the city center (Batalha 2004: 151). These poorer immigrants do tend to draw from black influences, including black American rap, Angolan *kuduru*, *funa-*

ná, or Antillean *zouk*, but are, in general, only marginally assimilated into Portuguese society and they have few resources and opportunities for starting musical groups to play modern music. Wealthier Cape Verdeans in Portugal prefer the more traditional forms of Cape Verdean music, such as *morna* or *coladeira* (Batalha 2004: 73), and in their traditional forms, which may be why, despite the size and duration of the diaspora community, Lisbon has not been the center for innovation in Cape Verdean music.

The Cape Verdean diaspora in France is in much the same situation economically and socially as Cape Verdeans living in Lisbon; they tend to be lumped together with other African immigrants, and relegated to the impoverished suburbs of French cities, commonly called *banlieues* (Gross et al. 1994: 11). Due to anti-immigrant sentiments, they live very insecure lives, trying to earn a living and always on the verge of being deported (Rocha 1997: 15). Cape Verdean music *recorded* in France has played an important role, but has primarily been interpretations of traditional forms.

Additionally, despite the fact that France is historically the centre of recording for *zouk*, there is little chance that *cabo-zouk* will ever be heard on a French radio station because since 1996 federal law requires 40 per cent of all radio programming to be in French. The original intent of the law was to counter the hegemony of American music, and, generally, the other 60 per cent is dedicated to music in English. This is true in the Netherlands as well, where 40 per cent of all programming must be in Dutch or Frisian, but the same law also requires that 25 per cent of radio programming is directed toward minority groups. Despite the small size of the community, Cape Verdean music has received national exposure under the category of 'world music' due to the fact that other minorities are too small to justify their own television or radio programs (Romer p.c.).

The U.S.

It is doubtful that *cabo-zouk* could have been created in the U.S. because Antillean *zouk* itself had a lower level of popularity in the U.S., and even Kassav struggled unsuccessfully to make a mark in the U.S. market (Berrian 2000: 66). This may have been due to the issue of language, as it is well known that the U.S. market is resistant to foreign language recordings, making it doubtful that Antillean *zouk* would have come directly from the Caribbean to the Cape Verdean communities in New England. Although now much improved, in the past, Cape Verdean-American studios had a reputation for doing shoddy recording work with substandard equipment and engineers, who

would have been incapable of handling the technical complexity required to produce a high-quality *cabo-zouk* recordings. Since the late
1990s, there have been several, what one could call 'second-string'
cabo-zouk performers who have recorded in the U.S., and who are
clearly following in the footsteps of their counterparts in Rotterdam.

Supporters

Despite the large number of critics, there are several high-profile traditional musicians who have come forward to defend *cabo-zouk* and the
new generation of musicians. Vasco Martins, a respected and prolific
composer-musician living in São Vicente, who studied in Portugal and
France, does not agree with the idea that the addition of new ideas or
technology harms Cape Verdean culture. As evidence, he ardently cites
the innovations and foreign influences brought by key composers as
intrinsic to the evolution and vitality of Cape Verdean music (Martins
1993).

The composer Ney Fernandes, when asked what he thought about
the foreign influences from which Cape Verdean music was currently
'suffering', responded by pointing out that the criticisms were primarily geared to the composers in the diaspora and that he did not think it
was justified to claim that their music was not Cape Verdean, simply
because it was not traditional (Garcia 1998: 23).

According to Martins (1993), the current obsession with traditional
music in Cape Verde is the result of Cesária's success, and the vision
of world music promoters who have a clear idea of what they would
like to present to the world as Cape Verdean. There are those who are
anxious to make Cape Verdean music an international phenomenon
beyond Cesária. Obviously, since the world (or world music promoters)
loves her, more of Cesária – or those modelled on her style of music –
would bring prestige and international renown to Cape Verdean music
and, ultimately, Cape Verde itself. The current search for her 'replacement', and thus, who would be considered the next generation of
'authentic' music, would, ironically, not be decided by Cape Verdeans,
but by world music promoters. Paradoxically, *cabo-zouk*, which is considered 'inauthentic' by many, is unapologetically geared to Cape Verdean youth, and especially if other Lusophone countries in Africa were
included, has a larger market than most traditional Cape Verdean
music.

Conclusions

The roots of *cabo-zouk* lie in a combination of local and global factors that crossed paths at a particular time, in a particular place and answered a particular need – the popularity of Antillean *zouk* intersected with a community of musicians that related to its rhythm and the related dancing. That community had the economic and musical wherewithal to respond to its popularity by adapting it to their own language. Simultaneously, a new political party and economic system altered the path of Cape Verdean music and, perhaps unintentionally, for the first time in its history, created a need for music with more commercial appeal. At the same time, a generation unaffected by any direct effects of colonialism wanted to include themselves in a larger world and needed to set themselves apart musically from their parents. Antillean *zouk*, a community in Rotterdam, a post-independence generation, and the MpD, combined temporally, spatially and culturally to create *cabo-zouk*.

If the music itself is not very complex and meaningful, the issues it raises are; specifically, the boundaries of musical innovation and a transformation in the dialogue between homeland and diaspora. Depending on your view, one could say that *cabo-zouk* has either expanded what it means to be Cape Verdean or ignored it altogether. Its commercial nature is a result, in part, of ten years of a government geared to free market policies, resulting in a music that responds to market forces, not cultural needs. In the shifting negotiations between modernity and tradition that Cape Verde has experienced since independence, it squarely comes down on the side of technology, youth and outside influences that stand in direct opposition to those who see Cape Verdean music rooted strongly in its past. Ironically, *cabo-zouk* may actually promote traditional music as well because its very existence has sparked a strong, renewed interest in expanding and even evolving existing forms of music. Even if there are legitimate questions of ownership and appropriation, it cannot be denied that the language, the performers and the audience are Cape Verdean. All other issues aside, *cabo-zouk* may be Cape Verdean simply because an entire generation, spread throughout the world, claims it to be so.

Notes

[1] Also known as Cape Verdean *zouk* or *cola-zouk* (when combined with *coladeira*); slower versions are known as 'slow' or '*cabo love*'.

[2] Innovations to Cape Verdean music often emanate from the islands themselves as well, fostered by returning emigrants and their music. Pinpointing the source of any musical innovation is difficult because *all* recordings were, by necessity, made outside of Cape

Verde, thus the location of the recording itself says nothing about the source of musical features or the membership of the musicians to any particular diaspora.

[3]   With regard to a similar phenomenon in literature, see Moser's *Changing Africa: The First Literary Generation of Independent Cape Verde* (1992).

[4]   In the past, *badiu* referred to slaves who escaped to the interior of the island of Santiago; over time the term has come to include all who reside on the island of Santiago (Monteiro p.c.). *Sampadjudo* refers primarily to those who reside in the *Barlavento* (Windward) islands, and may also include residents of Fogo and Brava, but not generally, Maio, which is seen as culturally similar to Santiago.

[5]   My thanks to Lisa Åkesson, Huub Beijers and Jørgen Carling for their comments on this section.

References

Batalha, L. (2004) *The Cape Verdean Diaspora in Portugal: Colonial Subjects in a Postcolonial World*. Lanham, MD: Lexington Books.

Benoit, É. (1993) 'Biguine: Popular Music of Guadeloupe, 1940-1960', in *Zouk: World Music in the West Indies*, J. Guilbault (ed.), Chicago, IL: University of Chicago Press, pp. 53-67.

Berrian, B.F. (2000) *Awakening Spaces: French, Caribbean Popular Song, Music, and Culture*. Chicago, IL: University of Chicago Press.

Cabral, A. (1994) 'National Liberation and Culture', in *Colonial Discourse and Post-Colonial Theory: A Reader*, P. Williams and L. Chrisman (eds.), New York: Columbia University Press, pp. 36-52. [Originally from Amílcar Cabral, *Return to the Source: Selected Speeches of Amílcar Cabral*, New York: Monthly Review Press, 1973].

Fanon, F. (1994) 'On National Culture', in *Colonial Discourse and Post-Colonial Theory: A Reader*, P. Williams and L. Chrisman (eds.), New York: Columbia University Press, pp. 53-65. [Originally from Frantz Fanon, *The Wretched of the Earth*, 1967].

Fortes, T.S. (2001) 'Cabo Verde Show: O Desejado Regresso'. *A Semana*, Ano XI, August 31, p. 14.

Garcia, J. (1998) 'Ney Fernandes: Entre a Luz e a Sombra'. *A Semana*, Ano VIII, Magazine, April 24, pp. 22-23.

Gilroy, P. (1993a) 'Between Afro-centrism and Euro-centrism: Youth Culture and the Problem of Hybridity'. *Nordic Journal of Youth Research* 1(2): 82-97.

Gilroy, P. (1993b) *The Black Atlantic: Modernity and Double Consciousness*. Cambridge, MA: Harvard University Press.

Gonçalves, M. (2004) *Cape Verdean Kriolu in the U.S.* Boston, MA: Cape Verdean Creole Institute.

Gross, J.; McMurray, D.; Swedenburg, T. (1994) 'Arab Noise and Ramadan Nights: Rai, Rap, and Franco-Maghrebi Identity'. *Diaspora* 3(1): 3-40.

Guilbault, J. (1993) *Zouk: World Music in the West Indies*. Chicago, IL: University of Chicago Press.

Lopes, J.V. (1991) 'A Força Zouk'. *Voz di Povo*, Ano XVI, July 2, p. 9.

Martins, V. (1993) 'A Deriva Cultura (3)'. *A Semana*, Ano III, no. 109, June 28.

Mascarenhas, A. (1992) 'Emigrante Cabo-verdiano Promete Salvaguardar a Nossa Cultura'. *Voz di Povo*, Ano XVI, no. 1190, January 16, p. 5.

Moser, G.M. (1992) *Changing Africa: The First Literary Generation of Independent Cape Verde*. Transactions of the American Philosophical Society, Held at Philadelphia for Promoting Useful Knowledge. vol. 82, part 4. Philadelphia: The American Philosophical Society.

Reis, O. dos (2003a) 'An Interview with Carlos Matos, the Renaissance Man!' www.cvmusic-world.com, December 11.

Reis, O. dos (2003b) 'Governo de Cabo Verde não Apoiou a Vitória da Suzanna Lubrano. www.cvmusicworld.com, December 15.

Reis, O. dos (2003c) Cabo Verde Honours Suzanna Lubrano. www.cvmusicworld.com, December 24.

Rocha, I. (1997) 'Emigração em França: da Esperança à Incerteza'. *Emigrason*, no. 37, pp. 15-16.

Voz di Povo [Newspaper](1990) 'Eles Querem Destronar o Zouk. Finaçon: Entre a Sensualidade e a Rebelião'. Ano XVI, no. 1032, December 18, 1990, p. 7.

Interviews

Lopes, A. 2000. Personal Interview. Praia, Cape Verde.

Monteiro, J.M. 1997. Personal Communication. Praia, Cape Verde.

Moreira, R. 2000. Personal Interview. Praia, Cape Verde.

Neto, J. 2000. Personal Interview. São Vicente, Cape Verde.

Romer, R. 2005. Personal Interview. Rotterdam, The Netherlands.

Chapter 17
Managing Work and Care for Young Children in Cape Verdean Families in Portugal

Karin Wall

Introduction

Our main concern in this chapter is with the work and family lives of Cape Verdean immigrant families. By focusing on a very specific but crucial problem in family life – how to manage work and caring responsibilities for young children – our aim is to identify the strategies adopted by Cape Verdean immigrant families in Portugal in order to organise work and family life. From a broader perspective, however, we can say that an analysis of the work/life strategies of families will give us a privileged insight into the integration process of Cape Verdean families. If, as we know, immigrants face strong pressures arising from work (long working hours, atypical timetables), from economic difficulties, from racial and social discrimination and from contrasting cultural and family values, then the reconciliation of work and family life is likely to be a sensitive point revealing the specific tensions and vulnerabilities of the position of immigrant families in the host society. How do immigrant families deal with these patterns of 'vulnerability' and to what extent does the latter hinder accessibility to the care models of the receiving society? On the other hand, what are the main factors which influence coping strategies? Is the reconciliation of care and paid work strongly shaped by the family's social position and its migration pattern?

To explore these issues, our analytical framework looks at the processes of social care and work/life balance as well as those related to migration. With regard to the first, our primary focus is on social care practices, broadly defined as the assistance and surveillance provided by paid or unpaid, professional or non-professional caregivers (within the public or the private sphere) in order to help children or adults in their daily lives and activities (Daly and Lewis 1998). These practices are embedded in work/life patterns whereby families develop specific strategies to manage work and care responsibilities (Crompton 1999; Dulk et al. 1999). The latter may include cutting back on working hours, adapting parents' work schedules or delegating care to professional and informal caregivers. 'Reconciliation' and 'balancing' are the concepts currently used to analyse this process. They seem to imply that some form of conciliation or equilibrium between the two spheres is always achieved, and this represents an analytical drawback. In fact, one of the important issues in this work may be to question the idea that receiving societies always develop accessibility to a 'reconciliation' model in which the State, the family and the private and voluntary sectors come together to provide adequate care for young children. Reconciliation of work and caring may not always be possible and this may lead to alternative arrangements such as taking children to work or leaving them to fend for themselves. Therefore, although we shall sometimes also use these concepts in our work, in general we prefer the rougher and more neutral concept of 'managing' work and family life (Hantrais 1990).

Work/family strategies in the receiving society must also be seen in the context of migration. Reasons for migration, ethnicity, duration of stay (for example, belonging to a first or a second generation migrant family) and social integration in the receiving society may vary considerably and this will have an impact on work and family life.

In this work we will draw on the results of a qualitative research project, which sought to understand the work/family balance of immigrant families in five countries (Finland, France, Italy, Portugal and the UK).[1] One segment of the Portuguese sample consisted of 21 Cape Verdean immigrant families with young children (aged 10 or under) and working parents (full-time); it included couples with children as well as some lone parents. This is a small sample but it allows us, nevertheless, to carry out an exploratory qualitative analysis which examines the specific constraints faced by immigrant families as well as the main linkages between some contextual variables, such as migration patterns, ethnicity, or social networks, and the work/care strategies of immigrant families.

The interviewed families were collected via a variety of sources: immigrant associations, social care services, personal networks, social workers, organisations employing immigrant workers. In-depth interviews were carried out on the basis of a semi-structured interview guide that included the following major themes: family life course (family life in the sending country, family and marital trajectories); the story of migration (reasons to emigrate, migration trajectory, problems on arrival, integration in the host society); work and life in the host country; caring for children in the host country (caring obligations, typical weekday of the child, family division of work and care, support networks, main problems, gaps and tensions); the effects of caring (on professional work, on the personal health of family members).

Cape Verdean immigrant families in Portugal

The Cape Verdean sample of families was collected in the Lisbon metropolitan area, where most African immigrants are concentrated, and
includes 21 Cape Verdean families (14 couples with young children
and seven lone parents). Most of the interviews were carried out in socially deprived areas – in the new housing developments in the suburbs, as well as in an older slum area where brick houses have replaced
the wooden shacks – but a few took place in other suburbs where some
families had rented or bought flats. The sample is therefore homogeneous in terms of the sending country but also comprises some internal diversity from the point of view of family forms, reasons for migration, duration of stay and integration in the host society.

If we begin by looking at the general characteristics of these immigrant families and their life histories, three striking features can be
emphasised. First, the intensity of the migration phenomenon in the
sending country. Cape Verde is an archipelago of extremely arid islands
off the West African coast. Drought is severe and can last for several
years, leading to endemic famine and persistent emigration in search
of alternative or complementary means of survival. Thus the life histories of the immigrant interviewees all inform us about the continuous circulation of men, women, young people and children: of men
who inevitably went to sea or emigrated, of single young men and women who followed a relative on his or her migrations, of mothers and
children who stayed behind for many years, of young lone mothers
who emigrated on their own, leaving small children behind with a
grandmother or an aunt. A second feature is related to the organisation
of family life, which contrasts sharply with the 'nuclear family' model
that in Europe is still the predominant and preferred pattern of family
life with children, in spite of the increase in other family forms.
Shaped by the historical and social contexts of slavery, African roots,
migration and the struggle for survival, family life is more centred on
the mother-child unit, on cohabitation and lone parenthood instead of
marriage, and on considerable independence and sexual freedom of
both women and men. Fertility, motherhood and fatherhood (rather
than parenthood), and intergenerational support are basic family values
but they are channelled through bonds and types of households which
slip away from the nuclear family of couples with or without children.
As a result, family transitions follow specific and diverse patterns
which revolve around lone parenthood: a young woman will have her
first child outside marriage and then cohabit with her partner and have
more children, or she may never cohabit and have several children with
the same partner, or she may have children by different partners and
never cohabit with any of them, or she may get married after cohabit-

ing for some years and giving birth to one or more children. Having children and independent motherhood are strongly valued, even by second-generation young women who are now less in favour of having many children. As one single mother put it:

> It's like this, we are not like the Portuguese. We, the mothers have their children, right? By norm it's the mother who has the child and who takes care of the child. Of course, this means that I alone have the responsibility, and if anything happens.... (Daniela, 24, born in Portugal, secondary education incomplete, with two children aged four and two from the same partner, cohabited for one year between the two births).

The small sample of immigrant families collected in Lisbon thus contains family forms and trajectories that are quite varied and also experienced as ethnically different: many are lone parents (seven) and among the families of couples with children there are more cohabiting (eight) than married couples, and several are blended families with children from different fathers or partnerships.

Integration into the labour market is the third aspect which must be highlighted. Cape Verdean immigrants have traditionally worked in two main sectors: the building and public works sector (the men) and the cleaning and catering services sector (the women). Both have long working hours, with the building sector starting very early in the morning, often working overtime and on weekends, and on sites outside Lisbon which implies being away from home for weeks or months. The cleaning sector, on the other hand, also has long or atypical working hours and very low salaries, compared to male wages in the building sector.

It is also important to underline the fact that African women are often confined to a certain sector of the labour market, to firms that clean offices and public buildings at dawn and in the evenings. These women have more difficulty in obtaining the better-paid jobs in private homes or jobs as waitresses or shop attendants (jobs commonly taken up by Portuguese women or by white Brazilians or Eastern European immigrants). In the Cape Verdean families interviewed, all of the women except one were working full-time, nearly all in cleaning or catering services; one mother, eight months pregnant and with another child of two, had temporarily reduced her working schedule to part-time work.

These are some general features of Cape Verdean immigrant families which need to be mentioned. If we look closer at the sample, however, it is also important to emphasise some internal differentiation from the point of view of the migration trajectory. Some interviewees are first-generation migrants and others are what we call second-generation migrants: they came as young children with one or both parents and a few were born in the host country. This does not always mean that the social integration of second-generation families is very different. However, it sometimes implies a slightly higher educational level, a stronger family support network and having no plans of returning to Cape Verde; in a few cases, it also means acquiring some professional training and getting jobs with normal hours, outside the building/cleaning sectors. Although the majority of families are worker migrant families, the sample also included two cases of student migration and one case of 'employee' migration (an administrative employee, now a civil servant in a bank, who migrated to Portugal during colonial times).

Managing work and care for young children

Taking into account these differences, we were able to identify three main patterns of migration which influence families' strategies for managing work and care for young children.

Work/care strategies of first generation unskilled worker immigrant families

First-generation, unskilled worker migration is related to a long-term migration project that emphasises access to paid employment, to food and better living conditions and, savings permitting, the building of a new house in Cape Verde where to return to after retirement (or the buying of a house in Portugal). Some immigrants arrived in the late 1960s, at the time of the 'great famine' in Cape Verde, others in the 1980s or 1990s. Networks usually helped them to find work and/or temporary accommodation inside the slum. Usually the man came first and the wife and children later; but some years usually went by before enough money was saved to pay for the travel expenses of those left behind in the sending country.

José and Domingas (aged 50 and 44, cohabiting couple, both illiterate) are a typical example of immigration in the late 1970s. In Cape Verde, Domingas worked seasonally as a farm labourer and later as a maid looking after small children. She started working when she was eight and never learned to read and write. She went to live with José and his family when she was 15 and had her first child (one of five) aged 17, in Cape Verde. José emigrated soon after, lodged with a relative in a slum and started working in the building sector. A few years later, after 'nailing together' a shack, he sent for his wife and child and, later, for his mother and brother. José gradually transformed the wooden shack into a brick house, but the family is still waiting for a home in a housing development project.

First-generation immigration in the 1990s is not very different from this model. António, a bricklayer (earning 650 euros per month) had already been working in Portugal for a few years when he met Dulce in Cape Verde during his holidays. Like Domingas, Dulce (now aged 37, one year of schooling and cohabiting) also remained in the sending country for a few years, had her first two children there, and then joined her husband. She arrived in 1994 but left the two children in the care of her mother in Cape Verde, so that she could work harder. António had left the slum area by then and rented a small one-bedroom council flat nearby. This is where they still live today, with four children; the two elder children who came in 1998 and the two born in Lisbon (the 4 children, now aged 13, 7, 3 and 2 share the one bedroom). Dulce first got a cleaning job in a factory through Cape Verdean friends. Because it was very hard work she eventually moved to a cleaning services firm where she now works in two shifts (from 7 a.m. to 1 p.m. and from 6 to 9 p.m., earning 350 euros per month). It is difficult to manage work and care, but Dulce has always relied on her elder son to look after the other children in the morning; he takes them to school and day care at 8 a.m. (private non-profit, 69 euros for two children). During the day, this son is quite independent: for example, for several years now, he has been going home during lunch time to cook his own lunch. Dulce fetches the other children in the afternoon but then leaves them alone for a few hours as she leaves for work at 5 p.m. and her older son has school until 6.30 p.m. (Formal care with older child care and self-care, see table 17.1). Dulce and António would like to return to Cape Verde one day when they retire, and they have already started building a house there.

Table 17.1. *Work/care strategies of Cape Verdean immigrant families in Portugal (2002)*

Work/care strategy	N
Managing work and care through extensive delegation	
Extensive formal care	6
Extensive formal care and older child care	3
Grandparental care	3
Paid babysitter	2
Paid babysitter with some negotiation within the family	2
Managing work and care with some child negligence	
Formal care[1] and older childcare and self care	3
Formal extensive care and self-care	1
Formal care (school, no extras) and self-care	1
Total	**21**

Source: interview data, SOCCARE Project.
[1] Day care/school, no extras.

The work/care strategies in this family highlight the main problems faced by first-generation migrants with young children. Incomes are low, housing conditions are bad, working hours are long and atypical, and formal care services, even though they are fairly cheap, do not cover the varied and long care needs of the children. Low-cost extensive delegation, care by older children and child negligence are therefore the main strategies used. If a grandmother joins the family (only one case in this study), then informal extensive delegation becomes a logical option. However, in the absence of this option, the gaps in care (early in the morning; when primary school ends at 3.30 p.m.; late afternoon; working overtime on weekends) are usually managed by other means: primary school children look after babies and learn how to cook, young adolescents look after several children, children stay on their own. In some families, such as Dulce's family, the parents manage to cover almost all their care needs with the assistance of one older child.

Even when the children are all young, it is often the oldest child who takes on the child care responsibilities. For example, Anita, Maria's seven-year-old daughter, has school and then an after-school club during the day, but in the morning, between 6.30 and 8.30, she takes care of her three-year-old sister, gives her breakfast and dresses her (formal extensive and self-care, table 17.1). Maria works a cleaning shift from 5.30 to 8 a.m. and her husband works in the building sector and leaves for work at 6.30 a.m. (Maria also cleans a shop in the morning and is a daily in a private home in the afternoon and on Saturdays). Before Anita started going to school, the family used to pay for a babysitter to care for her in the mornings and then take the two children to day care (75 euros per month, when day care already cost 55 euros per child). As this was very expensive, they decided to 'try' and leaving Anita on her own with her sister in the early morning and on Saturday mornings when the parents worked overtime. Anita does not like staying alone; she can't sleep after the parents have left, so she usually watches TV. Maria and her husband have brothers and sisters who have also emigrated and are living in Lisbon but they all work long hours, so they have no time to help take care of the children either. As one interviewee put it:

> No one is available here, everyone has to work.... So, we the Cape Verdeans, cannot reconcile the education of young children with two homelands. Not me personally, since I have managed, but I am a drop of water in the ocean. But the Cape Verdean immigrant loses her child at age 10 and many lose them at a much earlier age. They really lose them. The children are used to being alone, they run around, they finish school and get

home hours later, they don't do their homework.... (Guida, school assistant with normal hours, 39 years old, arrived in Portugal aged 8 in 1971, two elder children aged 19 and 20 from first marriage, now remarried and with seven-month-old twins; care for the twins is managed through extensive informal delegation to a paid childminder and some sharing and negotiation between the mother, the father and the two elder children involving bringing, fetching and caring for the youngest in the early mornings and evenings).

When the first-generation migrant is a first-generation single mother, the pattern of social exclusion becomes even more pronounced. Rosário, aged 26, is an example of this: Rosário was a three-year-old child when she was left with an aunt in Cape Verde. Her parents separated and both emigrated and remarried; since then, she has only seen her mother once, when she was 13. In Cape Verde, Rosário completed four years of primary school and then worked odd jobs in restaurants and in private homes. She had her first child at the age of 20 but never lived with the father of her child. It was against this background that Rosário decided to emigrate, in 1995, hoping to improve her life and earn more money. She came on her own, leaving her one-year-old daughter with her aunt, and with no relatives in Portugal who might help her. As she herself states: 'When I arrived there was no one to receive me with open arms for me to feel at home'. However, she had a contact to find work and became a maid in a private home in return for lodgings and food. After six months, she went to work in another private home, but this time for a salary.

Some time later she met a new partner and had a second child. At first the couple lived with his parents and eventually found a small rented flat of their own. However, after two years, they separated and Rosário could not afford the flat. She was taken in for three months by a friend from work (also a lone parent) and then rented a room in another immigrant's house in the slums. Rosário is so ashamed of her room in the slum that she did not tell her work colleagues where she lives. She currently works for a cleaning services company from 8 a.m. to 5 p.m., earning 350 euros per month. With this salary and a small family benefit, she has to pay her rent (100 euros), a local childminder for her daughter (100 euros), transportation, food and clothing, and try to send money to her daughter in Cape Verde. Most of the time she cannot make ends meet and runs out of money for food. She does not receive any assistance from her former partner and she has not seen her older daughter, now aged seven, for six years. She is also worried about the fact that the childminder is unreliable and sometimes leaves the small children alone with an eight-year-old daughter. Rosário feels that she has been living in hell since her separation.

Work/care strategies of second-generation worker immigrant families

Second-generation worker families and emigrants who came as very young children have often been brought up in the types of care situations described above. They lived in shacks, income was low, care responsibilities and household tasks were distributed between the parents and the older children, and the pressure to work, in order to boost family income, was strong. Their individual and family/work trajectories, however, are not always the same. Some never finished compulsory schooling (six years until the late 1980s, nine years since then), started working when they were 12 or 13 and had children very early on. A few started working but managed to work and go to school at the same time, while others went back to school or occupational training courses later on.

Family support is another important factor in the work/life strategies of these second-generation families. Lone parents, and some couples with children, will often receive support from nuclear family members (parents or just a mother, brothers and sisters). Adolescent single mothers, if they do not leave home to cohabit with their partners, often end up in an extended family household, where brothers and sisters and a grandmother are available to help take care of the young children. This does not mean that there is no child negligence. But work/care strategies in second-generation families are more systematically associated with grandparental support or paid extensive delegation which covers the needs for child care, mainly due to parents' more normal working schedules. If we look at the work/care strategies of some second-generation families, we find the following typical situations:

(a) Grandparental care

Albina was born in Portugal (her father arrived in the late 1960s, her mother some years later) and has only had four years of school. She is 25 years old, lives with her partner, who is 32, and has two daughters, one aged 5 and the other 11 (born when Albina was 14 and still living at home). Like her parents, Albina works in the cleaning services sector from 8 a.m. to 2 p.m., Monday to Friday and her husband works in the building sector six days a week. The grandmother cares for the youngest child during the day and offers support in other situations as she is retired and lives in the same building. The older daughter goes to school on her own, but has lunch with her grandmother (who also 'keeps an eye on her' after school). The family used to live in a slum, but have since moved to two low-rent flats in a housing development project.

Another typical situation of grandparental care is linked to cases of single adolescent mothers who continue to live at home. Francisca (18 years old) is the daughter of a separated single mother with four children and is herself a single mother with a five-month-old baby. She found school work difficult, failed repeatedly and only completed the sixth grade. She began cleaning illegally as a young adolescent but has now signed a work contract in the cleaning services, earning 350 euros. She works from 9 a.m. to 5 p.m. during the week and 9 a.m. to 1 p.m. on Saturdays. Her mother (at home, with health problems) cares for the baby and another grandson (two years old) who is the son of Francisca's sister (23), another single mother living at home and working in the same firm as her sister. There are also two younger children, Francisca's brothers, who are 13 and 9 and still in school. Francisca wanted to live with her boyfriend but her mother did not allow it. They hardly see each other anymore and Francisca is disappointed that he never comes to see their baby. Her dream is to emigrate to Luxembourg.

(b) Extensive formal care

Dalila's parents arrived in the 1960s. Dalila, born in Portugal, is 25 and works as a media library co-ordinator in an activity centre for young people (9 a.m. to 5.30 p.m., earning 600 euros). She began work in the cleaning services sector when she was 13 to help her parents (who had five children). However, she was a good student and she decided to go to school in the evenings and managed to complete secondary school. She then had her first relationship, which only lasted a few months, but has lived for six years with her present partner (aged 40, metal worker, a first-generation migrant who has four other children in Cape Verde); the couple lives with the eldest stepdaughter, aged 19, who arrived to work in Portugal not long ago. Dalila's two-year-old son is in day care (private non-profit, open from 8.30 a.m. to 4.30 p.m., with extended care until 6.30 p.m. for mothers who need these extra hours like Dalila; it costs 52 euros per month). She brings and picks him up. Her parents live near her workplace and cared for the child until he was one year old; however, her mother has health problems, so Dalila decided to put the child in day care fairly early on.

(c) Paid childminder (with some negotiation within the family)

Jamila (25) and Dajaré (23) are a cohabiting couple with a six-month-old baby. They both came to Portugal as young children. Jamila was the eldest of four boys and he left school at 13 to start working; a year later, he went back to school at night and managed to finish elementary school (nine years) while continuing to work. He was employed in the army for four years and then trained as an 'activities co-ordinator'; at present he is taking another training course on educational intervention (from 9 a.m. to 5 p.m.), and will start working again in a few months. Dajaré (secondary education completed) has a more complicated timetable with two alternating shifts (10 a.m. to 7 p.m. for two days, 5 p.m. to 12 a.m. on the other days, weekends included) in a McDonald's restaurant; she has a responsible position and earns 575 euros. Both Jamila and Dajaré have parents who could look after the baby but they live too far away. Their son is cared for by a childminder during the week (120 euros) and by Jamila in the evenings and on weekends when Dajaré is working. As a child, Jamila learned how to perform household chores and care for his younger brothers.

Work/care strategies of student immigrant families

The last profile involves student migration (as well as a case of 'employee migration' where the immigrant family managed to send their second-generation offspring to university). The work/family lives of these migrants contrast sharply with the patterns of vulnerability we have examined thus far. Independent motherhood is still strongly emphasised but the difficulties of atypical working hours and very low salaries no longer influence the work/care strategies. Dores and Rosa are good examples. Dores came to Portugal with a scholarship to go to university. She got pregnant two years later, had her child as a single mother, started working part-time (giving private lessons), and managed to finish her degree. She had a second child by another partner 11 years later. At the time of the interview, she was living with her two children and working full-time selling advertising space (earning 1,000 euros; she also gets child support from the father of her eldest child, a medical student she met at the university). The youngest child goes to a private nonprofit primary school (9 a.m. to 7 p.m., 95 euros); he is taken by his mother in the morning and usually picked up by his sister in the evening (extensive delegation and older child care, table 17.1). Dores has no close family members to offer her support and she is socially isolated.

Rosa came to Portugal as a young child. Her mother works as a secretary in a bank and her father, now retired, was a seaman. She studied law at Lisbon University and became a single mother when she was 32 (she never cohabited). At the time of the interview, she was living in her own flat, quite near her parents' house, and her five-year-old son was in a private sector nursery (225 euros/month), from 9.30 a.m. to 7 p.m.; occasionally, if she has to work late, a family member will babysit. She is strongly supported by her family and does not feel isolated.

To summarize, Cape Verdean immigrant families portray specific patterns of vulnerability that influence work/care strategies. Unskilled worker migration, associated in this case with strong ethnic contrasts (racial and familial) and social exclusion (segregation in terms of housing and the labour market), shapes work/life patterns in which parents work full-time with difficult schedules and low salaries. Extensive delegation, both formal (low-cost private non-profit) and informal, is the main care solution but it does not always cover all the care needs; in other cases, the costs are too high and this leads to extreme poverty. To deal with the care gaps, families rely on the older children for care-giving whenever possible but they also ask their younger children under 10 to remain home alone or to look after even younger children. These strategies reproduce work/life patterns from previous, rural or migratory, contexts or experiences and as such as they are recognised as 'normal' solutions, which does not mean that families do not feel constrained and concerned.

Families also complain of social isolation, especially first-generation immigrants. Family support for child care rarely exists in first-generation families and, while immigrant networks are important for finding work and lending an occasional helping hand (with house repairs, for example), time for regular child care is a rare resource in all of the families and the social networks just cannot deal with this need. Finally, family life, more centred in Cape Verdean families on lone motherhood, is another factor that intensifies the pattern of vulnerability. Women in unskilled jobs tend to earn less than men and they often have atypical working hours or shift work. Unskilled first-generation single-mother families thus emerge as the most vulnerable type of immigrant family: they are seldom entitled to any special benefits;[2] family networks are absent and they work in low-paid jobs with long working hours.

Conclusion

Cape Verdean immigrant families adopt a variety of work/care strategies in order to reconcile work and care for their young children. Apart from two predominant strategies – managing work and care through informal or formal 'extensive delegation' – families also rely on the regular help of an older child, leave children in the country of origin, and leave children under age 10 at home alone (self-care). Almost all of the immigrant families analysed in this exploratory research suffer from the low availability of close kin support networks, due to the extreme pressures of work, and from one or various integration problems: these are usually related to social isolation, bad housing and problems arising from low-paid, unskilled jobs with long and atypical working hours.

However, patterns of vulnerability and work/care strategies vary according to the migration pattern of the immigrant families. Unskilled worker-migrant families, especially first-generation migrant families, seem to be the most vulnerable. Pressures to work and from work – such as the migration project, low income, atypical or long hours and the pressure to not miss work – are the main constraints on family/work life and care strategies for children. Given their low incomes, these families must find low-cost formal care arrangements with long opening hours at either public or private day care facilities, or informal care based on childminders or family members. However, although most labour migrant communities have important social networks which provide support in some situations, interviews show that these informal networks often fail to provide support for child care. This is because time is scarce for all of the labour migrant families involved, and also because grandparents, the main child care providers (see Wall et al. 2001), are often absent. As a result, work/care strategies in Cape-Verdean first-generation immigrant families fall systematically into three main categories: informal extensive delegation to paid childminders (usually cheaper and offering more flexible hours but not always reliable), extensive delegation to formal day care services, providing it is affordable and available, and care strategies that rely on older children to care or on self-care (leaving children below age ten alone), usually before and after school hours or on Saturdays when parents are both working overtime.

Family structure (couples versus lone parents) is another important factor in the more vulnerable types of migration, such as first-generation unskilled-worker migration: it is here that single parents with young children are more exposed to social exclusion and to child negligence.

Second-generation migrant worker families often suffer the same type of constraints as first-generation families, such as pressures from long or atypical working schedules, low qualifications, poor housing, and few resources. Nevertheless, findings show that they seem to be more consistently associated with grandparental care and less associated with child negligence. Slightly higher qualifications, more normal working hours (of at least one family member) or some family support are often sufficient to produce work/care strategies that manage work and care without child negligence.

Student migration and 'employee' migration present patterns of vulnerability that are less striking compared to labour migrant families. Work/care strategies also emphasise the formal extensive delegation of care but higher qualifications and resources make access to day care centres, schools and after-school activities easier, thereby ensuring that younger children are cared for even if their parents are working long hours.

A final comment relates to some policy implications of these findings. First, it is important to underline the need to take into account the diversity of immigrant families. Within this broad category, there are many different worlds: different migration projects and trajectories, diverse family patterns and work/life strategies, variable resources to cope with the difficulties of managing work and care. However, if we focus on the most vulnerable immigrant families – unskilled-worker migrant families as well as single parents within this category – findings seem to point to the still inadequate regulatory functioning of the welfare state in the protection of these families with low-paid jobs and child care responsibilities. For example, in terms of child care, it is important to analyse the types of facilities provided by public or publicly-subsidised child care and schools. These are often inflexible, have gaps in their opening hours or close early. Labour migrant families usually need low-cost as well as responsive child care services which take into account their income and family-unfriendly working hours.

Another policy implication relates to the problem of close-kin networks. Although the social networks of economic migrant communities cannot respond to the families' child care needs, some families are able to bring close kin to help care for their younger children. Interviews show that this latter solution is not always easy to implement and thus, in the future, will mainly depend on family reunification policies that facilitate the participation of elder relatives.

Finally, another major challenge in terms of social policy lies in gender inequalities in terms of care pressure within the family and in terms of the labour market. Gender inequality in immigrant families with low-paid jobs is not easy to tackle. It involves looking at women's training and educational opportunities, their access to the labour market (and to legalised work) when they arrive in the host society, the wages and working hours in the employment sectors in which they work as well as the support mechanisms concerning child care. Policy development with regard to working-immigrant single mothers, particularly in Portugal, where single parents do not receive any extra attention and support, is also an important issue.

Notes

[1] In this chapter, I use the results of the SOCCARE Project (New Kinds of Families, New Kinds of Social Care). The project was coordinated by Jorma Sipila and subsidized by the EC within the Fifth Framework Programme. The Portuguese team included Karin Wall,

José de São José and Sónia V. Correia. National and Synthesis Reports of the project may be found at: www.uta.fi/laitokset/sospol/soccare.

[2] In Portugal, single parents with young children have some extra tax benefits but no special allowances. This means that single parents are expected to work. They indeed have a very high rate of employment (in 2001, 73 per cent of single mothers were employed).

References

Crompton, R. (ed.) (1999) *Restructuring Gender Relations and Employment*. Oxford: Oxford University Press.

Daly, M.; Lewis, J. (1998) 'Introduction: Conceptualising Social Care in the Context of Welfare State Restructuring', in *Gender, Social Care and Welfare State Restructuring in Europe*, J. Lewis (ed.), Ashgate: Aldershot, pp. 1-24.

Dulk, L. den; Doorne-Huiskes, A. van; Schippers, J. (eds.) (1999) *Work-family Arrangements in Europe*. Amsterdam: Thela Thesis.

Hantrais, L. (1990) *Managing Professional and Family Life. A Comparative Study of British and French Women*. Aldershot: Dartmouth Publishing Company.

Machado, F.L. (2000) *Contrastes e Continuidades: Migração, Etnicidade e Integração dos Guineenses em Portugal*. Oeiras, PT: Celta.

SOCCARE project, National and Synthesis reports: www.uta.fi/laitokset/sospol/soccare.

Wall K.; Aboim, S.; Cunha, V.; Vasconcelos, P. (2001) 'Families and Support Networks in Portugal: The Reproduction of Inequality'. *Journal of European Social Policy* 11(3): 213-233.

Wall, K.; São José, J. (2004) 'Managing Work and Care: A Difficult Challenge for Immigrant Families'. *Social Policy and Administration* 38(6): 591-621.

Chapter 18
Cape Verdeans' Pathways to Health: Local Problems, Transnational Solutions

Huub Beijers and Cláudia de Freitas

Western societies are developing into 'health societies' (Kickbusch 2004), where health is increasingly defined both as a public good, dominating the social and political discourses, and as an individual right and a personal goal in life. Each and every individual is expected to become an active partner in the drive toward health and is held accountable for securing his/her well-being (Rose 2001). This implies a re-organisation of the rights and obligations of citizens with regard to health and the rise of new modalities of citizenship (Abraham and Lewis 2002), connected to the vitality of the healthy body (and brain) and the biologisation of politics.

In this work, we address the pathways to health employed by Cape Verdean immigrants in the Netherlands in relation to their medical citizenship experiences. Taking on Scheper-Hughes' (2004) concept of medical citizenship[1] we discern three constitutive elements of this 'new modality' of citizenship in the Netherlands, on legislative, social systemic and personal levels: (1) legally defined citizens' rights, as defined in the political and administrative domain; (2) the transformation of the absoluteness of medical expert systems into a 'system of balances'; and (3) attitudinal, behavioral and cognitive abilities and skills required to effect this citizenship.

The exercise of medical citizenship demands 'tools' that can facilitate the realisation and enforcement of the rights and duties it entails. These tools include care users' participation in health care services and 'health literacy', defined as 'the ability to make sound health care decisions in the context of everyday life – at home, in the community, at the work place, the health care system, the market place and the political arena' (Kickbusch et al. 2005).

Cape Verdean immigrants are among the ethnic groups making the least use of available mental health services (Dieperink et al. 2002), in spite of their own perception of having a poor health status and a higher level of psychosocial problems (Huiskamp et al. 2000). This is a consequence of limited access to care, resulting from poor information about health care services, incompatibilities in relationships with health professionals and difficulties in negotiating health care (Beijers

2004b; Freitas 2006). Here we argue that Cape Verdeans also experience limitations to their medical citizenship in the Netherlands. The full exercise of medical citizenship among Cape Verdeans is not just thwarted; it requires a more holistic approach to health and health care provision at the legislative and social systemic levels and further development of fundamental personal competences. We support this argument in the light of our findings concerning transnational health-seeking practices, non-matching health beliefs and the inability to address social inequalities in the context of health promotion and health care. We follow the argument of Wimmer and Shiller (2002) that many studies of migration are biased by 'methodological nationalism', in which nationally bounded societies are taken to be naturally given entities of study. In this line of thinking, the concept of medical citizenship can be disputed, because of its intrinsic reference to the relevance and legitimacy of the nation-state. Transnational practices of Cape Verdeans are not compatible with this assumption and in many respects lead to exclusion within the context of the (Dutch) nation-state. They impede the improvement of care (Kickbusch, Maag and Saan 2005) and the acquisition of required skills and knowledge to make the local health care system work. This is a pragmatically and ideologically inspired argument: pragmatically because it concerns the practicalities of dealing with health care; ideological because it questions the presuppositions of biomedicine. Our reservation is that the concept of medical citizenship has the potential to enforce better health and promote the empowerment of the community, by taking into account both these pragmatic and ideological considerations.

The findings presented derive from a review of literature concerning Cape Verdean history and migration and from two studies conducted in the Netherlands between January 2001 and December 2003 (see Beijers 2004a; Freitas 2006), with Cape Verdean immigrants who experience psychosocial distress.[2] In this work we first provide a description of Cape Verdean health beliefs and idioms of distress. An analysis of the pathways to health employed follows, which addresses both local and transnational networks of support. We conclude with an analysis of medical citizenship as experienced by Cape Verdean immigrants in the Netherlands.

Health beliefs and idioms of distress

The inability to exercise medical citizenship to its full extent can be understood as a consequence of incompatibilities of cultural and social representations, of physical or psychological distress, and of personal factors. The way health problems are phrased and treated is inspired by health beliefs and by interpretations and attributions within the context in which the suffering emerges. They reflect social injustice or social imbalances and can be understood as 'idioms of distress' (Nichter 1981; Kleinman 2005b). Both health beliefs and 'idioms of distress' are the building blocks for a better understanding of the pathways to the health of Cape Verdeans.

Health beliefs and practices of Cape Verdeans are traditionally colored by the belief in witchcraft, spirits and the evil eye, as causes of illness (Like and Ellison 1981). These beliefs contrast with the dominant biomedical system in which medical citizenship in the Netherlands is conceptualized. Cabral (1980) describes how many Cape Verdeans live in ongoing struggle between good and evil on a spiritual and supernatural level, for example, between the 'guardian angel' and the devil, in a universe where vagabond spirits seek weakness and try to bring evil. Although these beliefs are abjured by many 'modern' Cape Verdeans, it is without doubt that spiritual experience and the conviction that supernatural phenomena remain relevant in everyday life and constitute important points of reference for giving meaning to health problems and in choosing pathways to health (Cabral 1980; Vasconcelos 2004, 2005). If you don't believe in them, be sure not to scoff at them either. In the Cape Verdean understanding of the origin of psychosocial distress, three interrelated factors can be discerned (Beijers 2004b):

1. Personal vulnerability, for which you can bear personal responsibility, by leading a good and responsible life, work hard and take care of your family.
2. Negative influences, which come from outside (either spiritual, interpersonal, biomedical or socio-economic). These influences can be avoided, resisted, analyzed and treated.
3. The inevitable, the ordeals that come to you, which you have to endure and bear. These ordeals can be hereditary or based on evolutionary debt. In a wider historical context, it is possible to postulate a social dimension: ordeals of climatological crises and famines on the Cape Verdean islands, and of colonial oppression and slavery.

The complex of health beliefs of the Cape Verdean immigrants in the Netherlands should be seen as a Christian-spiritual 'repertoire' in which the values of suffering and endurance for the sake of getting better, of charity and mutual responsibility, and of fear and respect for the inevitable, can flourish. It is a fate carried with pride and sometimes seen as a shared Cape Verdean dedication; as 'a mission' (Beijers 2004b). The Cape Verdean fate is to bear spiritual responsibility, and suffer, for the well-being of others. By taking personal responsibility and through the working of individual (spiritual) potencies, they are able to contribute to a better world (Vasconcelos 2004, 2005). These observations should not be mistaken as a statement that there is a single clear-cut Cape Verdean set of health beliefs or strong standards in explanatory models (Kleinman 2005a). There are dynamics of competing, co-existing and sometimes mutually strengthening discourses about the origin, understanding and treatment of psychosocial distress, and these are congruent with different pathways to health. The various positions are clarified by Suzana, a young professional.

> In the Netherlands I got overworked. I went to the community mental health centre and now a psychologist treats me. I can do that because I am integrated, I can express myself. [...] But most people do not look at it as an illness. So you need a kind of cultural changeover, an awakening, that it is an illness. [...] They know that something is wrong. But because of shame and feelings of guilt they do not want to see it. Uhm...this has to do with African culture as well, those people often go to a kind of medicine man when they have mental health problems; it is a kind of voodoo, not to hurt someone, but for your own health. [...] And of course, this kind of man can totally disturb them. He may say: 'Well now I know what's wrong with you! It's your niece who's hurting you!' [...] But people will not admit they go to him, because they are ashamed [...].
>
> Interviewer: Are they seeing *curandeiros?*
>
> *Suzana:* Yes, yes.

Suzana's view should not be taken as just a reflection of a controversy between modernity and tradition. They reflect the dynamics and social stratification of the community as inspired by current socio-political dynamics within the Dutch community, but certainly also in relation to the political situation in Cape Verde (Graça 1999; Silva 1997). They range between 'modern' and 'knowledgeable' (second-generation) versus 'traditional' and 'authoritarian' (first-generation). First-generation immigrants mention that they are hovering between their Cape Verdean origins and the Dutch present time. Second-generation adolescents have learned how to work the health care system.

The contextualisation of suffering and the component of injustice regarding the health problem is something patients experience and try to communicate, expecting to receive an intervention in this social or moral domain. The way health problems are experienced and expressed by Cape Verdeans provides insight on their social situation, where gender-related problems, poverty, discrimination and social defeatism emerge.

Mrs. Soares suffers from delusions and although she talks incoherently, her views on discrimination and the lack of appreciation she has experienced as an immigrant are clear.

> No, it is all here in the Netherlands. But my problems are all in my head. Because this voodoo started with evil.... I say this is jealousy. Sir, I am, I was a beautiful woman. I was beautiful when I was born and I always kept my beauty. Everybody has the evil eye on me. That is the problem. They want to kill me with voodoo. It's bad, isn't it? [...] Because this is jealousy, discrimination. Jealousy and discrimination. I do not think this is normal. This is bad for everybody, not just for the people involved, but for everybody. It was here a year ago; it caused cancer, with this man of that woman there [she points to one of her neighbors].

Ana and Graça, two single mothers (and depressed) touch upon gender-related problems.

> *Ana:* I had a cleaning job, which is heavy work, and then delivering and picking up the child all the time. I do not agree with that. I work outside the house and then I have to do everything inside as well. Sometimes he took care of the child, but he says he's doing me a favour when he does. He never did anything for us; when I asked for something I always get in trouble. I was very depressed and crying at the doctor's. [...] I came here for my husband, but he didn't want a wife, he wanted a robot.

> *Graça:* What I see here is that women really are victims of the situation. I'll give you an example: here Cape Verdean men have five or six women. They do not have a house, but... [makes a circling movement with her arms]... round: today I sleep here, tomorrow there, I eat there. They live the life of playboys. They really have a good life. A friend of mine says: 'Here Cape Verdean women grow old early'. And those men, when they are fifty, they look like they are thirty-five, because they go to the gym all day long... no responsibility.

Paula talks about migration-related disintegration:

> When I was 16 months old, my mother left for Italy. Four children stayed behind in Cape Verde and were brought up by my mother's mother. When the oldest child was ten years old she was brought to the Netherlands. When I came to the Nether-

lands I was twenty years old. I had seen my mother only once in the period between 16 months and 20 years of age.

Miguel, who is on a disability allowance and suffers from abdominal complaints, talks about the persevering poverty and the sense of 'social defeat' that he feels since he migrated to the Netherlands.

> I worked here for 30 years, so I thought I should not go backwards, but earn more over the years. And that hasn't happened. Now I get an allowance that goes directly to the bank. I wait because sometimes it does not come on time. And then you pay health insurance, rent and things like that and after that you talk about food, and that does not come. At that moment you get stuck in that situation. [...] Now I get 600 euros, and I spend 800 euros, so there is a deficit of 200 euros every month.

The way health problems are phrased and uttered does not always lead to a health care intervention, and when a health intervention is solicited, the doctor does not always respond as expected, i.e., with a social intervention. It is not surprising that besides doctors, lawyers are among the most consulted professionals in cases involving health problems. Doctors are sometimes addressed as lawyers, but a lawyer serves in many cases as a balm to the soul.

Pathways to health

Community-based solutions

When a health problem emerges, people help each other and help is arranged in an informal way, without appointments, without delay, and based on mutual personal commitment, and implicit agreements regarding repayment. This mutual support ensures a common understanding of the situation and keeps the problem within the community, discussed and treatable, and it 'writes' and 'inscribes' the shared experience and memory of Cape Verdean immigrants. Mutual support is evident and deliverable until the seriousness of the problem forces reliance on external intervention.

Cape Verdeans' health beliefs are based on a Christian-spiritual repertoire and churches or houses of worship are among the most important community-based points of reference for dealing with health problems. Religion provides people with a cosmology, symbolism and the rituals that allow them to comprehend and treat their problems, and the institutional context to profess them (Bhugra 1996; Geertz 1973). Three denominations are particularly relevant: Roman Catholicism,

Charismatic Pentecostalism and Christian Rationalism. The latter is practiced in the *Centro Redentor* (centre that brings salvation) (cf. Beijers 2004b; Vasconcelos 2004, 2005). Rotterdam has two 'houses' and Cape Verdeans gather there three times a week in crowded public sessions known as *Limpeza psíquica* or 'psychic cleansing'. This brings relief and comfort and is a place for reflection, a community you belong to, which empowers and helps them to survive everyday hardships. The Rotterdam *Igreja Universal do Reino de Deus* [IURD] (Universal Church of the Kingdom of God) is a real Cape Verdean church, charismatic Pentecostal, growing, and often depicted as controversial (Oro and Semán 2001). The majority of Cape Verdeans in the Netherlands however are Roman Catholic and the Cape Verdean parish *Nossa Senhora da Paz* in Rotterdam has a pivotal role in supporting and strengthening the community, both in times of prosperity and adversity. Professional social workers and community workers in the parish actively organise self-help groups. *Nossa Senhora da Paz* is part of the community, a place where people meet, experience their unity, where they exchange the latest news and hear from the homeland. It is the parish's policy to strengthen the community and its own specific cultural characteristics, like language, as a way of interacting and being together (Graça 2005). Political differences are overcome.

Relief from interpersonal and spiritual induced health problems can also be found among the indigenous healers. Information about their work, however, is limited. People do not want to be associated with *curandeiros* or *feiticeiras* and *bruxas*, because this can raise the suspicion that they are engaged in something evil. Acknowledgement is incompatible with the image of civilisation and modernity that people want to uphold (Cabral 1979). But Cape Verdeans are acquainted with *curandeirismo*. In our contacts with the community, many admitted that they used to consult healers, either in the Netherlands, France, Portugal or Cape Verde, but generally they insist that they abjure this type of help. Reluctance to talk about this sort of complementary treatment does not apply to Dutch fortune tellers, aura readers and herbalists who Cape Verdeans consult now and then.

These community-based places of consolation, support and worship are all evidence of a limited social capital (Graça 2005; Horta and Malheiros 2005). The Cape Verdeans in the Netherlands constitute a multiplex community: social roles are highly overlapping (Beijers 2004b) and common ground or interfaces between the Cape Verdean community and the rest of Dutch society in the field of health beliefs are lacking. The community remains shy and medical citizenship is not an issue. Exceptions are the Roman Catholic parish and the community-based mental health care project 'Apoio', which have well developed interfaces with mental health care and local politics.

Formal health care

In the Netherlands formal mental health care is only accessible when someone is referred by a general practitioner or social worker. Many Cape Verdeans have had dissatisfying experiences with mental health care. The need for prompt and unconditional help is often not satisfied. Patients report that they are frequently sent home with nothing more than a prescription for analgesics (Freitas 2006).

> *Paula:* When I go there [health centre] I only get ten minutes in the doctor's office. He doesn't check my blood pressure or my heart. He doesn't examine my body to see how I am doing. He only looks and listens to what I say, gives me my usual medication for Lupus and if I say I have some sort of a pain he gives me Paracetamol. That is all.

The prescription for Paracetamol is often used as a metaphor for ineffective treatment.

> *Dulce:* They [health care providers] are less interested in the patient and the treatments are not that effective. Here they give general treatment to everyone. They prescribe Paracetamol for everything and not everyone needs that.

Some Cape Verdeans realise that the generalised, dismissive and inappropriate 'Paracetamol treatment' can be replaced by more appropriate treatments. This, however, entails the ability to convince health professionals of the 'genuineness' of their complaints and need for care.

> *Judite:* The first times I went to see my current doctor he was difficult. Even when my children needed examinations.... In Portugal, if you feel something, the doctors immediately send you to a specialist. Here you need to go to the doctor several times and talk to him very seriously and explain that you are not feeling well.

The need to prove your complaints is interpreted as a direct confrontation with one's integrity, credibility, and legitimacy as a patient. When they eventually succeed in entering the health care system they are confronted by the compartmentalisation and fragmentation that characterises the Dutch health care system.

> *Miguel:* Sometimes the doctor will examine your problem. And
> sometimes the causes are not easy to find. This is an important
> issue in the case of doctors in the Netherlands and Cape Verde.
> In Cape Verde a doctor does everything. [...] But in the Nether-
> lands you have to go to a variety of doctors.

Miguel considers this specialisation time-consuming. It breaks down
the experience of bodily, biographical and social integrity and comes
with an annoying bureaucracy.

A way to bypass the system's gatekeepers consists of accessing health
care via the so-called 'American by-pass', which is used by many immigrants in the western world (Bhui and Bhugra 2002). They access the
more specialised services or emergency services directly, or end up receiving health care via the criminal justice system. It is based on re-
quests for instant-help, in escalating or multiproblem situations, often
coupled with interventions and mediation of non-mental health professionals (e.g., police). What is considered an irregular way of accessing
health care in one country, however, may be perfectly normal in another, as we will see later.

The difficulties people encounter in the health care system are sometimes attributed to a lack of knowledge or information, but are often
perceived as inadequacies in the 'quality of care'. Health care providers
in the Netherlands are depicted by many Cape Verdeans as non-atten-
tive, conditional, ineffective, generalizing, and dismissive. In their opinion, a good doctor is someone skilled, with prompt and problem-sol-
ving expertise, who has good communication skills (alert, personal,
takes the time, is caring and supportive) and who centers his/her medical practice on the patient (reaches out, is protective and focuses on the
patient's goals) (Freitas 2006).

We found that the most important breaches in communication concerning health care are found at an interpersonal level (between doctors and patients), but also at an institutional level where regulations,
intentions and orientations of health care are misunderstood (Beijers
2005). Furthermore, problems also occur at an interpretative and affec-
tive level: is there insufficient mutual understanding and insufficient
relationship building? The moral or social dimensions of problems are
left unattended. Doctors are no longer perceived as undisputed experts
or social authorities. And they feel they are not accountable for treating
the social dimension of health problems. Health care is transforming
social suffering into illnesses and diagnoses, while often denying the
social and moral origins and implications of the suffering. Feelings of
rejection, vulnerability and discredit emerge among patients, clearly
undermining the establishment of good relationships with health care

and its professionals thus reinforcing their perceived lack of legitimacy as people needing care.

Is the development of medical citizenship an instrument to counter this? Kickbusch et al. (2005) define reflexivity as one of the key features of health literacy, which refers to the skills necessary to deal with the instability of the conditions and presuppositions of the health care sector. This reflexivity can evolve into an ideologically driven strategy to change the dominant way in which a health condition is understood and treated. This is not just a process of personal emancipation but also involves the participation of users in mental health care, and of community-empowerment in which immigrants regain control over their bodies and rethink biomedical treatments so that migration, culture and their everyday social circumstances are considered factors of relevance.

Transnational health care seeking

Historically, solutions to the problems of people in Cape Verde have more rapidly emerged from within the local community and the diaspora than from the nation-state. During colonial times, Portugal often neglected the Cape Verdeans in periods of severe need (Meintel 1984; Patterson 1988; Lobban 1995) and diasporic solidarity (e.g., remittances) remains an indispensable resource for the republic to this very day. Following a two-century-long history of migration (Meintel 1983) virtually every Cape Verdean resident has contact with relatives and friends around the world, which is maintained more easily nowadays with the help of cheap transport and new communication technologies.

These transnational connections maintain personal relationships and provide alternative 'systems of reference'. Contrary to the examples of other migrant communities (Messias 2002; Murphy and Mahalingam 2004), transnational health care seeking is not limited to the home country, but spans across numerous countries of the diaspora. This deterritorialised perspective regarding health and health care use is astutely expressed by Manuel.

> In Cape Verde there are doctors that speak our own language but health has no borders. When a person has a health problem and seeks help there are no borders. If you know there are good doctors in Switzerland you go there. If you are in Portugal and you hear that there are better doctors in Spain, you go to Spain. When you're searching for health care there are no borders. You go where you have to.

Dulce, a 54-year-old Cape Verdean woman who had lived in Portugal and in France before settling in the Netherlands, discusses her experiences with illness and health care.

> In Portugal, I had to make an appointment for the specialist... sometimes that would take a month before I got my consultation. In France, I could see the doctor immediately. One month is long enough for me to make it a crisis. I know my symptoms very well and I know if I need to see the specialist directly. [...] Here [the Netherlands] I always have to go to the family doctor [GP]. I cannot decide by myself to go directly to the specialist. [...] When I feel I'm about to have a crisis because of my illness [sickle cell anemia] I go there. Sometimes I don't even go to the doctor here. If I'm well enough I get on a plane and go to the doctor in France. I can make a direct appointment with the specialist there. [...] I need to do a lot. I need to go to the dentist but I'm not doing it here. I'm waiting until I can go to France. [...] I still pay for my social security in France and I'm entitled to care there. I won't stop paying it because here I can't get the care I need. So I'll take my time and take care of my health there.

In seeking health care in the Netherlands, Dulce was confronted with the need to negotiate a referral to a specialist with her general practitioner (GP). The diagnosis of a chronic illness at an early age, however, has turned her into an expert regarding her illness and different sorts of health systems and professionals. She deliberately chose the French system of care because specialised services can be accessed more rapidly. This alternative pathway enables Dulce to articulate her right to take control of the management of her illness. By maximizing her transnational resources she is able to bypass the 'Paracetamol treatment', reaffirming her legitimacy as a patient and, ultimately, reasserting her state of well-being.

Resources from which advice or help is sought span a broader spectrum than merely the care provided by registered doctors. References are made to the transnational use of medication, requesting social support and care from family members, and consulting complementary healers.

A social support and presence was reported by Lucinda who recounts how her mother took her back to Cape Verde.

> I came here in 1982, but then I had some problems. My mother visited me on holiday and when she saw I was in a bad state, she took me back to Cape Verde. [...] I was ill and had problems with my brother, so my mother preferred taking me with her....

[In the Netherlands I had] psychological problems, many problems I couldn't solve.... I couldn't speak the language. I couldn't talk, was not able to use a bus or subway and didn't know where other Cape Verdeans lived. In Cape Verde, I received help from my family and a doctor, and they gave me medication. After that they sent me to a mental health facility [...] in Santiago. [...] But there [in Cape Verde] I had other problems such as poverty. When I returned there in 1982, I completely collapsed. My mother brought me back against my will and when I saw all these bare mountains and kids without proper clothing, I broke down. I have been back in Europe for four years now.

Lucinda's story reveals how transnational pathways to health are not always a positive and voluntary choice. Family members intervene in an assertive way, and success is not always guaranteed. Lucinda found herself hovering between different loyalties, unable to make a choice.

The use of transnational medicines constitutes another strategy. Marta describes how this process is put into practice. Given her legal constraints that prevented her from leaving the Netherlands because of her debts, she resorts to medication found in other countries.

When I had an abortion they said my ovaries weren't well but the doctor here always claims there's nothing wrong. I take medicines from Portugal and they help me sleep and eat. But if I take a pill today I feel pain in my ovaries tomorrow. No one prescribed this medicine... but many people take it. Almost all Cape Verdeans use it. It helps you with everything. If you have problems and you are angry, you can take it and you will sleep well. I asked a friend to get it for me in Portugal. I have been aware of it since I lived in Cape Verde.

These medicines are taken without medical supervision. They are validated by their common use among Cape Verdeans and the general appreciation of Portuguese health care, which is seen as reliable and familiar. Besides this aspect of familiarity and acquaintance, the need for additional and more holistic explanations of health problems can also play an important role in the choosing of care. Helena consulted a Brazilian doctor in Paris. He is a *vidente* or a clairvoyant doctor: 'He treats you in a totally different way. [...] When I came in he looked at me and told me: you suffer from itchiness, cold feet and a feeble mind.'

Cape Verdeans in Rotterdam organise bus trips on a monthly basis to see this doctor in Paris. *Curandeiros* are also consulted in Portugal, in Cape Verde or in France. The use of these transnational strategies – even when this is only feasible through indirect channels such as the 'importation' of medicine – signifies the determination of trying to assure good health and a refusal to comply with the limited medical citizenship encountered in the Netherlands. This dedication and the pathways used are the result of both individually and collectively organised initiatives. When Cape Verdeans are unable to travel abroad, due to their limited incomes, debilitating illnesses, legal constraints to free movement, inability to navigate foreign health care systems, or less resourceful networks abroad, the importing of 'good doctors' to the Netherlands emerges as a viable strategy to ensure better health care. Doctor 'Joep', a Belgian doctor, used to visit the Cape Verdean community in Rotterdam regularly. People would wait in line at his residence. He died recently. Consulting these traveling doctors or healers is not coincidental, but is considered a highly valued form of alternative care, which is not even discouraged by the uncertainty regarding reimbursements and continuity of care.

Resorting to transnational health care, nevertheless, has some drawbacks. Additional resources have to be available: knowledge about the intricacies of foreign health systems, travel planning, leaves from work, and financial resources. These demands are met in various ways, i.e., through the maintenance of previous health insurance policies, by keeping spare money for emergency situations or by soliciting financial help. The occurence of 'emergency' situations is unpredictable. If they occur often enough they can pose a real financial burden that can be difficult to overcome, leading to debts and placing one's subsistence at stake. Concerns emanating from these situations are often referred to as an important source of psychosocial distress. As Dulce pointed out, she is sometimes forced to postpone necessary treatment.

Social networks are the prime facilitators of support and have contributed to the formulation and enforcement of life strategies, which are not restricted by the borders of the home or receiving countries, but may arise in other social spaces of the diaspora. Potential solutions to health problems can be found in a variety of sources, which frequently stretch across a number of countries. The participants in our studies made it clear that when they seek health care, what matters most is quality, and not so much geography or politics. Transnational health care resources broaden the scope of treatment choices for participants, allowing the re-establishment of autonomy and agency in selecting care. They bolster self-confidence and reaffirm one's legitimacy as a patient. However, they contribute to a persistent distance from one's local health care services, inhibiting the acquisition of the necessary skills needed to navigate the health care system.

Conclusions

As in other Western countries, medical citizenship in the Netherlands is conceptualised and expected to be exercised within a biomedical approach to health and ill-health, regulated by the state together with increasingly powerful market forces. Although entitlement to 'alternative' health care has not been entirely ruled out, its access is dependant on the knowledge, lobbying skills and pressure exerted by users and of a complex process of negotiation with insurance companies. The circumstances in which 'care-dealing' occurs emphasise the ever-more visible paradox between the directives for promotion of demand-oriented care, which implies individualisation, and directives for the maximisation of available resources and efficiency, which imply standardisation. Furthermore, it highlights the need for the 'citizen in health' to become both a managerial and entrepreneurial actor (Scourfield 2005).

As we have shown, Cape Verdeans' explanations of health and ill-health differ significantly from the dominant biomedical framework, particularly where psychosocial distress is concerned. Their Christian-spiritual repertoire of health beliefs encompasses multiple pathways to health, often employed in syncretic fashion, and ranges from formal health care to complementary medicine (bypassing statutory access paths to health care) and transnational health care seeking. The medical citizenship granted in the Netherlands accommodates only one of these pathways – formal care according to a biomedical model. It does not permit a holistic approach to health care needs.

Within this context, Cape Verdeans' limited access to formal health care becomes of striking concern. Restricted access to formal care tends to undermine the full exercise of medical citizenship, which makes the access to good quality care problematic. The outcome of these mutually reinforcing processes of exclusion is not dismissal without treatment but rather the provision of treatments perceived as inappropriate (e.g., the 'Paracetamol treatment'). This form of exclusion is particularly hazardous. Although less visible and palpable than full exclusion (after all, 'treatment' is not denied), the responsibility for negotiating change, creating alternatives and enforcing one's rights becomes more easily transferable and ascribable to the individual in need of care. By providing a 'treatment', albeit one perceived as inadequate, the system ensures the achievement of what it is liable for – producing a potentially appropriate response.

The emancipation and 'proto-professionalisation' (Swaan 1990) of users thus become essential characteristics for the attainment of rights and good quality care. The development of these characteristics and the exercise of medical citizenship are directly linked to the accessibility of care and to the mastery of two fundamental and interrelated tools –

health literacy and user participation. Neither of these tools is sufficiently within the reach of Cape Verdeans in the Netherlands. Health literacy appears low as a consequence of the underprivileged socio-economic position of many Cape Verdeans, the limited amount of information available to the local community, and the relatively limited interaction with other ethnic groups in the host country. User participation is increasing but remains weak. The lobbying for customised care by and for the Cape Verdean community is thus consistently overshadowed by the interests of other, more vocal, groups. The incorporation of the roles of consumers, voters and social actors, advisable and expected within the health society (Kickbusch 2004), is thus highly compromised among many Cape Verdeans and with it the maintenance of their health.

This is particularly dramatic in an age where public health responsibilities are being massively transferred to the individual (Scourfield 2005). The over-valued independence and entrepreneurship (reinforced by the erosion of solidarity and marginalisation of people who are ill) are, for the most part, only within the reach of influential segments of post-modern health societies: unhealthy citizens are increasingly likely to become underprivileged, quasi-citizens. These developments appear linked to public health authority concerns and strategies for promoting efficient health care. Yet, their overall effects must not go unnoticed: equity is being increasingly 'sacrificed for efficacy' (Farmer 1999). Inequalities and limited access to good quality health care and medical citizenship are not characteristic of disadvantaged migrant groups alone. They are not solely due to ethnicity but spill over these boundaries and affect the poor, less-literate, gender-disadvantaged, stigmatised and racially discriminated segments of Europe's contemporary societies. The realisation of, and intervention in, the socio-economic foundations of health problems are essential if exclusion is to be tackled rather than reproduced and social suffering combated rather than perpetuated.

Recent developments in health-related European Community law have granted European citizens the right to seek health care in other member states when treatment options are lacking in the home country (Commission of the European Communities 2004). The Cape Verdeans in the Netherlands constitute a good example of the 'new' mobile health citizens, although still in an informal context. To counteract the increasing risks of health deterioration imposed by limited access to care and sustained by limited medical citizenship in the host country, Cape Verdeans resort to transnational spheres of social support that assist them in accessing good quality care. This strategy demonstrates their perseverance in ensuring a state of well-being, thus fully incorporating their individual responsibility as 'citizens in health'. It also displays the failure of the Dutch health system in enabling system navigation facilitations suited to guiding the whole of its multicultural population equally through the maze of health service provision.

One final consideration regards the dualistic nature of transnational networks of support in terms of their outcomes on the promotion of medical citizenship. While visiting a health professional in a foreign country might allow Cape Verdean users to reassert their legitimacy as patients and control the management of their illness, it can nevertheless place a barrier before the realisation of medical citizenship in the host country. Transnational health care use, when perceived as the only reliable treatment option, can lead to a significant decrease in contact with Dutch health care services. This impairs the acquisition of fundamental skills to learn about and figure out the local system. Participation and health literacy run the very real danger of remaining dormant, and with them the development of customised health care alternatives and the full exercise of medical citizenship.

Notes

[1] Scheper-Hughes (2004: 69) defines medical citizenship as the increasing awareness and claims made by health care users and user advocacy groups of their rights as citizens and as medical consumers to free access to medical information, to informed decision making regarding the participation in experimental drug-testing procedures, and to control over one's treatment regime and over the management of one's illness and death.

[2] We use Nichter's definition of psychosocial distress as 'a broad range of feeling states including vulnerability, apprehension, inadequacy, dissatisfaction, suppressed anger, and other anxiety states which might otherwise take the form of other untenable social conflict or rebellion' (1981: 403).

References

Abraham, J.; Lewis, G. (2002) 'Citizenship, Medical Expertise and the Capitalist Regulatory State in Europe'. *Sociology* 36(1): 67-88.

Beijers, H. (2004a) 'Onderscheiden wat van God komt'. *Maandblad Geestelijke volksgezondheid* 59(1): 71-75.

Beijers, H. (2004b) *People with a Mission: Meanings of Psychosocial Distress of Cape Verdeans in the Netherlands.* Amsterdam: University of Amsterdam.

Beijers, H. (2005) Within the Cape Verdean Community You Always Come to a Solution: Meanings of Psychosocial Distress and Experiences with Mental Health Care of Cape Verdean Immigrants in the Netherlands. Paper presented at the International Conference on Cape Verdean Migration and Diaspora, Lisbon, ISCTE/CEAS, April 6-8.

Bhugra, D. (1996) 'Religion and Mental Health', in *Psychiatry and Religion, Context, Consensus and Controversies,* D. Bhugra (ed.), New York: Routledge, pp. 1-4.

Bhui, K.; Bhugra, D. (2002) 'Explanatory Models for Mental Distress: Implications for Clinical Practice and Research'. *The British Journal of Psychiatry* 181(1):6-7.

Cabral, N.E. (1979) 'Notes sur le catholicisme aux îles du Cap-Vert'. *Revue française d'études politiques africaines* 14(165-66): 108-117.

Cabral, N.E. (1980) *Le moulin et le pilon, les Îles de Cap-Vert*. Paris: l'Harmattan – ACCT.

Chrisman, N.J. (1980) 'The Health Seeking Process: An Approach to the Natural History of Ilness'. *Culture, Medicine and Psychiatry* 1(4): 351-377.

Commission of the European Communities (2004) *Communication from the Commission – Follow up to the High Level Reflection Process on Patient Mobility and Healthcare Developments in the European Union*. Brussels: Commission of the European Communities.

Dieperink, C.J.; van Dijk, R.; Wierdsma, A.I. (2002) 'GGZ voor allochtonen. Ontwikkelingen in het zorggebruik in de regio Rotterdam, 1990-1998'. *Maandblad Geestelijke volksgezondheid* 57(1): 87-98.

Farmer, P. (1999) 'Pathologies of Power: Rethinking Health and Human Rights'. *American Journal of Public Health* 89(10): 1486-96.

Freitas, C. de (2006) *Em Busca de Um Bom Médico: Quando a Saúde Não Tem Fronteiras. Percepções dos Cabo-verdianos Sobre profissionais de Saúde na Holanda*. Lisbon: Alto-Comissariado para a Imigração e Minorias Étnicas.

Geertz, C. (1973) 'Religion as a Cultural System', in *The Interpretation of Cultures: Selected Essays*, C. Geertz, New York: Basic Books, pp. 87-125.

Graça, A.A. da (1999) *Een nieuwe horizon, een onderzoek naar de organisatorische dynamiek van Kaapverdianen in Nederland*. Amsterdam: University of Amsterdam.

Graça, A.A. da (2005) Associativismo Cabo-Verdeano em Roterdão e Integração Política. Paper presented at the International Conference on Cape Verdean Migration and Diaspora, Lisbon, ISCTE/CEAS, April 6-8.

Horta, A.P.B.; Malheiros, J. (2005) Social Capital and Migrants' Political Integration: The Case Study of Capeverdean Associations in the Region of Lisbon. Paper presented at the International Conference on Cape Verdean Migration and Diaspora, Lisbon, ISCTE/CEAS, April 6-8.

Huiskamp, N.; Vis, H.; Swart, W.; Voorham, T. (2000) *Gezondheid in Kaart Allochtonen, gezondheidsproblemen en preventiemogelijkheden in kaart gebracht*. Rotterdam: GGD Rotterdam en omstreken.

Kickbusch, I. (2004) 'Health and Citizenship: The Characteristics of 21st Century Health'. *World Hospitals and Health Services* 40(4): 12-14.

Kickbusch, I; Maag, D.; Saan, H. (2005) Enabling Healthy Choices in Modern Health Societies. Background Paper, European Health Forum 2005, Gastein, 5-8 October.

Kleinman, A. (1988) *Rethinking Psychiatry: From Cultural Category to Personal Experience*. New York: The Free Press/MacMillan.

Kleinman, A. (2005a) *Culture and Psychiatric Diagnosis and Treatment: What Are the Necessary Therapeutic Skills?* Utrecht: Trimbos-Instituut.

Kleinman, A. (2005b) 'Tussen lichaam en samenleving: de sociale en politieke wortels van ziekte en lijden'. *CMG* 2(1): 2-9.

Krikke, H.; van Dijk, R.; Beijers, H. (2000) *Thuis is, waar de ander is. Allochtone cliënten in de geestelijke gezondheidszorg en de cliëntenbeweging*. Rotterdam: Basisberaad GGZ.

Like, R.; Ellison, J. (1981) 'Sleeping Blood, Tremor and Paralysis: A Trans-cultural Approach to an Unusual Conversion Reaction'. *Culture, Medicine & Psychiatry* 5(1): 49-63.

Lobban, R. (1995) *Cape Verde: Crioulo Colony to Independent Nation*. Boulder, CO: Westview Press.

Matos, L. de (1986) *Het Christelijk Rationalisme*, Eerste Nederlandse uitgave. Rio de Janeiro/Rotterdam: Centro Redentor.

Meintel, D. (1983) 'Cape Verdean-Americans', in *Hidden Minorities: The Persistence of Ethnicity in American Life*, J.H. Rollins (ed.), Washington D.C.: University Press of America, pp. 236-56.

Meintel, D. (1984) *Race, Culture and Portuguese Colonialism in Cape Verde*. Syracuse, NY: Syracuse University.

Messias, D.K.H. (2002) 'Transnational Health Resources, Practices, and Perspectives: Brazilian Immigrant Women's Narratives'. *Journal of Immigrant Health* 4(4): 183-200.

Murphy, E.J.; Mahalingam, R. (2004) 'Transnational Ties and Mental Health of Caribbean Immigrants'. *Journal of Immigrant Health* 6(4): 167-178.

Nichter, M. (1981) 'Idioms of Distress: Alternatives in the Expression of Psychosocial Distress: A Case Study from South India'. *Culture, Medicine & Psychiatry* 5(4): 379-408.

Oro, A.P.; Semán, P. (2001) 'Brazilian Pentecostalism Crosses National Borders', in *Between Babel and Pentecost*, A. Corten and R. Marshall-Fratani (eds.), London: Hurst and Company, pp. 181-196.

Patterson, K.D. (1988) 'Epidemics, Famines and the Population in the Cape Verdean Islands, 1580-1800'. *International Journal of African Historical Studies* 21(2): 291-313.

Rose, N. (2001) 'The Politics of Life Itself'. *Theory, Culture & Society* 18(6): 1-30.

Scheper-Hughes, N. (2004) 'Parts Unknown: Undercover Ethnography of the Organs-trafficking Underworld'. *Ethnography* 5(1): 29-73.

Scourfield, P. (2007) 'Social Care and the Modern Citizen: Client, Consumer, Service User, Manager and Entrepreneur'. *British Journal of Social Work* 37(1): 107-122.

Silva, A. (1997) *Heimwee naar het eigene: de werkelijkheid achter de zoektocht van de Kaapverdianen naar de 'eigen identiteit'*. Doctoraalscriptie, Amsterdam: Faculteit der Sociaal-Culturele Wetenschappen, Vrije Universiteit Amsterdam.

Swaan, A. de (1990) *The Management of Normality: Critical Essays in Health and Welfare*. London: Routledge.

Vasconcelos, J. (2004) 'Espíritos Lusófonos numa Ilha Crioula: Língua, Poder e Identidade em São Vicente de Cabo Verde', in *A Persistência da História: Passado e Contemporaneidade em África*, C. Carvalho and J. de Pina-Cabral (orgs.), Lisbon: Imprensa de Ciências Sociais, pp. 149-190.

Vasconcelos, J. (2005) 'Langue des esprits et esprit de São Vicente (îles du Cape-Vert)'. *Terrain* 44: 109-124.

Wimmer, A.; Schiller, N.G. (2002) 'Methodological Nationalism and Beyond: Nation-state Building, Migration and the Social Sciences'. *Global Networks* 2(4): 301-334.

Chapter 19
Cape Verdean Diasporic Identity Formation

Gina Sánchez Gibau

Diasporic communities traverse the two or more states to which they belong, which they influence, and which reproduce them. This bipolar identity is the cornerstone of the diasporic experience. (Laguerre 1998: 9)

The importance of the concept of 'diaspora' as an explanatory paradigm stems from its malleable qualities given that it can apply to diverse communities. Dissociated from the historical experiences of a defined group of people, it becomes a universal nomenclature applicable to displaced groups of people. (Barkan and Shelton 1998: 5)

The concept of the African diaspora has its intellectual roots in traditional Pan-Africanist activities conducted in the U.S., the U.K. and in the Caribbean during the 19th century. Since that time, theories of the African diaspora include both support and criticism of the idea of Africa as the primary site of identity formation (Appiah 1992; Drake 1982; Gilroy 1993; Gordon 1998; Padmore 1956). The evolution of the literature ranges from past conceptualisations of the African diaspora as a conglomerate with traceable ties to Africa, to more recent attempts at de-essentializing this connection in order to analyze and emphasise the African diaspora as a dynamic process. The Cape Verdean diaspora population in Boston exemplifies both of these theoretical and political trends.

This chapter examines the concepts of diaspora, race, ethnicity and culture as intellectual frameworks through which to understand Cape Verdean diasporic identity formation. These concepts serve as analytical tools that reveal how Cape Verdeans define the parameters of their 'racial' and 'ethnic' identities while simultaneously constructing multiple ideas of what constitutes 'Cape Verdeanness.' This process of diasporic identity formation is complicated by the fact that Boston's Cape Verdean diaspora community is decidedly fragmented at this moment in time. The community is divided, in generational terms, into Cape Verdean and Cape Verdean-American segments that have a limited amount of contact with each other. Situating Cape Verdeans within the context of the larger African diaspora, as 'Black transnationals', illustrates their historical, social, political and economic experiences in the U.S.

Defining diasporas

The concept of diaspora is often characterised in terms of the phenomenon of displacement. In the popular imagination, diasporas are conceived as communities that emerge as a result of forced expulsions from a particular place of origin. This place or 'homeland' is believed to remain ever present within the collective consciousness of the diaspora community. Theoretical work examining the formation of diasporas tends to focus upon the impact that dispersal, relocation, and historical memory have on the development of transnational identities (Brah 1996; Clifford 1994; Cohen 1996; Gilroy 1993; Gopinath 1995; Helmreich 1992; Safran 1991; Scott 1991).

Geographical dispersion as a defining feature of modern diasporas can be understood in terms of what Marshall Sahlins (1985) calls a 'structure of conjuncture', an historical event or moment that occurs which facilitates social change and alters the course of cultural history thereafter. For the African diaspora of the Americas, this defining moment has been identified as the tragic Middle Passage, the historical memory of which links people of African descent to a common experience of slavery and racial terror across space and through time. An emphasis on the processes involved in the formation of African diasporic populations is analytically useful in the study of identity politics, racial formation, and community, especially as it pertains to the Cape Verdean diaspora.

For the Cape Verdean diaspora, the event of physical displacement is multidimensional. Perhaps the most significant defining moments were the initial migrations that occurred via the whaling industry. Relocation was also predicated on the forced labour migrations to São Tomé and Príncipe. Finally, significant movements occurred during the 19th and 20th centuries as Cape Verdeans sought to improve their socioeconomic conditions by migrating to Europe, Latin America and the U.S. in search of employment. The common experience of relocation serves as a basis for solidarity among Cape Verdeans in different locations, and even different countries. They are conjured up in casual conversations and in traditional songs as a means of connecting one's life experience to that of all Cape Verdeans. The trope of departure – of leaving *nha terra* (my homeland) – is evoked as a defining moment in the development of Cape Verdean diasporic peoplehood.

The concept of diaspora also encompasses a myth of return to the homeland. The return is considered mythical precisely because it is an illusive prospect. Diasporic populations usually cannot return to the homeland due to the persistence of poor ecological, economic and political conditions. As a result, they are relegated to 'dwelling-in-displacement' within a particular 'host' society (Clifford 1994). Yet, modern diasporas are distinguishable on the basis of continued contact with and/or interest in the homeland (see Carling 1997; Laguerre 1998; Safran 1991). Michel Laguerre qualifies diasporas further, characterising those who maintain actual ties to the homeland as an 'active diaspora', and a 'passive diaspora' as one that maintains only symbolic ties (1998:8).

With respect to the Cape Verdean diaspora, there exist both active and passive components, with some descendants of earlier Cape Verdean migrants retaining a symbolic connection to the islands. Although they may not have been born there nor have ever visited, Cape Verde is still revered as an imagined homeland to be claimed. Similar to African-Americans visiting the continent of Africa for the first time, Cape Verdean-Americans, after experiencing the initial culture shock involving contact with a population from which they are several generations removed, often experience a homecoming feeling upon first visiting the islands. Other Cape Verdean-Americans have attempted to engage in social and economic development projects in the islands, albeit with great frustration. More recent Cape Verdean immigrants in the U.S., on the other hand, may speak to their relatives by phone on a weekly basis. Others send money 'home' on a monthly basis. Still others arrange to have their relatives flown in from Cape Verde at least once a year. Whether maintaining an 'active' or 'passive' connection, Cape Verdeans still conceptualise the Cape Verde Islands as a defining cultural symbol in their identity construction.

Given that the present state of international migration is dictated by economic trends within an increasingly globalised marketplace, the concept of diaspora can no longer be conceived solely in terms of ties to a homeland or geographical dispersion. 'Diaspora' must now be understood in relation to local and global phenomena, whereby the 'here' and 'there' are no longer mutually exclusive but are in constant dialogue. With the improvement of airline transportation and communications via telephone and the Internet, contemporary diasporic populations now have a greater opportunity to maintain actual ties to the homeland than their predecessors. Diaspora, then, is now conceived as including less-than static movements or relocations, such as that of migrant workers, immigrants, refugees, asylum seekers, exiles, deportees and other marginalised citizens (Safran 1991). Moreover, it does not

preclude a definite forced dispersal. It is at once a voluntary and involuntary formation.

Laguerre utilises the term 'dispersed nation' to define a diaspora as a
transnational community – a nation of people constructed beyond the
confines of a territorialised nation-state or homeland (1998: 8). Diasporic populations can therefore be understood as straddling both the
home and host societies, as belonging and not belonging. The Cape
Verdean diaspora is one among many populations who acquire this
type of nationalistic 'double consciousness' (Du Bois 1903). This is the
case not only for the newer arrivals but also for those born on the islands and who have been living in the U.S. for the past fifteen to
twenty years. These Cape Verdeans are simultaneously attached to two
societies. They are living and participating members of the American
system and yet they still refer to Cape Verde as their home. Many Cape
Verdeans, for example, have told me of their desire to return 'home'
once they retire from their jobs here in the U.S. Laguerre refers to
these more transnational migrants as 'sojourners' who often 'return
home and use their money and social capital to help themselves and
others in their homeland' (1998: 7). The U.S., then, is understood as a
home-away-from-home in the minds of Cape Verdean-born members
of the diaspora.

The commonsense understanding of the African diaspora has been
criticised for essentialising a common African ancestry (i.e., African
blood) and ties to an African homeland (i.e., the homeland). In actual-
ity, the African diaspora is much more complex than mere geography
and genealogy may dictate. Appiah (1992), Gilroy (1993), Clifford
(1994), among others, offer alternative conceptualisations of the African diaspora that emphasise the historical and cultural processes involved in the formation of new and dynamic collectivities. This perspective of the African diaspora serves as a critical tool through which
to explore globally and in historical perspective the mobility of labour,
the development of transnational networks, and the social construction
of identities among people of African descent.

Although postmodern critics do not give primacy to Africa as a site
of imagination for the African diaspora, Africa, nevertheless, serves as
an important aspect of diaspora consciousness for some African-des-
cended groups. Emphasis on the role that Africa plays in historical
memory also highlights the particularity of subjectivities and experiences, which can often be obscured by general conceptualisations of
diasporic identity that privilege multiple identities and hybrid cultures.
The African diaspora experience is very different from that of the
Southeast Asian diaspora, for example. This revised model of the African diaspora is useful for theorizing Cape Verdean identity formation

as a contemporary Black social formation that takes place within the confines of the U.S.

Diaspora as an 'imagined community'

In the last two decades, theorists have relied heavily on Benedict Anderson's (1991) concept of imagined community to understand the processes by which a social group becomes a community (Alonso 1988, 1994; Brow 1990; Brueggemann 1995; Cohen 1985; Gillis 1994). Anderson's imagined community is one in which a group of people share a sense of connectedness, yet 'may never know most of their fellow-members' (1991: 6). Although Anderson originally invoked the term in his interpretation of the nation as a politically derived, historically specific community, an imagined community is still useful as a concept through which to understand the dynamics of various communities enjoined by a sense of belonging together (Brow 1990: 1).

Defining diasporas as imagined communities involves the idea of a community sharing a collective, historical memory as embedded and embodied in social practice. Perhaps the best example that can be offered to illustrate this sense of connectedness in relation to Cape Verdeans is the Smithsonian's 1995 Festival of American Folklife. One of the featured programs that year was devoted to Cape Verdean and Cape Verdean American culture. Cape Verdeans from various parts of the world felt an overwhelming sense of nostalgia and euphoria as they converged onto the national mall and interacted with each other. Cape Verdean Americans cried as they hugged islanders who only spoke Kriolu. Although this scene may appear overly romanticised, it is nevertheless an unexaggerated example of how the Cape Verdean diaspora has expressed this sense of imagined community.

The marker of heritage itself plays a tremendous role in the construction of Cape Verdean identity. A person can be accepted almost automatically as a member of the community by virtue of his/her Cape Verdean parentage. Similarly, two Cape Verdeans from different states may experience an acute sense of connectedness upon meeting each other for the first time, especially if they meet in a locale where Cape Verdeans are in the minority. This was the case for my uncle who experienced a chance meeting with a Cape Verdean man who resembled his cousin at the airport in Amsterdam. After closely scrutinizing each other, the two men attempted to engage in a dialogue – my uncle speaking French and the Cape Verdean man speaking in Kriolu – about island ancestry. Indeed, this is a common practice among diasporic Cape Verdeans attempting to delineate (and often finding) kinship connections.

The role of historical memory

For many diasporic populations, Cape Verdeans included, a sense of community has meant a belief in essentialised notions of common (biological) origin, homeland, language and cultural traditions that define the ties that bind. The commonsense aspect of communalisation is often manifested in cultural practices that evoke sentiments of the past in the present. The concept of diaspora illustrates the way in which the imagining of community is linked to the idea of that community sharing a collective, historical memory.

John and Jean Comaroff (1987) have focused on the unique histori-cal, social, political and economic experiences of groups that aid in the reconstruction of individual and collective consciousness. The Comar-offs define 'practical consciousness' as 'an active process in which ac-tors deploy historically salient cultural categories to construct self-awareness' (1987: 205). In other words, self-awareness is constructed through the commonsense recollections of the past upon which people rely to construct themselves as members of a present collectivity.

Historical memory, then, plays an integral role in the formation of a sense of peoplehood. Historical memory involves a reinvention of the past, 'mythical' or otherwise, through present reinterpretation. How-ever, the past as grasped through memory 'is always subject to selective retention, innocent amnesia, and tendentious re-interpretation' (Brow 1990: 3). In reconstructing the past, many people tend to highlight cer-tain aspects while obscuring others (Alonso 1988: 39). This is often re-ferred to as 'selective amnesia' or conscious or unconscious remember-ing and/or forgetting (Frisch 1981: 12).

Commemorations, on the other hand, as practices that illuminate the intersection of history and memory, are considered to be conscious efforts 'to limit forgetfulness' (Fabre and O'Meally 1994: 7; see also Gil-lis 1994). Remembering the past involves not only conscious and un-conscious selective amnesia, but also a degree of accuracy that is often altered by embellishment and fiction. As John Gillis notes, 'we are con-stantly revising our memories to suit our current identities' (1994: 3).

The dispersed nation

The concept of transnationalism places the experience of immigration at its center, and has a particular relevance to African diasporic identity formation. In describing the Haitian diaspora of New York City, La-guerre employs the term 'diasporic nationalism' – 'the public or domes-tic patriotic expression of attachment that immigrants exhibit for the homeland' (1998: 60). Cape Verdeans in Boston also exhibit diasporic nationalism in various ways. For Cape Verdean-Americans, this connection to Cape Verde is visually expressed through the 'I'm Cape Verdean' flag-embossed bumper sticker on their cars. For Cape Verdean immigrants, this transnational patriotism is illustrated in their listening to the local radio program that broadcasts the news from Cape Verde in Portuguese and/or Kriolu. The existence of diaspora populations in post-industrial states reconfigures the nation as comprised of multiple nations, or as irrevocably transnational.

However, self-identification is often complicated by the capacity of nation-states to construct social categories and identities for its citizens (Alonso 1988; Menchaca 1993; Woost 1993). Foster makes note of the way in which the state exerts its power as a natural condition of everyday life, thereby rendering individuals and groups as imagined constituents of a community or nation, 'even if their place [within that community/nation] is one of subordination and exploitation' (1991: 247). The same can be said of Portuguese colonial rule in the Cape Verde Islands and its other colonies for some 500 years.

Paulo Freire and Donaldo Macedo (1987) note how colonisation affects the worldview of subjugated peoples, defining what is acceptable behaviour, and how it fashions one's tastes in clothes, food and other social aspects of life. The internalisation of colonial oppression and simultaneous acquisition of upward social mobility led lighter-skinned, privileged Cape Verdeans, some of whom served as administrators in mainland colonies, to identify more with the Portuguese than with the Africans. While 'racial democracy' exalted racial miscegenation for obliterating racial distinctions, it simultaneously promoted whiteness as the social and physiological ideal. Thus, the colonial legacy of Cape Verde created a concomitant legacy of the promotion of one's Portuguese heritage over one's African heritage (Meintel 1984; Batalha 2004).

The resultant social hierarchy in Cape Verde during its colonial era delineated a myriad of social distinctions based on a combination of ancestry, phenotype, skin tone, social class status, and island of origin. Such distinctions were manifested in status-differentiating behaviours exhibited by various sectors of society. Internal differentiation is also evident in contemporary island stereotypes. People from Fogo are considered more 'hot-headed' or 'fiery' (fogo is Portuguese for fire). Brava, on the other hand, is lauded for its beautiful, light-skinned women and soft-spoken men. Yet, many Cape Verdeans still contend today that social class status is the main marker of difference on the islands. Several Cape Verdeans have indicated this to me, stating that racism does not exist in Cape Verde, but discrimination based on class is indeed a common phenomenon.

Since some Cape Verdeans today still refer to themselves as Portuguese, practice Catholicism as do Portuguese-Americans, speak Portuguese (in formal settings), and have similar cultural traditions as Portuguese-Americans, they are often defined as more culturally congruent with the Portuguese. Yet, the experiences of Cape Verdeans living in the U.S. reveal that their identities are often articulated as a composite of racial and ethnic categories.

Racialisation does not happen without some input from immigrant groups. Initially, there may be resistance to the system of racial classification ascribing them a particular label. In such instances, immigrant groups hold steadfast to their nationalist identity, and adhere to nationalist discourses. However, many others become racial conscious after spending a number of years in the U.S. These people may have experienced racial discrimination in one form or another, or they may have been exposed to the social conditions dictating the lives of people placed in a particular category in which they may find themselves. Yet, racial consciousness may not imply the subsequent acquisition of a proactive stance toward social oppression. It may simply indicate that one is now aware or conscious of the fact that one is ascribed a racial label, casually and institutionally, despite one's own efforts of self-identification.

Cape Verdeans in Boston: a fractured diaspora

Immigration and migration have been used to describe the movement of people across geographic, temporal, and spatial borders. No longer limited to a matter of going to or coming from a specific place, immigration and migration can now be used to describe internal, circular, and return movements. Recent studies have focused upon the complexity of immigration and migration as linked to a global system of capitalist development that renders the relationship between sending and receiving societies dialectical and interdependent (Anthias 1992; Foster 1991; Basch et al. 1994; Sassen 1988).

Cape Verdean migration, forced or voluntary, constitutes a transnational movement warranting sociocultural adjustment upon settlement in a new locale. The Cape Verdean diaspora community of Boston can be described as a fractured or fragmented diaspora because it is at once emergent and constitutive of socio-historical events. Age, citizenship, and migration history are just some of the distinguishing features of this community. Within a single household, for example, one could find great-grandparents, grandparents, parents and children all living under the same roof. There are Cape Verdeans who came to the U.S. twenty years ago and others who have just arrived a few months ago.

Likewise, there are Cape Verdeans who were born in Boston fifty years ago and others just two years ago.

Perhaps the most outstanding feature, however, is a temporal split between Cape Verdeans who were born in the U.S. (Cape Verdean-Americans) and those born on the islands (Cape Verdean immigrants). The Cape Verdean-American sector of Boston was created from the internal migration from the smaller South Shore communities of Massachusetts, such as Taunton, New Bedford, and Cape Cod, since the 1950's. For Cape Verdean-Americans, Boston was the quintessential Big City. It became a place of refuge from the 'country towns' where the standard course of life was limited to graduating from high school, starting a family and working for minimum wage. Boston served as a place of transformation, a place where a person became conscious of the world and his or her place in it.

The Cape Verdean-American sector of the diaspora is linked by a shared historical memory of early immigration, the political economy of Cape Verdean labour history in the U.S., and by a common experience of racial and xenophobic oppression. Many members of the community who 'came up' during the 1960s became closely associated with the larger African-American community. In fact, many Cape Verdean-Americans in Boston have since identified themselves as Black and may not even disclose their Cape Verdean heritage upon casual meeting. The Mayor's cultural liaison to the Cape Verdean community confirms the difficulty in documenting Cape Verdean-Americans in Boston, many of whom have culturally assimilated and/or intermarried into the larger African-American community.

Contemporary Cape Verdean immigrants, although still witnessing the constraints of racism, assimilation and anti-immigrant sentiment, lead qualitatively different lives from their Cape Verdean-American counterparts. Indeed, the Boston community differs from the older Cape Verdean communities of New Bedford, Massachusetts, and Providence, Rhode Island, because of its large Cape Verdean immigrant population. There are more Cape Verdean immigrants living in the Boston area than second- and third-generation Cape Verdean-Americans, and a significant number of the immigrant population have not become citizens. Some are legally resident while others have overstayed a visitor's visas. This sector of the diaspora is linked to post-1965 and especially post-independence (1975) relocations to the area.

Most Cape Verdean immigrants are in close contact with their relatives on the islands. They send 'home' remittances on a regular basis. They speak with relatives by phone or in person when they visit. They continue to speak Kriolu in the home or when they patronize Cape Verdean-owned establishments. Each of these everyday practices, and the continuing influx of Cape Verdean immigrants into the area, contributes to the manifestations of Cape Verdean diasporic identities that are created, revised and recreated in various social contexts.

Cape Verdeans in Boston, and the immigrant sector in particular, by insisting on identifying themselves as Cape Verdean, have challenged societal ascription that would categorise them as Black or African-American on the basis of physical appearance. This resistance to the forces of assimilation and ascription is similar to that detailed by Laguerre in relation to Haitian immigrants in New York City during the 19th century.

> Their complete assimilation [in]to the social life and mores of the U.S. could not be achieved because of their attachment to their countries of origin, their unwillingness to become completely Anglo-saxonised, and their desire to speak their native languages and establish schools, churches, and newspapers that maintained their cultural identities and traditions (1998: 5).

For Cape Verdeans, the idea of authenticity becomes pronounced as the immigrant community distinguishes itself vis-à-vis the older Cape Verdean-American population. Indeed, the contemporary coexistence of these two sectors results in claims of legitimacy and authenticity as both sectors vie for equal ownership of the label 'Cape Verdean'. This contention has created an intracultural gap between the two sectors of the diaspora, one often marked by animosity and distrust (Greenfield 1976). Janice (pseudonym) provides an example of how Cape Verdean immigrant perceptions of Cape Verdean-Americans have been interpreted as an affront to one's sense of Cape Verdeanness; she often speaks discontentedly of 'those Portagees' (Cape Verdean immigrants) who 'think they're better than everyone' because they speak Kriolu and cook Cape Verdean food different than the way she was taught:

> They think... those who came from there know everything there is to know. And then it's like, you know, because we were born here and raised here and we're raised differently, it's like we're not really Cape Verdeans, you know, unless you *change up* and do this and do that.

By 'change up,' Janice invokes the conversations she has had with Cape Verdean co-workers who have urged her to learn Kriolu and to alter the culinary traditions that she learned from her parents. Indeed, the contestation over who is or is not authentically Cape Verdean is often played out against these specific cultural signifiers.

People of Cape Verdean descent living in Boston can be understood in relation to the larger U.S. African diaspora by the way they negotiate their social identities. Both Cape Verdean-Americans and immigrants employ key themes from African diaspora theory in the social construction and maintenance of their identities. Some Cape Verdean immigrants, for example, draw on the imagining of Cape Verde as geographically, culturally, and politically part of continental Africa. Cape Verdean-Americans, on the other hand, stress their affinity with African Americans as rooted in a common experience of racial discrimination and of reclaiming the racial categories of Black or African American as positive self-designators.

However, one aspect of Cape Verdean diaspora identity formation that cannot be excluded is the impact of Portuguese colonisation. The Cape Verdean diaspora has maintained a love-hate relationship with the Portuguese. In response to Cape Verdeans calling themselves Portuguese, Portuguese-Americans have distanced themselves historically from the Cape Verdean immigrants to avoid being classified as non-White. This has caused a long-standing rift and deep-seated animosity between the two communities (Greenfield 1976). In addition, it has had an impact on how Cape Verdeans have since identified themselves, particularly for those who have lived under the conditions of both colonialism and independence.

Conclusion

We have examined the concept of diaspora and how the discourses of 'diaspora', 'imagined community' and 'historical memory' have an impact on diasporic identity formation. The articulation of diaspora discourses has a particular relevance to the study of black immigrant groups. Theories of the African diaspora are particularly useful to this study in how they illuminate the processes through which Cape Verdean-descended people negotiate their identities as multiple and transgressive. In other words, the concept of the African diaspora highlights how Cape Verdean identities are manifested in diasporic and transnational experiences.

The concept of diaspora is useful as a means to effectively destabilise fixed notions of race and nation. It offers a more 'pluralised notion of race' that renders cultural difference 'multiple and complex' (Eisenstein 1996: 17). Moreover, it has the potential to de-essentialise and decenter claims to authenticity often equated with defining black subjectivities. Finally, given the fact that diasporic identities are often formed as a result of transnational movement, the concept of the African diaspora has the potential to serve as a critical tool to explore the processes of social, cultural and political (re)alignment related to Black immigrant settlement.

References

Alonso, A.M. (1988) 'The Effects of Truth: Re-Presentations of the Past and the Imagining of Community'. *Journal of Historical Sociology* 1(1): 33-57.

Alonso, A.M. (1994) 'The Politics of Space, Time and Substance: State Formation, Nationalism and Ethnicity'. *Annual Review of Anthropology* 23: 379-405.

Anderson, B. (1991 [1983]) *Imagined Communities: Reflections on the Origin and Spread of Nationalism.* New York: Verso Press.

Anthias, F. (1992) *Ethnicity, Class, Gender and Migration: Greek-Cypriots in Britain.* Brookfield, VT: Ashgate Publishing Company.

Appiah, K.A. (1992) *In My Father's House.* Oxford: Oxford University Press.

Barkan, E.; Shelton, M-D. (eds.) (1998) *Borders, Exiles, Diasporas.* Stanford, CA: Stanford University Press.

Basch, L.; Schiller, N.G.; Blanc, C.S. (eds.) (1994) *Nations Unbound: Transnational Projects, Postcolonial Predicaments, and Deterritorialized Nation-states.* Amsterdam: Gordon and Breach.

Batalha, L. (2004) *The Cape Verdean Diaspora in Portugal: Colonial Subjects in a Postcolonial World.* Lanham, MD: Lexington Books.

Brah, A. (1996) *Cartographies of Diaspora: Contesting Identities.* London: Routledge.

Brow, J. (1990) 'Notes on Community, Hegemony, and the Uses of the Past'. *Anthropological Quarterly* 63(1): 1-5.

Brueggemann, J. (1995) 'Class, Race, and Symbolic Community'. *Critical Sociology* 21(3): 71-88.

Carling, J. (1997) 'Figuring Out the Cape Verdean Diaspora'. *Cimboa: Revista Caboverdiana de Letras, Artes e Estudos* 4 (fall/winter): 3-9.

Clifford, J. (1994) 'Diasporas'. *Cultural Anthropology* 9(3): 302-38.

Cohen, A.P. (1985) *The Symbolic Construction of Community.* New York: Tavistock Publications.

Cohen, R. (1996) 'Diasporas and the Nation-State: From Victims to Challengers'. *International Affairs* 72(3): 507-520.

Comaroff, J.L.; Comaroff, J. (1987) 'The Madman and the Migrant: Work and Labor in the Historical Consciousness of a South African People'. *American Ethnologist* 14(2): 191-209.

Drake, S.C. (1982) 'Diaspora Studies and Pan-Africanism', in *Global Dimensions of the African Diaspora,* J. Harris (ed.), Washington, DC: Howard University Press, pp. 341-402.

Du Bois, W.E.B (1903) *The Souls of Black Folk.* New York: Dover.

Eisenstein, Z.R. (1996) *Hatreds: Racialized and Sexualized Conflicts in the 21st Century.* New York: Routledge.

Fabre, G.; O'Meally, R. (eds.) (1992) *History and Memory in African American Culture.* New York: Oxford University Press.

Foster, R.J. (1991) 'Making National Cultures in the Global Ecumene'. *Annual Review of Anthropology* 20: 235-60.

Freire, P.; Macedo, D. (1987) *Literacy: Reading the Word and the World.* South Hadley, MA: Bergin and Garvey Publishers.

Frisch, M.H. (1981) 'The Memory of History'. *Radical History Review* 25: 9-23.

Gillis, J.R. (ed.) (1994) 'Memory and Identity: The History of a Relationship', in *Commemorations: The Politics of National Identity,* J.R. Gillis (ed.), Princeton, NJ: Princeton University Press, pp. 3-26.

Gilroy, P. (1993) *The Black Atlantic: Modernity and Double Consciousness.* Cambridge, MA: Harvard University Press.

Gopinath, G. (1995) 'Bombay, U.K., Yuba City: Bhangra Music and the Engendering of Diaspora'. *Diaspora* 4(3): 303-22.

Gordon, E.T. (1998) *Disparate Diasporas: Identity and Politics in an African-Nicaraguan Community*. Austin, TX: University of Texas Press.

Greenfield, S.M. (1976) 'In Search of Social Identity: Strategies of Ethnic Identity Management amongst Capeverdeans in Southeastern Massachusetts'. *Luso-Brazilian Review* 13 (1): 3-18.

Helmreich, S. (1992) 'Kinship, Nation, and Paul Gilroy's Concept of Diaspora'. *Diaspora* 2 (2): 243-49.

Laguerre, M.S. (1998) *Diasporic Citizenship: Haitian Americans in Transnational America*. New York: St. Martin's Press.

Meintel, D. (1984) *Race, Culture, and Portuguese Colonialism in Cape Verde*. Syracuse, NY: Syracuse University Press.

Menchaca, M. (1993) 'Chicano Indianism: A Historical Account of Racial Repression in the United States'. *American Ethnologist* 20(3): 583-603.

Padmore, G. (1956) *Pan-Africanism or Communism*. London: Dennis Dobson.

Safran, W. (1991) 'Diasporas in Modern Societies: Myths of Homeland and Return'. *Diaspora* 1(1): 83-99.

Sahlins, M.D. (1985) *Islands of History*. Chicago, IL: University of Chicago Press.

Sassen, S. (1988) *The Mobility of Labor and Capital: A Study in International Investment and Labor Flow*. Cambridge: Cambridge University Press.

Scott, D. (1991) 'That Event, This Memory: Notes on the Anthropology of African Diasporas in the New World'. *Diaspora* 1(3): 261-283.

Woost, M. (1993) 'Nationalizing the Local Past in Sri Lanka: Histories of Nation and Development in a Sinhalese Village'. *American Ethnologist* 20(3): 502-522.

Chapter 20
The Resilience of the Cape Verdean Migration Tradition

Lisa Åkesson

This chapter examines the relationship between social conditions, processes of identification and experiences of 'homeland transnationalism' against the backdrop of the Cape Verdean culture of migration. The objective is to synthesise the different factors that together shape Cape Verdeans' desires to leave their homeland. As will be made evident, aspirations to migrate are about many things; they concern hopes for social mobility as well as people's view of themselves and their nation, and they are also related to the pervasive impact of transnational relations on everyday life in the homeland.

During the last decades, the Cape Verdean tradition of migration has been challenged by the tightening of immigration policies in destination countries as well as by people's increasingly critical assessment of what life abroad can offer. To portray the migration project as 'an illusion' is common in Cape Verde of today. Therefore, I also reflect on why the culture of migration, despite these challenges, is still reproduced in the homeland.

By showing that the aspirations to migrate are not simply motivated by material desires, I diverge from the conventional view of the migrant as a 'homo œconomicus' (Olwig and Sørensen 2002). The 'economism' which has characterised both behavioural and structural explanations of migration, needs to be complemented by other approaches. Desires to migrate are not simply generated by rational choices based on economic calculations, and neither can prospective migrants be reduced to passive objects manipulated by the workings of the world capitalist system. Agency needs to be restored to migrants and we have to appreciate the fact that mobility takes on meanings in particular ethnographical contexts. Desires to migrate are shaped in (trans)local processes that concern people's ideas about the good and right life. Migration is, indeed, a meaningful event.

The desire to leave

At one time or another, most people in Cape Verde will consider leaving. When I asked Sónia, a factory worker and single mother in her thirties, why she wanted to emigrate, she said:

> I've always been thinking about emigration, ever since I was 16 or 17 years old. I've tried to get a visa for Italy, for Portugal, for the Netherlands. Even when I was a child I dreamed of going abroad and making my life. Right now I'm trying to go to the Netherlands, but there are many problems with my documents... I will try again and again. I want to emigrate.

Throughout my fieldwork in Cape Verde, I repeatedly heard similar declarations.[1] For some of those I met, migration was more of a distant vision, appearing only at times of personal crisis. Conflicts with relatives, for example, could trigger an immediate desire to leave. For others, the wish to migrate influenced many of their everyday activities as well as their sense of self. The prevalence of a positive attitude towards migration is also mirrored in statistics (Instituto de Emprego e Formação Professional 2006). Today, however, the migration ideology, or the idea that departure is both a natural and necessary part of life as a Cape Verdean, appears to be challenged in a number of ways. Here, the intention is to show why so many Cape Verdeans continue to pin their hope for a better future on emigration, although they are frequently doubtful about the benefits of migration and have very limited chances of ever acquiring immigration documents.

In order to understand the new and more negative view of migration that is spreading in Cape Verde a transnational approach is necessary. People's desires to leave are not shaped in a bounded local community. Instead, they result from the long-distance interaction between those at home and those abroad. In the Cape Verdean context, discussions about the pros and cons of migrating take place in an environment in which the local has interacted with the distant for centuries. Voyaging across the Atlantic is a fundamental aspect of Cape Verdean life, and when people today discuss their dreams of a better life, the homeland repertoire is constantly weighed against what the migrants say and do. This article, thus, applies a homeland perspective to transnationalism, and this sets it apart from most other studies of transnational migration, which focus on the experiences of those who have actually migrated.

Closed borders and the illusion of migration

The first and obvious challenge to the continuity of Cape Verdean emigration is the restrictive immigration regimes in the countries of destination. Over the last 30 years, migration has become increasingly difficult for Cape Verdeans (Carling 2004), which implies that experiences of involuntary immobility are widespread among those remaining in the archipelago. Especially for young people, efforts to obtain immigration documents may dominate their everyday lives as well as their sense of self. The different strategies used in order to acquire a visa are often costly, both in terms of human and economic resources, and many Cape Verdeans fail again and again in their attempts to circumvent immigration restrictions. In short, this means that the aspirations to migrate are often thwarted even for those who put all their money and hopes into their pursuit of immigration 'papers'.

Another important challenge to the migration tradition is the repertoire of ideas that question the traditional representation of foreign countries as a 'paradise' where you can get all you want – if you are prepared to work hard. This new attitude is often expressed by young people when they discuss their future. It has become common to call migration 'an illusion', and I heard this many times during my fieldwork. People are not necessarily saying that it is impossible to leave, a conclusion that might easily be drawn given the difficulties of fulfilling the restrictive immigration regimes. Instead, the message is that the traditional image of foreign countries as a 'paradise' is delusional and naïve. It is an illusion, historically spread by returning migrants, who have wanted to bolster their own status (Dias 2000: 66). One of those who expressed this more negative view of life in the diaspora is a young woman named Lucy.

> *Lisa*: Last time we met, you said you didn't want to emigrate because you had a good life here. Now I would like to ask you, are there also conditions in the countries of destination that contribute to making migration more undesirable for you?

> *Lucy*: Yes. When foreigners come here they are all treated very well, but we, when we leave, we are treated badly. Above all, racism. Sometimes they give priority to those from their own country, with their own color and race.

> *Lisa*: Where have you learnt about this?

> *Lucy*: From others who themselves know what it's like. The things I know about foreign countries I've learnt partly from

emigrants, but I've also formed my own ideas. It's a thing that you understand immediately. It's not necessary to go there in order to confirm this. Before, the outside might have been better, it had everything. It was easier. Everything was cheaper, easier before. That attitude still exists. Sometimes there are people who know what it's like abroad, but still take the risk by leaving. They try their luck. You can't stay here, *paród* (stagnant), without doing anything. There, at least there are jobs that are well paid, and money is important for those who dream of leaving. You see, it is not worth becoming a slave in another person's land just to earn a few cents.

When Lucy says that 'everything was easier before' and voices her aversion to becoming 'a slave[2] in another person's land', this echoes a change in the representation of foreign countries. The unemployment and racism, which have had an impact on European immigrants especially since the beginning of the 1990s, are well known in São Vicente, and people often talk about these problems. Lucy states that her dark view of migration is something that she has 'partly' learnt from the migrants.

How, then, do Lucy and other Cape Verdeans 'learn' things from the migrants? In São Vicente and elsewhere people generally maintain their regular contacts with relatives and friends in the diaspora via the telephone. The importance of cheap and reliable telecommunications for improved contacts between migrants and non-migrants has been noted in many transnational settings (e.g., Al-Ali 2002; Levitt 2001; Mahler 2001). For Cape Verdeans, the creation of a nationwide telephone networks has greatly facilitated long-distance contacts. So has reduced tariffs for international calls, although these are still much more expensive in Cape Verde than in most diaspora countries, which means that it is mostly the emigrants who call home. Besides the improved access to telephone service, more and more Cape Verdeans communicate with the outside world via the Internet (see chap. 13). Due to, among other things, the opening up of charter tours to Cape Verde, more emigrants spend their holidays in the homeland, and this is another important form of contact between people at home and abroad.

Taken together, the total number of long-distance contacts has clearly intensified. This seems to have been conducive to more ambiguous notions about life abroad. Earlier generations of emigrants maintained contact with their homeland, mainly through letters that were generally highly stylised both in form and content, and therefore probably revealed little about their everyday experiences. If these migrants ever returned, they were supposed to come back loaded with expensive goods and full of stories about the wealth and magic of the foreign host countries (Meintel 1984). Today, the intensified global interconnectedness makes it harder for the migrants to maintain these kinds of one-dimensional images with their relatives in Cape Verde. More contact implies deeper and more nuanced understandings of each other's realities. The dark sides of life abroad cannot be concealed. As a result of this, there is a growing appreciation of the fact that migrants also encounter difficulties.

In my interview with Lucy, she stated that she not only has learnt about foreign countries from the migrants, but has also taken this knowledge 'formed her own ideas'. What I believe she means is that ideas and things from the outside world today, in many ways, permeate Cape Verde, and accordingly form part of her everyday existence. People in the homeland develop a more nuanced understanding of life abroad, as more and more non-Cape Verdean ideas, commodities and people enter the country. There is a steadily growing influx of tourists. Imported items, including food and clothes are much more common today. Items that were used to be exotic riches from the outside world are now on sale in Cape Verde. To Lucy, this means that she does not have to listen to the migrants in order to learn about life abroad.

The role of the media is important in this development. People can watch news from abroad on television. Violence, earthquakes and crimes flash across the screen. People react with repudiation and compare these pictures with the *sossegód* (calm, non-violent) life in Cape Verde. The discriminatory treatment of emigrants is also part of the reports from abroad, as are the poor living conditions in the urban neighbourhoods where many Cape Verdeans end up living. An example of this, which gave rise to much concern in São Vicente, were the reports broadcasted by the Portuguese television channel RTP África. The reports presented a very negative picture of the situation in the extremely poor sections of Lisbon, where many migrants from the former Portuguese colonies in Africa live.

The dramatic expansion of the school system in Cape Verde since independence also plays an important role in changing people's understandings of the outside world and migrants' conditions. Among the emigrants on holiday I met in São Vicente, a common opinion was that people in the homeland today are much more *sklaresid* (educated) than before and more enlightened and knowledgeable about life beyond the islands. A consequence of this 'enlightenment' is that notions of the outside world are increasingly shared between those living at home and those living abroad. The hard, painful and dangerous sides of life abroad are discussed and known by those in the homeland. As a consequence of their better understanding, the outside world appears less enchanting today. The dream of magic foreign lands where everything can be achieved through hard work is fading away even among those who have never left their natal island. Disenchantment with the Western world is taking place in Cape Verde.

Appreciating complexity

What all this demonstrates is that the Cape Verdean outward orientation is now contested. The paradise abroad has been shown to be an illusion, and if one still dreams of emigrating there it is increasingly hard to fulfill the restrictive migration policies. Why, then, is the culture of migration still being reproduced in Cape Verde?

One important finding is that the answer is complex. When trying to explain why people aspire to leave, scholars of migration have often focused on single variables. Some researchers have foregrounded individuals' or households' desires to maximise their incomes, while others have pointed to the importance of social networks in augmenting and sustaining emigration. In my interpretation of the Cape Verdean ethnography I have tried to understand migration as a culturally and socially constructed phenomenon, and this approach has made me believe that the continuity of the migration tradition depends on a complex dynamic.

In the following sections, I set out to clarify this dynamic by looking at social conditions as well as conceptualisations related to history, the nation and the individual. I will also argue that being a 'homeland transnationalist' strongly influences people's dreams for the future.

The stagnation of those who 'get by'

People's appraisal of their social and economic situation in the homeland is important to the desire to leave. As we shall see, living conditions are not only assessed with reference to the local society. Through contacts with the migrants, those who have stayed behind are constantly and forcefully reminded of other people's lives and alternatives. To move on and try to create a better life somewhere else has become an imperative in Cape Verde.

A driving force behind many São Vicentians' aspirations to emigrate is their powerful experiences of stagnation. In the local society, stagnation appears to be a key symbol of a failed existence. Stagnation, both in a social and spatial sense, is a metaphor for an undesirable existence, while mobility is linked to the good life. Both desperately poor people and those a little bit better off, i.e., people who are considered to be 'getting by', often complain about being stuck in a hopeless future. It is, however, those who 'get by' who make the most active attempts to leave. While the members of the small local elite manage this with comparative ease, the poorest have almost no chance of realizing their dreams of migration. But among those who 'get by' some actually succeed in leaving.

Those who 'get by' form the largest social group in São Vicentian society. Most of them live in decent houses, although many are sparsely furnished. They manage to send their children to school, and they do not go to bed with an empty stomach. An important negative aspect of this category is, however, the high rate of unemployment. In 2005, one-third of the inhabitants on the island of São Vicente were reportedly seeking work (Instituto do Emprego e Formação Professional 2006). For those lucky enough to be employed, the salaries are another major problem. Incomes are low, both in the private and public sectors, and rise slowly. Salary complaints are as common among teachers, who earn about 300 euros per month, as among domestic servants, whose monthly salary is as low as 40 to 50 euros. Both of these groups maintain that their incomes only allow a subsistence lifestyle. Furthermore, my impression is that people who 'get by' seldom, if ever, have an opportunity to work their way up in local society. They have left the ranks of the really poor, but they cannot move up any further in terms of social mobility. Lack of formal education as well as beneficial contacts among the political and economical elite exclude these people from most careers. In contrast to this stagnation, however, novel and attractive commodities are constantly entering São Vicente's market and are producing new demands.

My friend Maria is one of the many São Vicentians who 'gets by'. One day when I visited her at home, she voiced her feelings about the stagnation that afflicted so many people in this socioeconomic group.

> I go punctually every day to my job, but at the end of the month it's always the same thing. I receive the same miserable salary. The money is just for food, and you can't even buy the food you like, because everything is so expensive here. It is always the same thing, and imagine those who don't even receive a salary by the end of the month! We have to leave, to work abroad because of this. If you remain here everything stays the same (é tud na mesma). It's just one year after another, but always the same. I want to emigrate. That's the only possibility.

After having said this, Maria calmed down a bit, but when she began talking about her sisters who have emigrated her eyes brimmed with tears.

Sometimes they send something. But help me to leave, no! When they come home on holidays they bring clothes, shoes, money. But I don't want those, I just want to leave. They say that foreign countries are just an illusion. I say that I have to go there, to see the outside world for myself, experience the difficulties, have a bad time, bear the rain and cold. Because of all this, I have to struggle to get out. I am experienced; I can do all kinds of work.

Maria's voice and posture betrays an intensity and passion that makes me acutely aware of the depth of her feelings. In many ways, hers and the lives of others in São Vicente can be described as anything but lacking in change. People switch partners, move their homes, have new babies, bury kin and companions and acquire new friends and enemies at a rapid pace – at least compared to what I am used to. After the conversation with Maria, however, I could clearly see that people's lives were characterised by stagnation as much as by change. A state of constant flux that never leads to any improvements only intensifies their feelings of being stuck. This was most evident with regard to socio-economic conditions, even though the frequent changes of partners and friends could also be seen as being part of a repetitive pattern. Among the women and men I met, many had performed the same kind of work for 10 or 30 years and saw no prospect whatsoever of any improvements in their standards of living.

There are many São Vicentians who share Maria's feelings of social and economic stagnation. These feelings can be discerned among people with quite different standards of living. Compared to many others, Maria is lucky. According to local conditions, her income is reasonable and her job easy. Yet, Maria nurtures the desire to change her life. However every month she spends all of her money maintaining a standard of living she considers poor or even humiliating. She pays the rent, buys some basic foodstuffs, but there is nothing left for any improvements. This would probably have been less painful if her frame of reference had been limited to São Vicente. This, however, is not the case. Maria cannot avoid comparing her situation with that of her sisters who come home on holidays loaded with gifts and plans for the construction of a house in São Vicente. Maria deeply regrets her inability to improve her own material standards and to construct a permanent home for herself and her son, and she continues to believe that migration is the only solution. Maria does not care about the difficulties abroad because she wants to show her sisters that she, too, can make it. When I ask Maria about her sisters' unwillingness to help her, she raises her voice.

They are bad, really bad sisters. They are already there. They no longer care about what it's like here. One of my sisters I got to know when she was on holiday in Cape Verde, and she promised to send me papers [documents for sponsoring Maria]. Nothing! It's just talk. She never sent those papers, never. But one day they will see me in Spain. I have faith. One day they will see me in Spain.

Making a life

As Maria's case reveals, feelings of stagnation tend to be grounded in the very real lack of any opportunities for upward social mobility, but they are also often related to widespread ideas about the good and proper life. In order to construct this kind of existence, one needs to earn money. This means that an improved economy is not a goal in and of itself, but the means for creating an existence that is culturally defined as meaningful and enjoyable. In São Vicentian society, this means having the economic means to make the transition to autonomous adulthood in which one owns a house and is head of a household. Having acquired this, you have also made your life.

N kré fazé nha vida (I want to make my life) is a common way of formulating one's desires to leave. The meaning of the phrase is essential in understanding the migration culture. There is an inherent ambiguity in the expression, as *vida* signifies both 'a living' and 'life'. The primary definition of *vida* is to secure a living. Migration is seen as immediately linked to work and an enhanced livelihood. People who want to leave São Vicente often explain their aspirations in terms of economic factors, and some of those whom I asked translated *vida* as 'survival'.

Vida is thus most immediately associated with livelihood, but the ambiguity of the term becomes apparent when people talk about a person who has 'made her/his *vida*'. These people have not simply secured a living, but have also succeeded in building a desirable life. To construct a house is generally the primary life-making objective since ownership of a house is a prerequisite for setting up a domestic unit and this, in turn, is the key sign of social maturity and autonomy among others.

The construction of houses is closely related to domestic life-cycles. People between 20 and 30 years of age often live with their parents, even after they have children of their own. But this kind of existence cannot go on forever. Matters are often brought to a head when the owner of the house dies. Grown-up children are forced to move out and disagreements begin about the inheritance of the house. This kind of disputes is common in São Vicente, and houses often fall into decay while heirs fight for years over ownership.

For those who do not inherit a house, i.e., the majority of the young, it is difficult to construct a house with the money one earns in the homeland. As we saw with Maria, an average salary just barely covers the basic necessities, and leaves no savings to build a house. Not having a house of your own when you are just starting a family implies economic insecurity, dependence on others and, in some cases, also risks of mental and physical abuse. Although the atmosphere in many households is peaceful, others are marked by considerable tensions. Some houses are an arena for conflicts and even violence, and inside these houses we find people who are constantly complaining that their relatives are trying to *mandá na mi* (boss me). Young people living in these conditions understandably yearn to leave and set up their own households. Even those who grow up in a more harmonious household generally strive to build a house of their own when they reach adulthood. While this is totally out of question for the poorest, and the richest take a future house more or less for granted, the outcome of the house project is much more uncertain for those who 'get by', for those who are generally linked to dreams of migrating. This dream, then, is nurtured by the development of domestic life-cycles and by young people's hopes of gaining autonomy from others and becoming the heads of their own households.

Thus, the migration goal of 'making a life' has to do with setting up a new domestic unit that has the economic and social power to make its own decisions. In São Vicentian discourse, life-making through migration is connected to images of a normal life (*vida normal*). The idea that migration is a means of achieving a normal life indicates the centrality of mobility in Cape Verdean society. The view of migration as something that normalises and stabilises life also links up with a transnational perspective. It is often deemed impossible to achieve a proper Cape Verdean life by remaining behind in this tiny nation-state. Instead, life is made through relations with more than one place.

Building a transnational nation

The resilience of the migration tradition is, thus, linked to a culturally specific model of the ideal life, but it is also linked to people's conceptualisations of themselves as a nation. Cape Verdean children are already taught early on in school that 'we have always emigrated'. The history of migration is often told orally as well as via schoolbooks and other kinds of literature. Similarly, the pioneer migrants who departed on American whalers came back to play the role of cultural heroes.

They are seen as the first who dared to cross the Atlantic in search of a better life somewhere else. In their wake, a nation has gone abroad.

In Cape Verde, the past is imbued with leave-takings and departures. The history of constant out-migration deeply affects the way people look upon themselves and their nation. Each successive generation grows up seeing mobility as an intrinsic part of life, and leaving family and homeland for another country is portrayed as an inevitable component of Cape Verdean life. People are strongly aware of the fact that emigration has been widespread for generations and that separations are part of their common history. Accordingly, the destiny of migration not only affects those alive today, but it also includes their ancestors and those yet to be born. Similarly, I often heard people saying that Cape Verde 'can't survive without migration'.

The idea that migration is a destiny that unites the Cape Verdean people is widespread. At parties and other social gatherings people often start to sing together or encourage somebody with a good voice to perform some of the well-known songs deal with departure and longing (*sodad*). The ambience then suddenly becomes serious and emotional. When everybody in a crowd sings in unison about *ora di bai* (the hour of departure), for instance, it creates an intense atmosphere of community and common fate. Personal distress resulting from the separation from loved ones is not always openly expressed in everyday life. Through music, however, these experiences are transformed into a dilemma shared by the whole nation. This view of migration as a national destiny contributes to shape desires to leave into something natural and necessary. When people leave, they do not abandon their country. Instead, they live up to a tradition established by earlier generations of Cape Verdeans.

Being a 'homeland transnationalist'

I have shown that Cape Verdean aspirations to leave are integrated into processes of identification that concern the ideal life of the person as well as people's conceptualisations of themselves as a nation. The pervasive cultural orientation towards mobility is, however, not only an integral part of people's understanding of themselves, it is also reproduced in everyday discourses and practices. Living in the absence of and friends, and being dependent upon their loyalty, is central to the transnational condition. By talking about kin who have emigrated, people demonstrate their links to other sites. Maintaining close relations with people abroad signifies opportunities of migration; a hope that somebody on the outside one day will 'give entry', i.e., sponsor them for a visa. By virtue of these links, some in the homeland aspire to what may be called a 'transnational personhood'. Through their long-distance relations, those who remain behind also begin to embody the ideas and practices related to mobility.

In their daily lives, people are engaged in a myriad of activities associated with the emigrants. They wait for gifts, phone calls and letters from abroad, and they constantly talk to each other about the latest news from relatives and friends in Europe and the U.S. References to what a daughter in Italy has said on the telephone are as common as gossip about one's neighbours. Participation in transnational dialogues is thus an important part of daily social life. Money sent from abroad also plays a central role in the lives of many São Vicentians. Although people often complain about the lack of support from the diaspora, many simultaneously pin their hopes of rescue from diverse economic problems on remittances from relatives working abroad. Taken together, this means that life abroad is ever-present in the minutiae of São Vicentians' lives.

A practice that provides especially strong and long-lasting transnational ties is fostering a child. Today, Cape Verdean women and men migrate at similar rates, and migrating women often leave dependent children behind. This produces commitments both for them and for their female kin in the homeland. A refusal to provide a home for the children of a female relative who wants to go abroad is considered disloyal, as this would hinder her ability to 'make her life'. The mother, on her part, is expected to continuously send money home to support her children. A woman who neglects this duty is seen as an irresponsible mother. Thus, expectations are strong both on the child giver and the child receiver and, combined with the fact that the raising of children is a long-term practice, this means that child fostering produce enduring links.

Another long-term service afforded by those who remain behind is the supervision of the house-building projects of emigrants in the homeland. At least ideally, this practice involves mutual gains, as the supervisor should either be paid in cash or kind, or allowed to occupy part of the house upon completion. In São Vicente, the symbolical significance of the house-building by emigrants is powerful. Their houses are solid signs of the possibilities that migration offers. When somebody who left empty-handed manages to construct a house, this is seen as an individual achievement, but also as a proof of the positive connection between mobility and life-making. The houses of emigrants, then, function as permanent and tangible reminders of another life and other possibilities.

Holidays spent by emigrants in the homeland also strengthen Cape Verdeans' dreams of mobility. The presence of holidaymakers is especially conspicuous in August, but also during Christmas and New Year.

As described earlier, the migrants do not necessarily provide the home-land people a positive picture of life abroad. Nevertheless, the mere presence of all the emigrants at beaches, bars and family gatherings re-inforces the migration culture. The migrants on holiday have com-pleted the ideal trajectory. They have managed to leave, but also to re-turn to enjoy the sun and the social life of the homeland.

The many ways in which São Vicentians interact with their relatives and friends abroad affects most aspects of life in the homeland. Being a 'homeland transnationalist' means, then, that people, ideas and money located overseas strongly influence one's everyday social rela-tions and livelihood, as well as one's dreams for the future. Precisely because practices associated with mobility are so deeply entrenched in São Vicentians' everyday lives, aspirations to migrate take on a self-evi-dent character.

Conclusions

The case of Maria, and her desperate need to show her sisters that she could also make it to Europe, shows that feelings of socio-economic stagnation underpin desires to leave. And often, it is assumed in the social sciences that out-migration is simply motivated by desires to im-prove one's economic future and one's social status. The fact is, how-ever, that people throughout the Third World are being reduced to a life marked by stagnation and deprivation, but aspirations to emigrate are not always as prevalent as in Cape Verde. This implies that the resi-lience of the Cape Verdean migration tradition cannot by explained by referring solely to economic conditions. Experiences of stagnation and poverty are powerful motives for migration, but it is not tenable to ar-gue that they are the only driving forces behind the powerful tradition of migration.

As I have shown, the culture of migration in Cape Verde is inte-grated into processes of identification. The migration ideology is under-pinned by the construction of both the individual and the nation. The project of 'life-making', which I have briefly outlined, includes earning enough money abroad to construct a house and set up a new domestic unit. This, ideally, leads to socially recognised respect and autonomy. Desires to leave are connected to images of the good Cape Verdean life. This existence is stimulated by those who have returned from lives of working hard abroad and now enjoy an independent life in a nice house, surrounded by family and friends. Similarly, mobility is believed to facilitate an individual's progress along a trajectory that leads to-wards the realisation of an idealised self.

The ideal individual is, thus, realised through migration, as is the nation itself. To migrate is something one does in one's capacity as a Cape Verdean. The history of migration is central to conceptualisations of a common past. The sufferings of hunger and drought, which have consistently plagued the archipelago, have made it necessary to leave, and this forms a unifying backdrop to the national identity. The men who left onboard American whalers appear in schoolbooks and are elsewhere presented as the nearly mythological forerunners of the tradition to go abroad. In fact, when a Cape Verdean people emerges from the encounter between Europe and Africa, this people is paradoxically not characterised by its propensity to develop the homeland, but precisely by its propensity to leave it. In the discourse on the collective identity, being Cape Verdean means being predestined to mobility, and this destiny is seen as emerging out of the history of constant departures.

I have also argued that the Cape Verdean orientation towards the outside world is reproduced through a large variety of transnational practices. The orientation towards migration is a *habitus* (Bourdieu 1977), a disposition people acquire by living a Cape Verdean life. In a society where so many important institutions, ideas and practices are associated with mobility, desires to go abroad continue to constitute a collective disposition that is not easily changed. The authority of the migration ideology, which leads to the representation of mobility as both natural and necessary, is linked to the fact that migration has pervaded Cape Verdean society for such a long time. Since this has been going on for generations, the search for a better life has been moulded into an established order that produces its own self-evidence.

Having identified these different elements that together shape the resilient dream of a better life somewhere else, it is also easy to understand why the present restrictions against immigration will do little to stop Cape Verdeans from attempting to leave. Mobility is, simply put, an intrinsic part of both identity constructions and everyday practices. Moreover, when discussing the closed borders in Europe and the U.S. with friends in Cape Verde, they consistently underline that it has been difficult throughout the history of emigration to gain the right of living outside the archipelago. 'Emigration has always been hard', I have been told again and again. In saying this, people refer to the various obstacles that were imposed by the Portuguese colonial regime against Cape Verdean emigration, as well as to the fact that countries of destination, since the beginning of the 20th century, have consistently created obstacles for immigrants. To my ears, however, what they also imply is that 'we will continue to go abroad, no matter what'. The tradition of migration has proven to be resilient, and my belief is that whatever the powerful countries of destination do they can do little to stop Cape Verdeans from being what they are, that is, a people on the move.

Notes

[1]   My information is based on a total of one year of anthropological fieldwork in the town of Mindelo, island of São Vicente, between 1998 and 2004 (Åkesson 2004). Following local linguistic usage, I will call Mindelo 'São Vicente', and I will refer to the island as 'island of São Vicente'.

[2]   The word 'slave' has a particularly sinister meaning in Cape Verde, which derives from the country's historical experience of slavery.

References

Åkesson, L. (2004) *Making a Life: Meanings of Migration in Cape Verde*. Ph.D. thesis. Department of Social Anthropology, Gothenburg: Göteborg University.

Al-Ali, N. (2002) 'Loss of Status or New Opportunities? Gender Relations and Transnational Ties among Bosnian Refugees', in *The Transnational Family: New European Frontiers and Global Networks*, D. Bryceson and U. Vuorela (eds.), Oxford: Berg, pp. 83-102.

Bourdieu, P. (1977 [1972]) *Outline of a Theory of Practice*. Cambridge: Cambridge University Press.

Carling, J. (2004) 'Emigration, Return and Development in Cape Verde: The Impact of Closing Borders'. *Population, Space and Place* 10(2): 113-132.

Dias, J.B. (2000) Entre Partidas e Regressos: Tecendo Relações Familiares em Cabo Verde. Master's dissertation, Universidade de Brasília.

Instituto do Emprego e Formação Professional (2006) (www.iefp.cv, accessed 2006-9-13).

Levitt, P. (2001) *The Transnational Villagers*. Berkeley, CA: University of California Press.

Mahler, S. (2001) 'Transnational Relationships: The Struggle to Communicate across Borders'. *Identities* 7(4): 583-620.

Meintel, D. (1984) 'Emigração em Cabo Verde: Solução ou Problema?'. *Revista Internacional de Estudos Africanos* 2: 93-120.

Olwig, K.F.; Sørensen, N.N. (2002) 'Mobile Livelihoods: Making a Living in the World', in *Work and Migration: Life and Livelihoods in a Globalizing World*, N.N. Sørensen and K.F. Olwig (eds.), London: Routledge, pp. 1-19.

Subject Index